RICHARD WRIGHT

A Collection of Critical Essays

Edited by

Arnold Rampersad

Assistant Editors
Bruce Simon
Jeffrey Tucker

Prentice Hall, Englewood Cliffs, New Jersey 07632

Library of Congress Cataloging-in-Publication Data

Richard Wright : a collection of critical essays / edited by Arnold
    Rampersad.
        p.   cm. — (New century views)
    Includes bibliographical references (p.).
    ISBN 0–13–036120–8
        1. Wright, Richard, 1908–1960—Criticism and interpretation.
    2. Afro-Americans in literature.   I. Rampersad, Arnold.
    II. Series.
    PS3545.R815Z815   1995
    813'.52—dc20   94–19515
                                                          CIP

Acquisitions editor: Anthony English
Editoral/production supervision and
    interior design: Joan Powers
Copy editor: Elizabeth Durand
Cover design: Karen Salzbach
Buyer: Mary Ann Gloriande

 © 1995 by Prentice-Hall, Inc.
A Simon & Schuster Company
Englewood Cliffs, New Jersey 07632

Printed in the United States of America
10 9 8 7 6 5 4 3 2 1

ISBN 0-13-036120-8

Prentice-Hall International (UK) Limited, *London*
Prentice-Hall of Australia Pty. Limited, *Sydney*
Prentice-Hall Canada Inc., *Toronto*
Prentice-Hall Hispanoamericana, S.A., *Mexico*
Prentice-Hall of India Private Limited, *New Delhi*
Prentice-Hall of Japan, Inc., *Tokyo*
Simon & Schuster Asia Pte. Ltd., *Singapore*
Editora Prentice-Hall do Brazil, Ltda., *Rio de Janeiro*

Contents

Introduction

Arnold Rampersad

Richard Wright's reputation as a writer has risen and fallen over the more than six decades since he began publishing his work in 1931, when he was twenty-three. The appearance of *Native Son* in 1940 undoubtedly made him the most famous African American author in the United States, a position he consolidated with the publication of another bestselling book, his autobiography *Black Boy*, in 1945.

In 1948, however, Wright's reputation as an artist came under attack by James Baldwin, whose essay in *Partisan Review*, "Everybody's Protest Novel," assailed the notion of *Native Son* as an outstanding work of art that reflected the complexities of African American life. Baldwin found Wright's work typical of propaganda in its diminution of the identity and humanity of its central character, Bigger Thomas, and, by extension, African Americans. The publication of Ralph Ellison's *Invisible Man* (1952), with its elegantly restrained modernist structure, its lyricism and humor, in contrast to the violence and general grimness of Wright's fictional world, did nothing to arrest the slide in the latter's reputation.

The arrival of the most tumultuous stage of the Civil Rights Movement in the early 1960s, followed by the rise of the Black Arts and Black Power Movements, saw a turnabout in the general perception of Wright's art. The depiction of Bigger Thomas, especially, with his hatred of whites and his contempt for the passivity of blacks, including the religiously devout, was hailed by many observers as a militant racial gesture. Still later, the explosion of violent crime in the cities, associated increasingly with young black men of the "underclass," as this stratum of black society came to be called, made *Native Son* and Wright seem remarkably prescient. Then, starting mainly in the 1980s, Wright's reputation suffered once again when his work was scrutinized by feminist literary criticism, perhaps the most dominant single intellectual movement of the age in American and African American literary study. Many feminists understandably found the body of his work less than appealing; Wright's fiction offers few examples of women, especially black women, who might be admired for intelligence or strength of character. Indeed, in his fiction he sometimes seems to fear and dislike black women.

Nevertheless, his body of work, large by African American standards, moves into the twenty-first century on solid ground. Among African American writers he is perceived certainly as one of the landmark authors in the two-hundred-year history of the literature. In American literature, from one perspective he is seen as a kind of appendage to the major phase of naturalistic writing, of which writers such as Crane, London, Norris, and Dreiser were major exponents. However, the increasing prominence of race in the national discourse—a prominence likely to grow, rather than diminish, in the twenty-first century—has made Wright's work take on a significance that readers of previous generations sometimes missed. His achievement as a writer must also be judged on a global scale, especially as a variety of literatures in English around the world—in Africa and India, for example—begin to flower, and the interrelated phenomena of colonialism, neocolonialism, and decolonization take on new meanings and interpretations. Many American writers with national reputations greater than Wright's then seem less significant, more provincial; and a writer like Richard Wright, who clearly was conscious long ago of some of the international implications of domestic issues (as his books on Spain, Africa, and Asia attest) comes to the fore.

Most notably in *Black Boy*, Wright has chronicled the various stages in his emergence as an individual human being and a writer. By his own description, he suffered a bitter childhood in his native Mississippi, one designed to destroy in him all vestiges of self-confidence and independence. After his father, a sharecropper, deserted his family when Richard was five, the road was all stony and uphill. His mother suffered a stroke that left her and her two sons dependent on her family and especially on her own mother, a severe woman who (according to Wright) imposed her Seventh Day Adventism so harshly on the household that Richard thereafter hated religion. As Wright himself recalled, he was an imaginative and a sensitive child who loved to hear stories; unfortunately, his devout grandmother abominated fiction, even children's fiction, as fundamentally the telling of lies, the devil's work. The larger black communities in which Richard lived offered little or no support, and the white world was cold and distant when it was not brutal. In *Black Boy*, no one ever helps Wright in any significant way. Only his mother loves him; but she, incapacitated for much of her life by strokes, becomes a symbol for him not of love but of passivity, impotence, and suffering.

Although it has been argued that Wright's childhood and youth were less oppressive than he claims in *Black Boy*, his books suggest strongly that he was a harshly circumscribed child, one violated by the elements that ideally should have nurtured him gently. His identity as a writer, blunt and stark in its outline, was no pose but was deeply ingrained in his own personality. In creating fiction or writing essays, his fundamental sense of himself was as someone tough, challenging, even prosecutorial. While he could be flexible in his use of language, his instinct as a creator of narrative was for stories curled tightly around scenes of violence, of crushed heads and broken limbs. All his important heroes are male, and they are essentially solitary men, uncomfortable with women when not actually hostile, even murderous, toward them. In almost all of his most important pieces of fiction, his heroes are men deeply ashamed of their pasts and eager to seize the chance to begin all over again, in the delusion that they can remake themselves in some fundamentally different way.

Wright's aggressiveness was already entrenched early in his career—even as in 1937, with few publications and no book as yet to his name, he surveyed past black writing and identified its crucial failings. "Generally speaking," he wrote in his essay "Blueprint for Negro Writing," "Negro writing in the past has been confined to humble novels, poems, and plays, prim and decorous ambassadors who went a-begging to white America . . . dressed in the knee-pants of servility. . . . For the most part these artistic ambassadors were received as though they were French poodles who do clever tricks." His own writing, he was certain, would never be humble, prim, or decorous; he would beg no one for favors, or an audience. Already reading deeply in European and American literature, he would nevertheless disdain imitation of all but the most vigorous and progressive of the writers, and then only as a means of finding his own voice. As an artist, he would not do clever tricks.

As Wright told it, his sudden exposure to the iconoclastic writings of the Baltimore journalist H. L. Mencken (whose celebrated essay "The Sahara of the Bozart" in 1917, attacking white Southern culture, had enraged whites there) first gave him a glimpse of his future. Mencken had showed Wright how, in the hands of a vigorous manipulator of language, words could be used as "weapons" against even the most powerful adversaries. Next Wright discovered through his first extended reading of fiction the peculiar power of narrative art, as opposed to the polemical writing of which Mencken was a master. In the realists and naturalists of the late nineteenth and early twentieth centuries, mainly in America, Wright discovered a kinship between his experience of life and certain literary and philosophic methods and approaches. "All my life had shaped me for the realism, the naturalism of the modern novel," he would write in *Black Boy*, "and I could not read enough of them."

Before he could begin to write fiction in the same vein, he passed through an initial phase as a radical socialist writer, composing verse in which radical rhetoric is further inflated and yet humanized by a democratic fervor learned almost certainly from Walt Whitman. However, even as a member of the Communist Party, Wright was hearkening to a less conventionally militant, more deeply unorthodox drummer. In the novel initially called *Cesspool*, then eventually published after Wright's death as *Lawd Today*, he first showed a close correspondence between his sense of the spirit of his life, especially his youth, as he had lived it and his wide reading in fiction and philosophy. *Lawd Today* is the story of one day (Lincoln's birthday) in the life of a black male postal worker in Chicago and three of his coworkers and friends, also black men. Consciously modernist in its borrowings from James Joyce and James T. Farrell, among others, the novel emphasizes the crude sensuality of the main character, Jake, who lives only for food, drink, sex, gambling, and displays of vanity; his three friends are hardly any better as human beings. The novel ends with Jake robbed and beaten by other blacks, then struck in self-defense with a broken piece of glass by his wife Lil after he begins to abuse her. As she sobs unhappily, he sinks into unconsciousness: "Outside an icy wind swept around the corner of the building, whining and moaning like an idiot in a deep black pit."

In *Lawd Today*, despite Wright's connections as he composed the novel, there is no glimmer of revolutionary consciousness among these four blacks or among any blacks at all. Indeed, revolution is simply not a category within the novel. As a group, although dimly seen, the whites are clearly superior to the blacks and purposeful, but their world seems inaccessible to the blacks. Clearly present here in this early work, in characteristically problematic form, is the question of Wright's relationship to black culture, to his fellow blacks, and the troubled yet empowering interplay between his feelings on this subject and his larger philosophical and cultural views. At least one gifted commentator has remarked on Wright's apparent inability, in his fiction, to imagine a black character as intelligent or as sensitive as he himself was.

Did Wright view himself, as he often seems to do in his fiction, as an exception among blacks, different and superior by virtue of intelligence, sensitivity, and moral vision? The answer appears to be, yes. This is not to suggest that Wright never identified, even sentimentally at times, with black Americans. Still less is it to suggest that Wright was a weaker artist for having this sense of difference and superiority. Out of this distance would come unprecedented explorations of aspects of African American and American culture lost entirely to more timid black writers who may have felt Wright's sense of distance but could not bring themselves to admit, much less proclaim it. His most memorable narratives are haunted by a profound sense of lovelessness, homelessness, and alienation, as well as by a related sense of black American culture as spiritually and culturally emaciated. On the other hand, such feelings typically exact a tremendous psychological toll, and Wright was no exception here. He would find it increasingly difficult to continue to write fiction about black Americans, and this difficulty would both shape his career and lead to further psychological turmoil that would leave its mark on his writing.

It might be argued, in the light of Wright's more optimistic reading of African American culture in *12 Million Black Voices*, which appeared shortly after *Native Son*, that he despised mainly the bourgeois or petty bourgeois elements of black culture. However, that qualification is really insupportable. Although Wright flirted with an admiration of the blues and other forms of black folkways, he appears to have disliked black American culture, especially in the South, almost as thoroughly as he despised white Southern culture. Both were mere cultures; as such, they were opposed in his mind, as *Black Boy* makes clear, to civilization, which existed in parts of the North and flourished in Europe. In addition, *Lawd Today* illuminates fairly clearly the extent to which Wright was embryonically an existentialist long before he heard the term or met some of the stars of the movement, such as Sartre and de Beauvoir in Paris after his emigration there in 1947. The gloom of the novel in part reflects Wright's pessimism about black culture, and in part reflects his assimilation of naturalism as an idea; but it decidedly also reflects his deeply rooted sense of the bleakness that undergirds life even in its most sophisticated forms, as well as the necessity of shaping individual identity and collective culture alike by the force of will.

Why so many major publishers—about half a dozen—rejected *Lawd Today* is a mystery. It is doubtful that anyone really thought it too poorly written to be published. At least in its final revised form, the novel is not poorly written, although even today some critics take their lead from its checkered publication record and call it deeply flawed. Some publishers may have been repelled by the spectacle of black male sexuality in the book, which at one point even turns its gaze on white womanhood. Quite possibly, others may have found the book too pessimistic—too pessimistic about black American culture, in the first place, but also too pessimistic by implication about the United States, on the one hand, and the chances of radical socialism, on the other.

Indeed, when Wright's breakthrough in publishing came, it was in the form of a radical socialist story, "Fire and Cloud," which is distinctly contrary in spirit and structure to *Lawd Today*. The story features a black preacher in an economically ravaged town in the South who finally stands up to the mayor, the chief of police, and the Chamber of Commerce over the right of the people to march in protest against conditions there. For a long time intimidated by these powers, the preacher finds the strength to defy them when he turns at last to the people, black and white, who march together at the end of the tale. "Fire and Cloud" was so highly regarded that it won the main prize ($500) for Wright among 600 entries in a contest organized by *Story Magazine*. It probably led directly to the publication in 1938 of Wright's first book, *Uncle Tom's Children: Four Novellas* (a fifth novella, "Bright and Morning Star," was added in the revised edition of 1940).

Apart from "Fire and Cloud" and "Bright and Morning Star," however, *Uncle Tom's Children* is not an ideologically obsessed collection. "Big Boy Leaves Home" is a harrowing account, replete with the killing of a white man and the lynching of a black boy, of one black youth's rite of passage into manhood through an ordeal of violence. In "Long Black Song," a neglected country wife, succumbing to the importuning of a white itinerant salesman, drives her enraged husband to murder and suicide. "Down by the Riverside" tells of a black sharecropper and his heroic but doomed effort to save his pregnant wife during a great flood; he steals a boat belonging to a white family but later must help rescue that family. His wife dies, and he himself is shot and killed trying to escape his white accusers.

Steering between a radical socialist esthetic, on the one hand, and another conceived more liberally, on the other, *Uncle Tom's Children* presents a somewhat schizoid face to the reader. Perhaps no one was more keenly aware of its tensions than Wright himself. In 1940, writing about the genesis of *Native Son* after it had become a bestseller, he professed to have been dissatisfied with the reception of *Uncle Tom's Children*. When he found out that the collection was "a book which even bankers' daughters could read and feel good about," he swore that the one that followed would be different. He would make sure that "no one would weep over it; that it would be so hard and deep that they would have to face it without the consolation of tears." In part, Wright was alluding to the communist stories, with their strained orchestrations; but he might have been disturbed as well by the other, more liberally conceived novellas. In their emphasis on the trials of a youth, a woman, or a man wrestling with a flood, they may have seemed to Wright curiously limited—although these are certainly among the most unforgettable stories in all of Wright's work.

What separates these tales from Wright's major works of fiction is, among other things, the extent to which (in the tales) the central characters are held relatively unaccountable for their lives and their fates, the extent to which they are neither blamed nor given credit for what they have become. The central characters of the novellas are, on the whole, acted upon; and the central consciousness of these stories (to deliberately borrow a term from Henry James, with whose theories of fiction Wright was already familiar), for all of the violence featured, is suffused by a sentimental lyricism that triumphs over horror in the end. In Wright's next venture in fiction, communism and sentimental lyricism would both undergo the harshest scrutiny.

Native Son certainly was unlike any book in African American literature before it. (It was also the first genuine bestseller by a black American. Already in page proofs at Harper and Brothers in 1939, the book was picked up by the Book-of-the-Month Club, which made Wright purge certain passages from the text and brought out the revised volume as one of its two main selections early in 1940. Almost 250,000 copies were sold that year.) In other books, there had been episodes of violence by blacks against whites, and intimations of the depth and inevitability of black hatred of whites; but the raw power of Bigger Thomas's sense of alienation from blacks and whites alike, as well as from his family, religion, education, and the law, had never been previously glimpsed.

The sheer emptiness of Bigger's sense of his self, to be filled finally by two brutal killings of innocent women for which he refuses to repent, had also never been seen. For some readers, Bigger Thomas might just as well have come from another planet—except that he was, as Wright announced, decidedly a native son, a pure product of America. Wright depicts him as a product of American racism and capitalist greed, which sometimes masquerades as benign liberalism but is the ruthless instrument that squeezes humanity and hope from its victims, the poor. In the end, at his trial, Bigger stands between the forces of racism and reaction, on the one hand, and communism, on the other, and is understood by neither. His communist lawyer Max comes closer, of course, than the State's Attorney; but Max's final response to Bigger is shock and horror at realizing that Bigger, emerging from the depths of his despair, actually cherishes his killings as the only reliable sign of an interior life on which he might build a humane identity: "What I killed for must've been good! . . . It must have been good! When a man kills, it's for something. . . . I didn't know I was really alive in this world until I felt things hard enough to kill for 'em."

Wright's harsh feelings about black American culture, so evident in *Native Son*, were much less in evidence in his next book, *12 Million Black Voices: A Folk History of the Negro in the United States* (which also features photographs selected by Edwin Rosskam). This volume is indeed anomalous in all of Wright's work because of its relatively positive portrait of the African American world. With reference to a broad range of the agrarian black experience in America, and in harmony with the evocative photographs of blacks in a variety of situations and moods, Wright attempted to render a complex and yet favorable record of the African American world, its history, social structure, art, and psychology. The resulting image of the black world is, on the whole, plausible. Why did Wright take this approach? He had not seen the photographs, which are even more suggestive of dignity and heroism, when he wrote the text. Perhaps he wanted to counterbalance the dreary, pessimistic image of black life he had offered in *Native Son*. In any event, the relatively heroic portrait would not be seen again, except in even more diminished form in his last novel, *The Long Dream*, as his career developed.

Four years later, indeed, Wright's next book, *Black Boy: A Record of Childhood and Youth*, offered a searing indictment of black culture, as well as white culture, in the South. The limitation of the book to Wright's southern experience was the result of a decision not by Wright but by the Book-of-the-Month Club, which bought the book (already in galleys at Harper and Brothers) on condition that Wright drop the entire second part of the manuscript, which dealt with his life in the North, and especially his experiences with the Communist Party. (*Black Boy* sold more than a half million copies in 1945 alone.) If the spirit of the author is the defining aspect of an autobiography, then *Black Boy* epitomizes individual determination and independence. Wright's emphasis here is on his absolute indomitability in trying to make something of himself, notably as a writer, in the face of a world bent on his destruction. Unlike characters in his fiction who are ashamed of their pasts, Wright here confronts his own past for the purpose of indicting it and, at the same time, underscoring his triumph over it.

In a book of many shocks and harrowing episodes, probably the key moment in its exposition comes at the end of the first chapter when Wright, breaking the chronology of his story, writes of a meeting with his father twenty-five years after Nathan Wright had deserted his family. This meeting confirms their estrangement. "Though I could see a shadow of my face in his face," Wright insists, "though there was an echo of my voice in his voice, we were forever strangers, speaking a different language, living on vastly different planes of reality." The next chapter barely begins when Wright launches the bitter attack on black American culture already mentioned, in which he recites a litany of his people's shortcomings ("how unstable was our tenderness, how lacking in genuine passion we were, how void of great hope, how timid our joy, how bare our traditions, how hollow our memories, how lacking we were in those intangible sentiments that bind man to man, and how shallow was even our despair . . .").

This renunciation of home deliberately echoed Henry James's infamous catalog of the inadequacies of America in Hawthorne's day—and, implicitly, James's own; at the end of his essay "How Bigger Was Born" five years before, Wright had alluded knowledgeably to James's biography of Hawthorne. Wright's renunciation had, however, far more consequence for himself. James could fit easily into British society; Wright himself would always be a conspicuous alien in Europe, for which he left two years after *Black Boy* appeared. The challenge to Wright thereafter, growing in intensity with each passing year, was how to make a literary career out of this radical rootlessness, this sense of having been driven from home—the South, the United States, the African American community—by blacks and whites alike. In some respects, this challenge was only an intensification of Wright's original challenge as a writer. Now, however, he did not have radical socialism, or the party, or philosophic naturalism, to lean on.

Eight years passed before Wright's next book. In 1953, his novel *The Outsider* showed the extent to which he had turned for solace and illumination to the existentialists, to Heidegger and Husserl, as well as to Sartre, de Beauvoir, and Camus (notably in *The Stranger*). His central character, Cross Damon, undoubtedly the most intellectual and well-spoken main character in Wright's fiction, nevertheless is like most of the others in his almost total disaffection from society. Unlike in *Native Son* and *Black Boy*, race is almost inconsequential in *The Outsider*. The most urgent issues in the twentieth century, as Wright sees them here, transcend race. Fleeing his wife, his mistress, and his mother, all of whom he finds suffocating, Damon takes advantage of his supposed death in a subway wreck in order to start life over under an assumed identity. What to make of this freedom, how to understand and use it, is the crux of the novel—with Damon's individual freedom standing for human freedom in general.

The highly improbable plot of the novel brings him into contact in New York with members of the Communist Party, on the one hand, and the embodiment of fascist intolerance in the person of a landlord, on the other. Cross Damon himself believes in nothing. To preserve his new "freedom," he murders four people, black and white, communist and fascist, and causes the suicide of the one person to whom he is genuinely attracted (a white woman, she is an abstract artist married to a communist leader). In killing agents of communism and fascism, Damon expresses his contempt for both positions, which he sees as fundamentally alike in that, for all their claims, their adherents are interested above all in power, in the ruthless domination of all others. The ancient restraints on the will to power, such as myth and religion, no longer obtain in the twentieth century. Thus Damon justifies his acts of violence.

The Outsider is Wright's most freighted (one might say burdened) meditation on the interplay between politics and culture in the modern world. Coming in perhaps the coldest period of the cold war, it takes a resolute stand against communism but also vilifies fascism, which it identifies with white racism. The novel is certainly astute in its prediction of a worldwide revival of religious fundamentalism (Christian and Islamic fundamentalisms come to mind) in response to the dehumanizing effect of power politics. Wright clearly hopes for a more secular opposition, although his novel chooses to underscore the sheer difficulty of such a struggle. In the end, Cross is killed by Communists mainly because they fear his independence and detachment. Before he dies, he answers the key question posed by the novel, about the meaning of freedom to the individual. "Alone man is nothing," Cross declares. "I wish I had some way to give the meaning of my life to others . . . To make a bridge from man to man. . . . We must find some way of being good to ourselves . . . Man is all we've got."

Wright's thesis of the interdependence of people everywhere is one thing; the unmitigated bleakness of his fictional world in *The Outsider* is another, and in itself almost repudiates the ideals asserted at the end of this thesis-driven novel. Bleakness of spirit and social texture continued to dominate his fiction in his next book, *Savage Holiday*, which appeared the following year, 1954. Race and racism, downplayed as factors in *The Outsider*, vanished altogether here. All of the characters are white, including the main figure, a psychopath who inadvertently causes the death of a boy, marries the boy's mother out of guilt, and then, caught in a maelstrom of uncontrollable emotions that include guilt, sexual desire, and shame, stabs her to death.

With this novel, Wright reached something of a dead end on the road he had been traveling steadily away from home virtually from the start of his career. Essentially he had only two ways to turn if he wished to remain a serious writer— to satire, which was impossible in any sustained way for Wright, or to nonfiction, to books and essays of cultural and political commentary. In fact, this latter area had been the most important secondary aspect of Wright's career all along, with the autobiography *Black Boy* its most distinguished work.

In addition to *Savage Holiday*, four books of political, social, and cultural commentary appeared between 1954 and 1957. In 1954 came a book about a visit in the summer of 1953 to West Africa, *Black Power: A Record of Reactions in a Land of Pathos*. Wright's subtitle captures something of its spirit of skeptical distance not only from Africa but also from appeals to racial solidarity, common ancestry, and the like, which Wright tended to regard as romantic and weakminded. Proud of himself as a Western intellectual, he found Africa too primitive, too ridden by myth, fetish, and symbol, for his taste. He blamed European colonialism for many of Africa's problems, but expressed no clear confidence in the indigenous cultures. *Black Power* is at once anti-colonial and patronizing of Africans, a fact that made it popular with almost no one.

A visit in 1955 to Indonesia to attend the landmark Bandung conference of non-aligned nations, one of the most prominent steps in the road away from colonialism for the peoples of Africa and Asia in particular, led to *The Color Curtain: A Report on the Bandung Conference* (1956). Wright was favorably impressed by the spirit and goals of the conference, which virtually ratified the concept of the so-called Third World, and raised the real possibility that a political, economic, and cultural force was rising independent of capitalism and communism. *Pagan Spain*, the result of extensive travels and many interviews in that country, emphasized what Wright saw as the pagan rather than Christian basis of Catholic Spain. Once again Wright fastened on the irrationality beneath the surface of ostensibly civilized society despite its moral pretensions, which were acute in Franco's

Spain. His volume *White Man, Listen!* (1956) collected essays based on the texts of various lectures delivered by Wright in the 1950s. Perhaps the most interesting of these is a venture in literary history, "The Literature of the Negro in the United States," in which Wright offers a detailed survey of the literature and stresses the extent to which social and political factors shaped black American literary expression.

The last major work published by Wright in his lifetime (the collection of stories *Eight Men* and the novel *Lawd Today* came posthumously) was the novel *The Long Dream*. This was the beginning of what he hoped would be a trilogy designed to show "the extent to which 'racial conditioning' remained strong among blacks even after they had left the environment that engendered it." *The Long Dream* is mainly the story of Fishbelly Tucker, whose life is traced from its earliest phase to his young manhood. The most important relationship is between Fishbelly and his father, Tyree Tucker, a prosperous undertaker and brothel owner in a small Mississippi town who is killed by the local chief of police in order to suppress evidence of the chief's corruption. After his father's death, Fishbelly himself is jailed through the conniving of the chief; once he is released, Fishbelly abandons Mississippi, and is last seen on a plane headed for France.

The Long Dream, clearly an attempt to return to the basic material that had inspired *Uncle Tom's Children* near the start of Wright's career, is unusual in certain respects. Neither Tyree nor Fishbelly is profoundly alienated from life; neither is portrayed in a relationship with a woman—wife or mother—who personifies suffering and passivity to the same extent as in *Lawd Today*, *Native Son*, or *The Outsider*. Fishbelly is not violent; indeed, outside of the stories in *Uncle Tom's Cabin*, he is the most "normal" of Wright's heroes, neither particularly intelligent nor sensitive but only reasonably bright and clearheaded, and about as principled as one could expect under the circumstances. Wright narrates his story in fairly expert fashion, but the novel suffers because of the lack of depth or complexity in its main characters. The central element of the novel is not a particular personality but the peculiar environment of the South and the lives of its whites and blacks blighted by segregation, racism, shabby standards of education and culture, brutality, and petty corruption. The result in Fishbelly is a young man stunted in intellectual and emotional growth but not driven by the terrible forces that energize other characters in Wright's work. Certainly a work of realism, *The Long Dream* also exemplifies a mild brand of naturalism, as well as Wright's move away from the various dogmatisms that had previously engaged his attention.

About this time, Wright prepared for publication a collection of stories, *Eight Men* (1961). Patterned probably after Theodore Dreiser's *Twelve Men*, the book broke no new ground. "The Man Who Was Almost a Man," about a boy who ineptly shoots a mule, reflects the world of *Uncle Tom's Children* but without either political or racial passion. The most powerful story is "The Man Who Lived Underground," which Wright had started around 1941 as a novel. In its emphasis on the spiritual despair of its central character, a black man, Wright showed the extent to which he had already anticipated some of the main concerns of *The Outsider.*

In 1960, at the age of only fifty-two, Wright died unexpectedly in an obscure Paris clinic. His body of work, like that of almost any fairly prolific writer, is unquestionably uneven in quality. Within American literature, however, it occupies a significant place because of the extraordinary light he cast on the question of the place of blacks in the national consciousness. He approached the subject from the perspective of black America but he did so without defensiveness or diplomacy. In his artistic meditations, he spared neither black nor white, and the result was an unprecedented degree of truth about America as a whole. In African American fiction, he was perhaps the most significant and influential author of this century. Certainly few later writers have matched Wright in the fearless and uncompromising nature of his essential vision, or created works of art as decisive in defining what history has made of the African American character.

The Violence of
Native Son

Jerry H. Bryant

Throughout his adult life, Richard Wright was preoccupied with the nature of a healthy society. He believed that only when people acknowledge each other's need for warmth, sympathy, and understanding can they build a social structure in which all can feel at home. These qualities were conspicuously absent for the black American of the 1930s, who, as Wright sees it, never felt at home in his own land. Certainly Bigger Thomas did not. Bigger is a representative black victim of white racism. More importantly, he is a representative modern man—at least one type of modern man. Closed off from self-fulfillment and self-expression, isolated from the world around him, he turns to violence, becoming, like his contemporaries of the same stamp, a threat to the civilization that produced him.

The murders that Bigger commits in *Native Son* break most of the rules of civilized behavior. Wright believes in those rules, and he does not allow us to applaud Bigger as an incipient revolutionary stoutly defending his manhood. Nor does Wright try morally to justify Bigger's actions. He presents them as reprehensible. Bigger smothers the white girl who tries, however clumsily, to befriend him, and then hacks her head off to fit her into the furnace to burn the evidence of his crime. He smashes the skull of his own black girlfriend after he has forced her to make love to him, and then throws her body down the air shaft of a deserted Chicago tenement, where the freezing night finishes her off. Both acts have an element of cowardice in them, committed against women who, physically weaker than Bigger, have entrusted themselves to his keeping. Both are connected directly or indirectly with Bigger's loveless appetite for sex—the white girl a forbidden object, the black girl one nobody cares about. Both acts are performed, at the most vulgar level, to save Bigger's skin, which he and his motives make us doubt is very much worth saving.

Wright shows us how Bigger could do these things, the life he leads that produces so vicious a behavior. Bigger has been cramped by his environment, limited in his education, and prevented from developing his native understanding and sensibility. He can think only in the crudest terms and react only in the most basic ways. When Mary Dalton's blind mother enters her daughter's bedroom and

Reprinted from *The Southern Review* 17.1 (Spring 1981): 303–319. By permission of Jerry H. Bryant.

nearly touches the terrified Bigger standing by the bed, his mind can handle only two alternatives—whether he will or will not get caught. To avoid getting caught, his slow mind finds only one course of action: to prevent Mary from rising up in her drunken stupor and speaking to Mrs. Dalton. But with an excess that characterizes most of his behavior, Bigger unintentionally kills her, becoming a perfect victim of a racist and capitalist environment.

During this scene, Bigger's behavior seems out of proportion to the apparent danger. It is impossible to imagine, for example, Jan Erlone, Mary's white boyfriend, suffocating Mary in her own bed in order to remain undetected, even though her parents emphatically disapprove of him and his Communist affiliation. But the excessiveness of Bigger's reaction is part of Wright's point. The intensity of his feelings expresses the entire set of circumstances that has shaped Bigger's response. He is seized by "hysterical terror," dominated by "frenzy," and he acts "frantically." The reason for these extreme feelings is condensed in the figure of blind Mrs. Dalton. She is the white world, deceptively fragile, but immensely threatening to the young black man, for she carries with her, for all her seeming weakness, the implacable power of a white world that hates blacks and makes them feel ashamed and guilty. Bigger is "intimidated to the core" by her as she enters. His conditioning has taught him that to be caught in the bedroom of a drunken white girl is tantamount to being convicted of rape, and rape falls under the most powerful taboo of all those that govern the relations between black and white in America. Bigger has absorbed that taboo and is terrified by its implications. The prosecuting attorney at Bigger's trial quite understands the powerful anxiety the taboo creates in both black and white, for he invokes it as an almost certain way to gain a conviction: "Mind you, Your Honor, the central crime here is rape!"

Part of Bigger's terror comes from the fact that he is indeed guilty of rape, at least in his mind. At the moment Mrs. Dalton enters Mary's bedroom, Bigger is caressing and kissing Mary, trembling with an emotion he has never felt before. For black men, white women are the ultimate danger, and Wright has placed Bigger between two of them, about to commit the ultimate black crime. The extremity of his reaction to Mrs. Dalton is in direct proportion to the completeness with which he has internalized the taboo.

Wright does not summon up this background to put us on Bigger's side. He simply asks the reader to face the full "hard and deep" horror of Bigger's act. While we may be brought to recognize the forces that shape him and lead him to the murders he commits, we must not think of him as more sinned against than sinning. He is an American black man, and he hates with a virulence that Wright daringly, for the time, insists upon acknowledging. Thus, Wright does not stop with the relatively mild scene in which Bigger smothers Mary with her pillow. To hide his crime, he must resort to greater horror. The conditions for escaping the notice of Mrs. Dalton dictated his suffocating Mary. When he gets the girl's body to the furnace room, new conditions require that he decapitate it. The blazing furnace, melodramatically evoking the fires of hell, must receive her body and become, also melodramatically, her crypt and the womb from which Bigger will emerge newly born. He does not accomplish the deed unfeelingly, or with a relish of revenge against the white race. He does it out of desperation for safety. But he is nearly overwhelmed by the frightfulness of what he is doing, by the smell of Mary's body, the blood that flows from her throat when he attempts to cut off her head with his knife. His thoughts are frantic: "He wanted to run from the basement and go as far as possible from the light of this bloody throat. . . . He wanted to lie down upon the floor and sleep off the horror of this thing."

Bigger is not the brute of the newspaper stories. Nor is he the rolling-eyed jelly-knee of the cinema stereotype who runs from ghosts. Such creatures do not feel with Bigger's intensity—the fear, the frenzy, the frustration. His muscles as well as his will, under the Poe-esque gaze of the Daltons' white cat, are assaulted by a larger sense of guilt than the racial, and by the recoil against the physical abuse of another member of his kind. But he is impelled by the even more basic human need to save himself, which takes precedence over his revulsion at what he has done to Mary's body. Above all his horror he remembers that "he had to burn this girl . . . he had to get out of here."

Bigger did not plan this murder, or the grotesque means of getting rid of the body. He is no Raskolnikov, killing to prove a principle. He reenacts the fate of the black American male. The circumstances of a racist culture put him at a certain place at a certain time and force upon him a choice that can have no safe outcome. Without time to think Bigger reacts according to his simplest instincts. It turns out that they have not been completely determined by his social conditioning. American racial conventions require that the fear Bigger feels toward whites should cause him to think of the white taboo before anything else. When Mrs. Dalton appears, he might have collapsed in paralysis, like a minstrel Step 'n Fetchit, allowing the white world to penetrate the last protection of his sense of self-worth. Instead, he saves himself, giving priority to his own existence over the racial values of white America and conferring a value upon himself that he had never been conscious of before. In the days following the murder, Bigger gets a firmer grip on that consciousness. Waiting in his cell to be executed, he understands what he has done: "What I killed for I am." It is not until he is called upon to make the choice between himself and Mary and her world that he recognizes the worth he has put upon his own life. "It must've been pretty deep in me to make me kill," he says. "I must have felt it awful hard to murder." Only a human being who senses the fundamental immorality of murder could use the act as a measure of the intensity of his own feelings. And though he does not realize the dangerous irony in his reversal of normal values, Bigger comes to believe that through his violent act he has replaced with self-esteem the feelings of shame, guilt, and fear that have dominated his life.

His new consciousness produces a more acute sense of being present in life. With a new sense of his own importance, his need to elude detection by the white world becomes more intense, too. He learns to plan, to project, to consider the future. He becomes more finely aware of his every move, the tone of his voice, the effect he is having on others. All his senses work with an exhilarating clarity that replaces the cloudy feelings of anxiety that weighed upon his thoughts about his gang and their petty crimes. Bigger now occupies stage center, alone, singled out by the spotlight of his heightened self-consciousness and his bracing new role as a man important enough to be wanted by the police. He has always been psychologically isolated from his family, as well as from his friends. Now that he has traveled into an experience so alien to his regular world, his differentness takes on a new tone. His friends seem to occupy "another life." He himself has gone into another country. He sees his cramped family apartment "for the first time." He holds in his mind a memory the others have no access to, and this gives him an unfamiliar strength. The strength is mixed with fear, and his exhilaration with horror, but just as he murdered Mary to save himself, now he accepts the deed. It means a new being. As he swaggers toward the pool room where the gang hangs out, he feels "like a man reborn."

Precisely what the killing of Mary Dalton means to him, though, becomes fully clear only after he commits his second murder. The motive behind his killing Bessie Mears expresses his deepest need. In spite of the fear he once again feels as he brings the brick down upon her skull, after it is over and he is sure she is dead, he experiences "a queer sense of power. *He* had done this. *He* had brought all this about. In all life these two murders were the most meaningful things that had ever happened to him. He was living, truly and deeply, no matter what others might think, looking at him with their blind eyes." Wright explicitly makes Bigger a representative modern man, defined by his seizing upon violence as a proof of his reality. In "How Bigger Was Born," Wright says,

> From far away Nazi Germany and old Russia had come to me items of knowledge that told me that certain modern experiences were creating types of personalities whose existence ignored racial and national lines of demarcation, that these personalities carried with them a more universal drama-element than anything I'd ever encountered before; that these personalities were mainly imposed upon men and women living in a world whose fundamental assumptions could no longer be taken for granted.

The attraction violence assumes for Bigger as a way of becoming a new and more effective person is explained by these personalities. They crave, as Wright describes it, sheer action, "animal sensation." Like drunkards needing more liquor to produce the desired intensity of feeling, they figuratively take a drink of "hard life" to get a "thrilling moment . . . a quivering sense of wild exultation and fulfillment that soon faded and soon let them down." To keep up this sense of being alive, they need ever larger doses of excitement. They seem to live "by violence, through extreme action and sensation, through drowning daily in a perpetual nervous agitation." Having inadvertently taken a drink of the heady liquor, Bigger craves more to sustain his high. His nerves become "hungry" to follow the newly opened avenue into a "strange land." He trembles; he gets "tremendously excited"; he anticipates more to come. Boris A. Max, his defense attorney, claims that Bigger "was impelled toward murder as much through the thirst for excitement, exultation, and elation as he was through fear! It was his way of *living!*"

Bigger is a modern paradox. Born of our civilization, he is a major threat to it. The type he represents is described by Jose Ortega y Gasset in *The Revolt of the Masses* (1929). Bigger is like Ortega's "mass-man," aching for sensation, ignorant of the complex elements of the new world, godless, valueless. He has been estranged, says Wright of Bigger, not only from the "folk," but from the past and from himself. Without work or faith or tradition to sustain him, Bigger and the "mass-man" find no soil to hold their roots or give them nourishment. They live a pale vicarious life watching others do the things they want to do. Bigger exhausts himself, says Wright, trying "to react to and answer the call of the dominant civilization whose glitter came to him through the newspapers, magazines, radios, movies, and the mere imposing sight and sound of daily American life." This is a dangerous man to society. The resentment he feels over "the balked longing for some kind of fulfillment and exultation," Max warns the judge hearing Bigger's case, "makes our future seem a looming image of violence."

Part of the meaning of Bigger's violence is not only that he is a black man striking out against the boundaries of racism, but that he is a man living a key modern experience. In his conviction that at the bottom of that experience is violence, Wright stands very close to two other American writers of the 1930s, James T. Farrell and Nathanael West. That Wright knew Farrell and absorbed some of his naturalistic techniques has been frequently demonstrated. Wright probably did not know West's work, but the two are alike in their reading of the modern spirit. In *The Day of the Locust* (1939), West gives us a picture of that spirit.

Tod Hackett, West's narrator, is working on a painting he calls "The Burning of Los Angeles." Hackett takes great pains to render precisely the "torchbearers" that lead the mob in its destructive frenzy. Bored by their jobs, by their leisure, by their social life, these are people who have come to Hollywood from all over America to seek fulfillment in the illusions of the movies and the lives of the false gods and goddesses the movie industry has invented. Like Bigger, they are separated from real life fulfillment by their fantasies, which they strive to actualize in the celluloid images of film and in the newspaper headlines that exaggerate every human misfortune into an exciting epic catastrophe. But they cannot stimulate their jaded senses into life with the false-front, movie-set world they reside in. So they engineer the ultimate excitement—the destruction of Los Angeles. Their demeanor is murderous but without passion or hate. Tod has an awed respect for them, and believes that, as Wright does of Bigger, "they had it in them to destroy civilization."

The similarly starved sensibilities that lead to such mindless sensation-seeking produce the Armistice Day frenzy in *The Young Manhood of Studs Lonigan* (1934). Like Bigger, Studs and his friends live lives of trivial fantasies and stunted goals, and have an appetite for violence. At the 1918 Armistice Day celebration in

Chicago, the bored urban youths behave like West's torchbearers, flowing about in aimless crowds, craning for a view of something real—sex, blood, violence—and behaving with impersonal brutality. Like cattle, they move from one atrocity to the next: gangs of Marines walking over the beaten, bleeding body of a drunk; a girl getting her dress torn off; a man falling through a plate glass window and nearly being decapitated.

Violence, these writers suggest, grows out of a stultifying American culture and a developing totalitarianism in Europe and Asia. Confronted by a sense of growing isolation, an increasing loss of self and respect for individual life, and an alienation of people from themselves, their work, and each other, the mass-man pursues violence in order to feel alive. However humanly intense Bigger's agitation is as he commits the crimes upon Mary and Bessie, it is a self-absorbed one. Like the mobs of Farrell and West, Bigger does not identify with the living person of his victims. Mary is "not real" to him, "not a human being." This estrangement from life is the foundation of the fascist character. Bigger likes "to hear of how Japan was conquering China; of how Hitler was running the Jews to the ground; of how Mussolini was invading Spain." He thinks dimly of a dictatorship in which a black man "would whip the black people into a tight band . . . make all those black people act together, rule them, tell them what to do, and make them do it."

This is perhaps the most disturbing thing of all for Wright—the use of violence for national and self-fulfillment. Ruling black people, forcing them into a fighting instrument, would be, for Bigger, "one way to end fear and shame." Bigger's motive here is not the simple and heroic one that makes him want to go down fighting, the brave black of Claude McKay's "If We Must Die." Bigger gets satisfaction from the power over others his violence gives him. It is on this basis that the dictatorships of Japan, Germany, and Italy appeal to him.

Today we speak of the "holocaust," and try to explain it. And we are still puzzling over the Moscow trials of the 1930s. Wright, without the full evidence of the ovens at Auschwitz and Buchenwald and probably unwilling to examine too closely what little news leaked out about the Communist purges, sensed something in the air of his time. He tried to combine the unformed image of some horror stalking the modern world with the well-defined image of the ghetto black man, seeing in them a dangerous similarity. Bigger was for Wright much more than a "bad nigger," or even a black revolutionary. He was a creature of the new world.

II

The mass-man is also something of an "existentialist," and so is Bigger. I use the word here not to define a technical philosophical position but to evoke the ideas behind the European movement of the late 1930s led by Jean-Paul Sartre and Albert Camus. Wright, so far as anyone knows, had not read anything by either

Frenchman when he wrote *Native Son*. Camus's *The Stranger* and *The Myth of Sisyphus* appeared in 1942 and were not translated and published in America until 1946 and 1955, respectively. Sartre's *Nausea* came out in 1938, but he did not become known in America until after World War II. The point to be made here is that Wright's understanding of the new world's tilt toward violence and totalitarian force and his experience as a black man in America lead him to explore some of the same problems and advance some of the same answers as do Sartre and Camus, but independently.

The common ground upon which these writers meet is the sense of a "contingent" world which is implacably *there*, "in the way" (*de trop*, as Sartre puts it), and fraught with injustice. Alone in this world, the human being is faced with the question of how he, as a free and undetermined individual, can deal with pain and evil, without recourse to the supernatural or worldly assistance beyond his grasp. In *Native Son*, Wright has whites appear as a natural force in the world. America for Bigger is not a country of human beings who treat each other with mutual respect. "To Bigger and his kind white people were not really people; they were a sort of great natural force, like a stormy sky looming overhead, or like a deep swirling river stretching suddenly at one's feet in the dark." Bigger does not face people who have feelings, but a dangerous world of "mountains, floods, seas," like the existential universe, indifferent to his individual fate. White people make up an environment that is inimical to black life, one that is chaotic, blind, like the plague in Camus's later novel, or the German occupation of France which some say the plague symbolizes.

Wright had already made forays into this theme in *Uncle Tom's Children* (1938), in which the natural and social details of his black characters' lives dramatize their helplessness against the white plague. Circumstances created by a racist social order, natural occurrences, and chance put the characters into an intolerable position that forces them to do something violent, final, self-destructive. Yet, their violent gesture, though it brings death to them, seems to be preferable to abject submission, spiritual enslavement, moral paralysis, denial of self—in the same way, perhaps, joining the Resistance against the Germans was preferable to passive survival, or fighting a hopeless battle against a baffling disease was better than expecting help from an unknown and hidden God. In these terms, Bigger's murder of Mary Dalton under the pressure of the intimidation he feels from Mrs. Dalton becomes an expression of rebellion against the ultimate encroachment upon the self of (in a human sense) an immoral world, one that says with Camus's rebel, "This far and no farther."

The similarities in the way Wright and his two French contemporaries respond to their experience produce similarities in their work as well. All of their protagonists grope for what is rudimentary to human existence: a sense of being someone, of existing, the need for a certainty that the self can verify. They seek to break through the assumptions and presuppositions that fix people in roles and stereotypes. When Roquentin, the protagonist of *Nausea*, does just that, he experiences a "nausea," an anxiety at being cast up on a strange shore without any way of accounting for it. His whole world takes on a disturbing unfamiliarity, for he discovers that all the old ways of making life intelligible and coherent are illusions. They prevent one from directly experiencing existence.

What seeps into Roquentin's world explodes into Bigger's. When he kills Mary Dalton, he blasts through the racial and social categories through which he has always experienced his life. He moves toward the self lying beneath the masks he has been forced to wear, finding it in a strange world bounded by new and different limits. Bigger does not experience nausea or anxiety, but excitement and impatience to get on with it. To be free of the old categories elates him; he feels for the first time that he is in control of his own life, that he can plan for what he might be.

Bigger is now the "stranger" in a way he never was as a black accepting his white limits. He has been to the abyss, done and seen things that shock and terrify those still blinded by the expected and the familiar. Indeed, blindness, as many have pointed out, has an important symbolic value for Wright. Most obviously, Mrs. Dalton's blindness is the blindness of all whites toward the humanity of blacks. But it is also the blindness in the explanations invented to comfort those who need to be assured that life is safely understandable. Wright says that this particular kind of blindness is not restricted to whites. Musing upon his own family after he has killed two people, Bigger thinks that they live

> without thinking, making for peace and habit, making for a hope that blinded. He felt that they wanted and yearned to see life in a certain way; they needed a certain picture of the world; there was one way of living they preferred above all others; and they were blind to what did not fit.

Native Son and *The Stranger* resemble each other even more strongly. Both novels make the point that "insiders" maintain a deliberate blindness toward the truth of the real world around them. Both novels proceed from a crime committed by their protagonist to the protagonist's imprisonment, followed by a trial and a period of contemplation, and ending in the protagonist's being left in his cell to face death alone. Both protagonists experience a deep change in their feelings about themselves and life. And in both novels, the protagonist is, for the middle-class majority, more than a murderer; he is a monstrous and grotesque outsider. Bigger is an animalistic brute; Meursault is a man who does not love his mother.

Both novelists focus their attention on violent acts by their protagonists. In their trials, Bigger and Meursault face judgment by the caretakers of middle-class morality—an Algerian jury and a white judge. Both are prosecuted by attorneys who play upon their judges' prejudices. Meursault's prosecutor tries him not for the murder of the Arab for which he is technically on trial, but for outraging conventional sentiment by not showing adequate grief at his mother's funeral. When it becomes known that a parricide will come up for judgment the next day, the prosecutor links Meursault's crime with that of the parricide, contending that Meursault "set a precedent" and therefore "is also guilty of the murder to be tried tomorrow in this court." State's Attorney Buckley makes Bigger's crime "rape," which has much greater shock value for white sensibility than mere murder. And at the coroner's inquest, the Deputy Coroner, inquiring into Bigger's guilt of Mary Dalton's murder, brings in the body of Bessie Mears to prove his murder of Mary.

Both novelists suggest that those who look at the world out of the eyes of convention only impose a connection upon otherwise disconnected events, avoiding an understanding of the real world and maintaining the illusion of a coherent and just world that serves their interests. The outsider, having seen the truth, knows those connections exist nowhere but in the controlled imagination of the insider. Out of their need to make their world familiar and unthreatening, insiders must brand the outsider with the mark of Cain, inherent guilt. Thus, the crowds that gather around the courtroom view both Bigger and Meursault with a loathing born of fear. The fact that they have killed is less important than that they are different. They have had the temerity to do what the crowd has not dared to do: to damn themselves.

But the existential protagonist refuses to be damned by the conventional morality. As Camus says of the "absurd" man, all he feels is "his irreparable innocence." Sartre gives this guilt-innocence discussion an illuminating form. In his version of the Orestes-Clytemnestra myth, *The Flies*, Sartre says that guilt is what the "gods" want humans to feel in order to retain control of them, not only of their actions but of their image of themselves. Zeus's means of making Electra feel guilty are the Furies, which come to attack her after she has helped Orestes murder Clytemnestra, as the Dalton cat stares at Bigger after he has killed Mary. Accepting the moral conventions that declare her guilty, she repents. Because she submits, Zeus "saves" her. Orestes refuses to feel any guilt, though he is the principal in the act of violence. He insists upon his freedom from Zeus and refuses to bow to the Furies. He takes responsibility for the murder of his mother.

Bigger assumes a similar responsibility. To become a whole man, he must deny the white world the power to judge him guilty for having a black skin. The gravity binding him to the awesome planet of white judgment is so strong that he must commit an extreme act to break free of it into his own space. He must do what Orestes does—affirm his natural act. When Bigger's friends and family crowd into his tiny jail cell, it becomes clear they consider him guilty—on all counts. Even his mother had constantly accused him of being "the most nocountest man I ever seen in all my life!" Now everyone feels sorry for him. His mother weeps. But as he witnesses this performance from his transformed world, he reacts like Orestes:

> Bigger felt a wild and outlandish conviction surge in him: *They ought to be glad!* It was a strange but strong feeling, springing from the very depths of his life. Had he not taken fully upon himself the crime of being black? Had he not done the thing which they dreaded above all others? Then they ought not stand there and pity him, cry over him; but look at him and go home, contented, feeling that their shame was washed away.

Referring to his killing of Clytemnestra and his violating the law of Zeus, Orestes speaks to the jeering crowd in similar language:

> You see me, men of Argos, you understand my crime is wholly mine; I claim it as my own, for all to know; it is my glory, my life's work, and you can neither punish me nor pity me. . . . As for your sins and your remorse, your night-fears, and the crime Aegisthus committed—all are mine, I take them all upon me.

Bigger lacks Orestes' regal confidence. In fact, there is something of the boasting juvenile in his words. But he declares his integrity as no black fictional character has done before him.

For both Wright and his European contemporaries, conventional religion would rob every person of that integrity. Religion preaches a pernicious hope that one might be exempted from the limits and the debts of the contingent world, if only one puts oneself into the hands of God. Both Wright and Camus bring a priest of God into the death cell of their protagonists. The priest urges surrender to the conventional morality and the admission of sin. But both Meursault and Bigger erupt in anger at the smugness of the priest and grow violent with him. Through their rejection of the priest's appeal, both achieve a "hopelessness" that gives them an exhilarating certainty. Both learn to take responsibility for their own acts. "Whatever he thought or did from now on," concludes Bigger, "would have to come from him alone, or not at all."

This conclusion lays the ground for the final stage of Bigger's development, in which he learns his true relationship with the world and his own meaning. Most students of *Native Son* have been so taken up with Max's long defense of Bigger and its ideological preachiness that they tend to pass over what happens to Bigger in the third book. He is forced by his incarceration from action to unaccustomed reflection. After the frantic movement of Books I and II, Book III is contemplative, but not peacefully so. Mentally, Bigger is as changeable as he always was. He swings back and forth from an existential "dream of nothingness" after he first gets caught, to hope when Mr. Max shows a genuine interest in him at their first interview. He struggles for self-control, for meaning and understanding, then succumbs to a sense "that it was all foolish, useless, vain."

These oscillations are different, though, from the wild changes he undergoes in the early part of the novel. In Book III, Bigger experiences the absurd opposition between the human need for unity and coherence, and the human realization that that need can never be filled by this world. For Camus, the absurd is largely a philosophical and epistemological problem. For Bigger, it is part of the grain of his life. He has tasted the freedom of self-awareness, but he cannot finally fill the gap between his desire for meaning and his fear that his life is meaningless. He seeks completeness in Mr. Max, that final answer to the puzzle of his new existence. True to what seems to be an instinct for the absurd, Wright has Bigger's final discovery, in one of its aspects, become something other than what he seeks. He searches for completeness, ultimate meaning. He gets a knowledge of emptiness.

When Mr. Max visits Bigger in his cell after an appeal to the Governor has failed, Bigger is more eager for some explanation of life than for saving his own. But the attorney does not understand what Bigger wants when the young black man begins putting odd, elliptical questions to him. Bigger wants to communicate. Max, too, however, has been conditioned by American racism and cannot fathom the depth or the nature of Bigger's need. But the distance between Bigger and Max is not simply the conventional one between black and white; it is the one between all human beings. Bigger must learn that we are all isolated, and the point makes the last book of the novel the climax to the evolution of Bigger's consciousness. Bigger has moved along two tracks during the novel. One has led him into himself, his own individual, concrete, immediate being. The other has led him to some outside assistance, a sort of Marxist Christ: "If only someone had gone before and lived or suffered or died—made it so that it could be understood!" But his own violence, his trial, and the final failure of Max to guess at what Bigger needs demonstrate the nature of the human condition—a lonely passage through a meaningless world in which the only salvation lies in the discovery and acceptance of one's own self.

In his last hours, shaped by his experience with the priest and Mr. Max, Bigger finds that *his* meaning does not come from others but from himself. His existence is the only thing he can rely upon, the one thing he knows for certain. That is the wellspring of his violence, and when he learns that, he undergoes a subtle but distinct change, and the reader comes to a new understanding. The murders of Mary Dalton and Bessie Mears bring to him the truth about himself and his world, and they affirm his own identity. "They wouldn't let me live and I killed," he tells Max in their final meeting. "Maybe it ain't fair to kill, and I reckon I really didn't want to kill. But when I think of why all the killing was, I begin to feel what I wanted, what I am." The essence of human life is not the heartbeat, but self-awareness, the sense of owning oneself, of being intensely in the world, making choices according to one's own integrity. As a human being and as a black man in America, Bigger feels this need with double volume.

But if there is illumination in this for Wright, there is also the horror that Bigger had to kill to learn this, the horror in discovering how far humans will go, when pushed, to save themselves. It is this horror that links the mass-man in Bigger with the existentialist and that is the foundation of Wright's critique of American racism and his analysis of the modern experience.

Our last glimpse of Bigger finds him alone in his cell, the doors closing behind the departing Max and echoing through Bigger's isolation. His jail cell and death sentence have forced upon him a knowledge of ineluctable reality. He cannot escape the death that is coming in the electric chair. He can accept it as the debt he must pay, and in doing so create his own meaning in a world that has no inherent meaning discoverable by humans. The result is an acuity of consciousness that leaves Bigger, not in the state of cleansed joy that ends *The Stranger,* but slightly sorry and a little bitter that the world could have been something else, but was not. But this is a condition far preferable to the false hope of the black preacher and

Bigger's family. Bigger's knowledge of his own truth and his strength in facing it show his worth as a moral being.

III

"In all my life," says Wright, describing his arrival in Chicago in 1927, "though surrounded by many people—I had not had a single satisfying, sustained relationship with another human being and, not having had any, I did not miss it." Loneliness is a Wright trait. Almost all of his major protagonists are isolated in some way, reflecting Wright's own feeling of being alienated from his family and friends when he was a child and from other blacks when he became a man. It is not a temporary feeling either. Just a few years before his death in 1960, he described himself in *White Man, Listen!* as a "rootless man" who did not "need as many emotional attachments, sustaining roots, or idealistic allegiances as most people." He even cherished "the state of abandonment, of aloneness," as the "natural, inevitable condition of man." It was this temperament, perhaps, that drew Wright toward the existential viewpoint before he was quite sure there was such a viewpoint, and that made it easy for him to feel more or less at home in the French intellectual world when he went to Paris after World War II. It was also this temperament that led him to weave into the character of Bigger Thomas a reflective quality that modifies the mindless violence of the mass-man.

A third side of Bigger also springs from Wright's temperament. Writing in *American Hunger,* the sequel to his autobiography *Black Boy,* Wright describes his inability to carry on a conversation with a young black woman with whom he was having an affair. He speaks of how angry he was "sitting beside a human being to whom I could not talk, angry with myself for coming to her, hating my wild and restless loneliness." It may be that Wright believed in the natural loneliness of the human condition. But the complement to that belief was Wright's need to get close to people, to form warm, gratifying ties. One of the more moving passages in *American Hunger* emphasizes the importance of such ties:

> The problem of human unity was more important than bread, more important than physical living itself; for I felt that without a common bond uniting men, without a continuous current of shared thought and feeling circulating through the body, there could be no living worthy of being called human.

This comes from the Wright that sought out the American Communist Party in the early 1930s both for its promise of sustained personal relationships and its offer of "the possibility of uniting scattered but kindred peoples into a whole." Along with the sensation-seeking mass-man and the existential solitary, the Marxist humanist takes its place in Bigger, who seeks membership in the collective even while he learns about isolation. But it is a Marxist humanism given Wright's very personal twist. Wright's main interest is neither class warfare nor the inevitable triumph of the working class, but rather how society can be organized and people motivated in order to promote the human harmony that preoccupied many of his non-Marxist contemporaries.

Bigger's need to become part of the human group drives him to question Max in the final hours of his life. In his pre-trial interrogations of Bigger, Max has opened some lines of communication unprecedented in Bigger's life. Both Max and Jan strive to convince Bigger that they care about him as a human being, and Max attempts to explain to Bigger that he, too, is a member of the human race because he acts and feels like others. But Max, the Communist intellectual, fails. He reacts in horror to Bigger's final affirmation of the crime that brought him new self-consciousness. He thinks Bigger wants comfort for the death he is about to face, not understanding that Bigger's real need is not only the self-understanding mentioned in the previous section but the satisfaction of being questioned about himself. It is now the reverse of the usual black-white relationship. It is Mr. Max who fails to make his way into Bigger's world. Bigger is physically imprisoned and isolated at the end, but he is psychologically free in a way that even Max is not, and he is ready to enter into the true human community. Max walks out of the literal prison back into the figurative prison of American society. Max's failure suggests that the Communist Party, like Mrs. Dalton, like Bigger's family, is blind, too.

Wright does not try to wring propaganda out of Bigger's new potential for human ties. He wants Bigger to remain unresolved as a character, one whose unity is, like Engels' dialectical organism, composed of irreconcilable forces. Therefore, he only fleetingly hints at the new Bigger in the last few paragraphs of the novel. As David Bakish has pointed out in *Richard Wright,* Max remains "Mr." to Bigger; but through Max, Bigger sends a message—a communication—to Jan Erlone, whose name suggests that he, too, is alone. It may be that aesthetically Jan is a cardboard character who displays virtually no sorrow or shock over the murder and mutilation of Mary Dalton, his sweetheart. It may be that he shows a superhuman capacity for forgiving the man who violated his loved one. We see from Bigger's point of view, and all Bigger sees is that Jan, too, has suffered, which qualifies him to become the first real communicant with Bigger's new world. The solidarity between them, established with such difficulty and over such tragedy, emerges when, as Bakish has noted, Bigger drops the "Mr." and uses the familiar "Jan." It is consolidated when Bigger says "goodbye" to Mr. Max, but asks Max to say "hello" to Jan. The climax of Bigger's life comes not when someone leads or pushes him into unity with others, but when he achieves the consciousness that permits him to forge his own bonds, and this possibility becomes a more powerful stimulant than violence.

Bigger's sudden grasp of what Jan means to him is strictly personal, and it suggests one of the main conclusions to be drawn from the novel. Personal sympathy is the basis of human community, not impersonal organizations. Violence, personal or organizational, destroys the bonds between people. But in *Native Son,* Wright shows a world in which people are placed in situations in which they have to kill if, paradoxically, they are to remain human. Given the nature of the human being—his thirst for understanding, for personal worth, for identity, for sensation—and the kind of world he lives in, killing becomes nearly inevitable. To say this is not necessarily to agree with Wright's view of the world or to accept it as a law of human life. Yet one suspects that no other view could have come out of Wright's own experience in America or the knowledge he had of the contemporary world. The pathos lies in his willingness to face the truth as he saw it, even while he craved the gentler way. He holds the pessimism of a man who sees no appeal from the conditions of the given world, and the hope of one who believes in the power of the self to take up ties with others, or at least dream of it. Bigger Thomas, in his own way, comes to a deep certainty of human limitations and a vivid sense of what might have been.

When we emerge from the violent world of *Native Son,* we have a sense of having traveled through the emotional climate of the 1930s, and not just the American racial climate, either. Wright, with his remarkable but undisciplined mind, tries to understand that climate. He is influenced by a tangled variety of ideas, which are not always smoothly or compatibly meshed. At the center of the 1930s milieu is an act of violence, which we come to understand in the several terms that Wright learned to think and feel in. The three taken up here do not exhaust the possibilities. But they display the rich intellectual and emotional density of the novel. *Native Son* evokes not so much the images of the era, or its sights and sounds, as the submerged stresses in the lives of real people and the historical events that carry them toward their uncertain futures.

Composing Bigger:
Wright and the Making of *Native Son*

Joseph T. Skerrett, Jr.

More is going on in *Native Son* than a merely intellectual synthesis of literary naturalism and Marxist political economy. In an early review Malcolm Cowley sensed a widening of Wright's sympathies since the stories of *Uncle Tom's Children*, "a collection of stories all but one of which had the same pattern: a Negro was goaded into killing one or more white men and was killed in turn, without feeling regret for himself or his victims." Admiring the stories, Cowley thought them "painful to read," for he felt that in them Wright's indignation was expressing itself in the revenge of "a whole series of symbolic murders." "In *Native Son* the pattern is the same, but the author's sympathies have broadened and his resentment, though quite as deep, is less painful and personal." This suggestion that the intellectualization of the violent relationships portrayed in the short stories was doing something *for* Wright as well as for the reader is bolstered by Saunders Redding's insistence that Wright himself was behind Bigger Thomas's inarticulateness. Redding broadly asserted that "in a way that is more direct than is true of most important modern authors of fiction, Wright's heroes were in naked honesty himself, and not imaginary creations that served to express his complicated personality." Stanley Edgar Hyman accounted for the great power of *Native Son* by concluding that in the novel

> the tensions and guilts connected with sexuality, openly and deliberately manipulated in the fiction, fled into the color imagery, and gave it a sexual resonance and ambiguity not consciously contrived, which powerfully reflected the social undercurrents of American life.

Despite these strong indications of alternative directions of inquiry, critics have been reluctant to release the by now comfortable grasp they have on the "protest fiction" aspect of *Native Son*. It has, I think, blinded them to the meaning of *Native Son* as the culmination of Wright's first phase as a writer. *Native Son* is not only Wright's most ambitious and most achieved work of art, but it is also the work in which he most completely—whether or not "openly and deliberately" as Hyman says—related the materials of his personal biography to his intellectual and aes-

Reprinted from *Richard Wright's* Native Son, ed. Harold Bloom (New York: Chelsea House, 1988), pp. 125–142. By permission of Joseph T. Skerrett, Jr.

thetic activities. In the working out of *Native Son* Wright objectified, in symbolic terms, the conflicts and passions arising out of his life up to that time. *Native Son* is rooted in the fertile soil of his personal psychosocial and psychosexual "situation," to use Kenneth Burke's term.

II

Wright began to work on the story before leaving Chicago for New York in the spring of 1939; one of his Chicago acquaintances at that time later told Michel Fabre that he could remember having seen a draft of early parts of the story shortly before Wright left for New York. In Chicago Wright had been living with his family—his ailing mother, his brother, and grandmother Wilson, who had joined them during the summer of 1934. If the emotional record of *Black Boy* is to be trusted, as I think it may, Wright must have felt the continual pressure of aggression and guilt and responsibility. Age had not tempered his grandmother's religious zeal and narrow-mindedness, and Wright's mother, though supportive, "was still partially paralyzed after a recent attack of encephalitis." Neither can have approved of whatever hint they got of Richard's involvement with the Communists. Wright respected his mother, Fabre says, "Because of her indisputable moral authority, [but] her devoutness irritated him more and more, along with her resigned attitude toward social injustice and hatred of communism." His dependent and seemingly indolent brother Leon did not contribute to the support of the family; "Wright spent increasingly less time at home in order to avoid friction between them." The intrafamiliar tensions so vividly described in *Black Boy* continued to exert pressure on Wright's life, even as, through his contact with the Communists, he was discovering a community which valued his rebellious attitudes. Wright's imaginative response to this complex "situation" was an equally complex one, for at the same time, at various stages of development, in 1934, 1935, and 1936 he was at work on the "objective" description of Jake Jackson's day in *Lawd Today*, the "ameliorative" and integrationist stories of *Uncle Tom's Children*; and the "revolutionary" attitudes of Bigger Thomas.

In "How 'Bigger' Was Born" Wright indicates that he sat down to his typewriter sometime in 1934 with the meaning and characterization of Bigger all "thought out." Whether this is true or not, the cathartic event in the process of committing Bigger to paper was Wright's new job at the South Side Youth Club. Here he was able to observe the rebellious urbanized and alienated black youths of whom Bigger is a composite and symbolic projection. But more importantly, at the Youth Club Wright began to identify with the passions of the delinquents and, as Fabre remarks, "for once, to give free reign to his own antisocial feelings." He felt that the job had thrust him into "a kind of dressed-up police work" and he hated the work of distracting these potential rebels with "ping-pong, checkers, swimming, marbles and baseball in order that [they] might not roam the streets and harm the

valuable white property which adjoined the Black Belt." Privately Wright identified with the damage and disturbance the boys caused when they left his club-
house in the afternoons, for it was a meaningful demonstration that "life is
stronger than ping-pong." This identification with the criminal rebellion of his
youthful charges enabled him to tolerate the work: "that was the only way I could
contain myself for doing a job I hated; for a moment I'd allow myself, vicariously,
to feel as Bigger felt—not much, just a little, just a *little*—but still, there it was"
("How 'Bigger' Was Born").

In giving rein to even this littlest amount of fellow-feeling with the boys and
with his own imaginative re-creation of them, Wright brought himself face to
face with his own inner tension about literary expression. He thought of literature as an essentially criminal activity, which had to be carried out under the
shadow of what he calls in "How 'Bigger' Was Born" a "mental censor—product
of the fears which a Negro feels from living in America." The fear of disapproval
from white audiences and black leaders, though he considers them in separate
categories, are really one and the same: fear of reprisal for the act of aggression
he knew the book to be. The writing of the novel became entangled with
Wright's deepest aggressive drives. His dissatisfaction with the response to
Uncle Tom's Children supports this contention, for he found that it inspired
more pity than terror.

> I found that I had written a book which even bankers' daughters could read and weep
> over and feel good about. I swore to myself that if I ever wrote another book, no one
> would weep over it; that it would be so hard and deep that they would have to face it
> without the consolation of tears.
>
> ("How 'Bigger' Was Born")

This feeling that the stories had failed was not a reflection of disapproval from
Wright's Communist friends: their approval had been unstinting. The disapproval arose from within: the stories did not do for Wright what he wanted from
them. So it was shortly after the completion of *Uncle Tom's Children* that Bigger
Thomas, spawned in Wright's memories of "bad" black boys in his Mississippi
home and developed in his observation of other boys in the Chicago slums,
made contact with Wright's deepest personal fears and obsessions and took possession of his imagination: the writing of the novel became a struggle of exor-
cism from the forces, both black and white, that attempted to censor Wright's
feeling of it.

> The more I thought of it the more I became convinced that if I did not write of Bigger
> as I saw and felt him, if I did not try to make him a living personality and at the same
> time a symbol of all the larger things I felt and saw in him, I'd be reacting as Bigger him-
> self reacted: that is, I'd be acting out of *fear* if I let what I thought whites would say con-
> strict and paralyze me.
>
> As I contemplated Bigger and what he meant, I said to myself: "I must write this
> novel, not only for others to read, but to free *myself* of this sense of shame and fear." In
> fact the novel, as time passed, grew upon me to the extent that it became a necessity to

write it; the writing of it turned into a way of living for me.

("How 'Bigger' Was Born")

III

Bigger Thomas's situation in the novel is an imaginative replication of Wright's own "situation." Trapped by the economics of the Depression and the resultant intensification of racial prejudice and discrimination, Bigger feels resentment against the demands of his family—his religious mother, his sister Vera, and his younger brother, Buddy—whose needs require that he submit to the near-slavery of the employment offered by the welfare relief program. Bigger struggles against the family strategies to control his actions without access to the violence that is characteristic of his behavior later in the story. His central counter-strategy is to numb himself to the family feeling within:

> He shut their voices out of his mind. He hated his family because he knew that they were suffering and that he was powerless to help them. He knew that the moment he allowed himself to feel to its fullness how they lived, the shame and misery of their lives, he would be swept out of himself with fear and despair. So he held toward them an attitude of iron reserve; he lived with them, but behind a wall, a curtain.
>
> (Native Son)

This denial is, of course, not without its cost. Bigger must repress his own impulses even more stringently. "He knew that the moment he allowed what his life meant to enter fully into his consciousness, he would either kill himself or someone else. So he denied himself and acted tough."

Like Jake in *Lawd Today*, Bigger hesitates to follow his occasional thoughts of rebellion. Each time he asks himself the question What can I do? "his mind hit[s] a blank wall and he [stops] thinking." Jake takes out his frustration and anger on his wife Lil, whom he blames for his troubles; Bigger is in many ways psychologically more sensitive. He has displaced his sensitivity and potential tenderness within the family circle in order to protect his ego from pain. Curiously, unlike Jake, Bigger has no symbolic outlet for his aggressive feeling, as Jake does in the elaborate verbal play of "the dozens" in which he engages his street buddy. Bigger's passion is too close to the surface, perhaps, to be assuaged by such verbal objectification. The engagement that excites him is the engagement with the whites, who have so suffocatingly circumscribed his life. Having revived the plan to rob Blum's Delicatessen, Bigger feels released from the numbed and half-dead existence that is normality to him.

> All that morning he had lurked behind his curtain of indifference and looked at things, snapping and glaring at whatever had tried to make him come out into the open. But now he was out; the thought of the job at Blum's and the tilt he had had with Gus had snarled him into things and his self-trust was gone. Confidence could only come again now through action so violent that it would make him forget.

The fear of the whites threatens Bigger's sense of manly self-control. Amongst the gang it is that fear which creates a brutal community. Bigger humiliates Gus, forcing him to lick the tip of Bigger's knife, in order to prevent the gang from carrying out the planned armed robbery of Blum's. He knew that "the fear of robbing a white man had had a hold of him when he started the fight with Gus." But, as this is a knowledge too costly to be admitted, Bigger's psyche represses it. "He knew it in a way that kept it from coming to his mind in the form of a hard and sharp idea. . . . But he kept this knowledge of his thrust firmly down in him: his courage to live depended upon how successfully his fear was hidden from his consciousness."

This attitude on Bigger's part, this holding his own consciousness at arm's length, is perhaps Wright's most original achievement in his characterization of Bigger. Unlike his creator, Bigger has, as his story opens, almost no access to his own symbolic imagination, his own creative consciousness. His almost formalized imaginative act is the role-playing game he engages Gus in—"playing white." The roles—general, banker, President—are satiric (and thus aggressive) but they are quickly abandoned when their nasty double edge is felt: the absurd pomposity and venality of the powerful whites control the boys' imaginations even in parody. Bigger has never experienced the fulfillment Wright got from the act of writing, that Jamesian sense of an invigorating self-integration and self-satisfaction that is the hallmark of a stable identity. In Francis Fergusson's terminology, the central "action" of the novel, dictated by Bigger's "purpose" in this story, is "to discover an identity." The search for the murderer that occupies the Daltons, the police, and the reporters, the search for motives and evidence by the attorneys, the search for a mode of acquittal by Max are all counterpointed with Bigger's increasingly conscious search for an integrated and satisfying consciousness of who he is.

This important aspect of Wright's exclusive use of Bigger's point of view has been at the center of the critical contention surrounding the novel's achievement. Some, like John Bayliss, see Bigger as merely pathetic in his struggles with consciousness, slow-witted and environmentally unsuited for urban society. More astute critics characteristically lose track of the fact that it is Bigger's point of view we are dealing with, and begin to attribute what Fergusson would call "the movement of the spirit" in the novel entirely to the author's, and not the character's, psyche. Thus Robert Bone notes that Wright succeeds in balancing the "stark horror" of the story with the "spiritual anguish" promised in the novel's epigraph from the Book of Job—"Even today is my complaint rebellious; my stroke is heavier than my groaning"—but he finally sees this anguish in terms of Wright rather than Bigger:

> This note of anguish, which emphasizes Bigger's suffering, is so intense as to be almost physical in character. It is sustained by a style which can only be called visceral. The author writes from his guts, describing the emotional state of his characters in graphic psychosomatic terms. It is a characteristic device which has its source in Wright's aching memory of the deep south.
>
> (*The Negro Novel in America*)

The observation, as this essay attempts to demonstrate, is essentially true. But it is no less true that the critic here—and later in his essay as well—refuses to deal with the nature of Bigger's individuality as it comes to grips with itself. He winds up summing the novel's themes thus: "Bigger is a human being whose environment has made him incapable of relating meaningfully to other human beings except through murder." Surely this does not give much room to that "movement of the spirit" which Wright's epigraph from Scripture suggests that we seek. Donald Gibson has addressed himself to this curious obtuseness of critics who fail to deal with the totality of the character, charging them with sociocultural blindness: "most critics of Wright's novel see only the outer covering of Bigger Thomas, the blackness of his skin and his resulting social role. Few have seen him as a discrete entity, a particular person, who struggles with the burden of his humanity."

Considered as more than a representative figure or pawn in a sociological murder-melodrama, Bigger's story extends from the brilliantly epitomic opening domestic scene to his dismissal of Max on the last page of the narrative, and not, as many of Gibson's "blind" readers would have it, from Mary Dalton's murder to Boris Max's defense. Bigger's purpose, the action which this novel imitates, is the search for identity, an identity denied him by both his social milieu and his family situation. Bigger seeks a world in which he is not an alienated being, a world in which he can be "at home." Bigger's severe alienation from his human environments is matched by a sensual awareness (expressed in what Bone calls Wright's "visceral" prose style) which develops a nearly philosophical intensity. Thus, Wright manages to replicate, through the experience of Bigger, his own experience in coming to terms with his imagination as the "at home" identity that would save him from the familial and social threat that surrounded him. In Bigger's case it is not a mediated and formalized form of aggression that is the instrument of liberation, but rather the unmediated, literal, and violent murders of Mary Dalton and Bessie Mears.

Given the conflict that characterized Wright's relationship with his family womenfolk, it is, of course, highly significant that both of Bigger's victims are women. It is perhaps a more significant fact that one is white, the other black. In Wright's short stories the black men were victims and the women either bystanders and supporters or burdens and betrayers. The image of black woman as heroine and Communist in "Bright and Morning Star" was an afterthought, an anomaly. In *Native Son*, with its central image of the black man in rebellion against the victimizing strictures and constraints that retard his development, the targets of the attack are women.

Now Wright's difficulties with women were not, of course, limited to childhood traumas and adolescent misunderstandings of motive. He gave the name "Mary Dalton" to Bigger's first victim at least in part because it was the "nom de guerre" of a Communist Party member in Chicago whom Wright disliked intensely. More importantly, at the time he was writing *Native Son*, Wright's sexual relationships with women had begun to reflect and fulfill the patterns that had been established in his new home life.

After moving to New York in 1937, Wright lived for a time with the Sawyers, a modest black family, on 143rd Street in Harlem. Wright became sexually involved with the daughter of the household, Marian Sawyer, and their engagement was announced in the spring of 1938. Early in May, Wright rushed into the apartment of his friends, the Newtons, "announcing that according to the prenuptial physical examination Marian had an advanced case of syphilis." Feeling "outraged that he had been deceived and relieved that he had escaped from such a grave danger," Wright immediately broke with the Sawyers and moved into the Newtons' new apartment in Brooklyn (Michel Fabre, *The Unfinished Quest of Richard Wright*).

Jane Newton quickly became a significant literary confidante; Wright read to her from his manuscript and respected her suggestions for changes. Before completing the novel (in early June of 1939), he had seriously courted two more women, both white. When Ellen Poplar hesitated to commit herself to a marriage within a month or so, Wright married Dhima Rose Meadman "at the beginning of August 1939, in the sacristy of the Episcopal Church on [Convent] Avenue, with Ralph Ellison as best man" (Fabre).

In the Marian Sawyer affair Wright can only have felt betrayed and nearly trapped by the sexual connection. Her illness, "advanced" or not, could only serve—as his mother's illness, so recently escaped—to limit or divert him. The whole business revived in him the sense of threat posed by women, a sense of threat deeply ingrained in him at home. A marriage, contracted in large part, it seems (judging by the precipitous and absolute rupture between the couple), on Wright's conventional sense of guilt and responsibility for the illicit sexual contact, is avoided when the woman is proven a "betrayer," threatening Wright with disease, disgrace, and/or the misery and limitation of continued guilt-ridden nursing duties. In the marriage, Wright seems to have been reacting rather than acting. The evidence suggests that while Dhima Rose Meadman was attractive to Wright, his strongest reason for marrying her was the apparent rejection of his proposal by Ellen Poplar. After an unhappy season in Mexico, Wright and Dhima separated and divorced. Fabre indicates that Wright "had never stopped blaming himself for his impatience and injustice" toward Ellen, and when they met at the Newtons' late in 1940 their union was quickly sealed. Benefit of clergy was bestowed in March 1941, after which the Wrights moved out of the Newtons' apartment and set up housekeeping on their own. Ellen Poplar's hesitation was a challenge to Wright's ego; the marriage to Dhima was his response, a demonstration of his independence and self-sufficiency, his worthiness and adequacy.

Wright felt a strong resentment of his need for sexual and human companionship from women. After the publication of *Native Son*, he engaged in an experiment with Frederic Wertham, a psychoanalyst, to discover whether there were any direct associations of Bigger's murder of Mary in Wright's background. Wertham and Wright probed for some connections between Wright's experience in white households in the South during his youth and the key scene of Bigger's smothering Mary in the presence of her blind mother. Wright began to recall working for a young couple who lived with the wife's mother when he was about fifteen years old. The woman was very friendly to Wright, "and he felt this was a second home to him." He tended the fireplace, lighting the day's heat on winter mornings. One morning he opened a door in the course of these duties to discover the young woman partly dressed; he was reprimanded and told to knock.

As a careful reading of *Black Boy* makes clear, in Wright's life the ego ideal derived from the mother and not the father. And Wertham notes that "the very symbol of the seeing eye that is blind fits the mother image." By extension, of course, all the blind, questing authorities in *Native Son*, who seek to punish Bigger for his transgressions against the two women, are derived from Wright's own mother. In the experience explored with Wertham, the patterns of response to female authority, sexuality, and affection which had been set at home, made themselves manifest in a situation that was also socially charged with threat: even at fifteen, Wright knew the danger of being accused of sexual improprieties with a white woman.

In the novel, the "outering" of these conflict patterns in the life of Bigger Thomas is more complex, I believe, than Wertham and Wright's little experiment demonstrated. For in considering the total action of *Native Son*—the psychic motive out of which the events are generated—as Bigger's effort "to discover an identity," the killing of white Mary Dalton, half-accidental and unconscious as it is, is secondary to the purposeful and free act of killing black Bessie Mears.

Mary Dalton's death is Dreiserian, determined by Bigger's social conditioning and the terrible pressure of the moment. Mary's clumsy efforts at social egalitarianism and Marxist comraderie with her father's new chauffeur make only for confusion in Bigger's mind. He recoils from their attempts at intimacy, for it sharpens his shame and hatred of his status.

> He felt he had no physical existence at all right then: he was something he hated, the badge of shame which he knew was attached to a black skin. It was a shadowy region, a No Man's Land, the ground that separated the white world from the black that he stood upon. He felt naked, transparent; he felt that this white man (Jan Erlone), having helped to put him down, having helped to deform him, held him up now to look at him and be amused. At that moment he felt toward Mary and Jan a dumb, cold, and inarticulate hate.

Bigger feels vividly his condition of being "cut dead" by his social environment; Jan's and Mary's efforts at being friendly only exacerbate and intensify Bigger's sense of shame, fear, and hatred. The unreal, dreamlike quality of the murder scene later, comes into the tone of the novel here, with Bigger's uncomfortable journey across the city in the car, squeezed between Jan and Mary, who are completely blind to his terror. After the killing, Bigger realizes the absurdity: "It all seemed foolish! He wanted to laugh. It was unreal. He had to lift a dead woman and he was afraid. He felt that he had been dreaming of something like this for a long time, and then, suddenly, it was true."

Killing Mary is thus clearly, for Bigger, a release of long pent-up aggressive tendencies that are both sexual and social. The act opens Bigger to a flood of realizations that he had managed all his life to repress with a half-conscious resistance. His vision cleared by his irreversible act, Bigger comes to grasp the essential blindness of both black and familial authority and white social authority. Having already grasped blind Mrs. Dalton's similarity to his mother and responded to it in kind, Bigger now sees that his own mother moves like a blind person, "touching objects with her fingers as she passed them, using them for support."

Bigger is elated by this perception of the essential blindness of all those who would censor and punish him for the as yet undiscovered murder. "His being black and at the bottom of the world was something which he could take with a new born strength. What his knife and gun had once meant to him, his knowledge of having secretly murdered Mary now meant." But this sense of power does not satisfy him. Bigger finds that he wants to tell the world what he has done:

> He wanted the keen thrill of startling them. . . . He wished that he could be an image in their minds; that his black face and the image of his smothering Mary and cutting off her head and burning her could hover before their eyes as a terrible picture of reality which they could see and feel and yet not destroy.

Bigger's sense of his act of murder as a creative expression, as an act which confers on him a meaningful identity in his own eyes, is incomplete, even though "the knowledge that he had killed a white girl they loved and regarded as their symbol of beauty made him feel the equal of them, like a man who had been somehow cheated, but had now evened the score." Something more is required. Full psychic liberation can come to Bigger only when the image of his self reflected back at him by others coincides with his own image of his self. Although the knowledge of having murdered Mary Dalton replaces in his mind the sense of security that carrying a knife and a gun had given him,

> he was not satisfied with the way things stood now; he was a man who had come in sight of a goal, then had won it, and in winning it had seen just within his grasp another goal, higher, greater. He had learned to shout and had shouted and no ear had heard him; he had just learned to walk and was walking but could not see the ground beneath his feet; and had long been yearning for weapons to hold in his hands and suddenly found that his hands held weapons that were invisible.

Charles James has pointed out that Bigger's girl, Bessie, "is the ear he needs to sound out the meaning of Mary's death. Through her, Bigger can gain some insight into his family's judgement of his act, without actually telling them." For Bessie is an oasis of motherly comfort in Bigger's world. Wright presents her and their essentially physical relationship in pastoral terms infused with stock female symbols—the "fallow field" and "the warm night sea" and the cooling and cleansing "fountain" whose "warm waters" cleared Bigger's senses "to end the tiredness and to reforge in him a new sense of time and space." This passive, maternal, all-accepting and sensually refreshing aspect of his mistress contrasts strongly in Bigger's mind with "the other Bessie," the questioning and censoring aspect of her which arouses in Bigger a desire "to clench his fist and swing his arm and blot out, kill, sweep away" all her resistance to his will and ideas.

Bessie's failure to understand and endorse the meaning Bigger has found in killing Mary Dalton dooms her. When Bigger tells her what he has done, she is terrified that she will be implicated. Her near-hysterical outburst of weak fatalism contains an explicit rejection of Bigger's very being—"I wish to God I never seen you. I wish one of us had died before we was born"—and makes Bigger realize that she can neither accompany him on his flight, nor be left behind to betray him. Bessie has proven herself to be like his mother: weak, limited, blind. "He hated his mother for that way of hers that was like Bessie's. What his mother had was Bessie's whiskey, and Bessie's whiskey was his mother's religion." Bigger begins to conceive of killing Bessie as a free act, "as a man seeing what he must do to save himself and feeling resolved to do it."

Killing Bessie, Bigger comes closer than in killing Mary to direct expression of Richard Wright's own primary inner conflict, the desire to strike out against the women who limited, repressed, censored, and punished his rebellious initiatives. Having killed Bessie with a brick, Bigger feels at last "truly and deeply" free and alive. The killings have given him a sense of freedom, and he is now able to make a direct contact with that consciousness he had for so long held at arm's length: "he had killed twice, but in a true sense it was not the first time he had ever killed. He had killed many times before, but only during the last two days had this impulse assumed the form of actual killing." His elation now is larger than the pride and sense of power he derived from killing Mary. This time, with this murder, he is brought to the brink of a philosophical consideration of his identity. As Charles James provocatively puts it, having "symbolically 'wiped out' the progenitive elements of the two things he hates most [the white societal oppressor and the black, submissive oppressed]," Bigger is free to begin thinking as an existentially liberated person:

> But what was he after? What did he want? What did he love and what did he hate? He did not know. There was something he *knew* and something he *felt*; something the *world* gave him and something he *himself* had; something spread out in *front* of him and something spread out in *back*; and never in all his life, with this black skin of his, had the two worlds, thought and feeling, will and mind, aspiration and satisfaction, been together; never had he felt a sense of wholeness.

Killing Bessie Mears puts Bigger in the position of a questor, consciously searching for an identity—"a sense of wholeness"—that will enable him to "be at home" in his society, "to be a part of the world, to lose himself in it so he could find himself, to be allowed a chance to live like others, even though he was black." From this point forward no other action has greater meaning. After the newspaper headlines announce "AUTHORITIES HINT SEX CRIMES," Bigger feels alienation settle down around him again: "Those words excluded him utterly from the world." He knows now that the meaning of his acts will be denied by the

whites in their blind fury to capture and kill him. The accusation of sexual violation denies the individuality of his action, "cuts him dead" again. He knows that
white society will refuse to see and confirm his new sense of identity, his real self,
which he created by murdering Mary and Bessie, the dual images of his psychosocial oppression. Murdering Bessie, Charles James argues, "is Bigger's acknowl-
edgement of his own impending death. He knows he must be caught, so from
that moment his energy is devoted to salvaging 'spiritual victory.' "

The ambiguity of Mary Dalton's death required, for Wright's satisfaction, an
unambiguous and legitimate murder, for which Bigger can confess and be punished. Lest he again create a story that bankers' daughters might tearfully enjoy,
he wedded the American, Dreiserian naturalist tradition and the Russian,
Dostoevskian existential tradition to make Bigger's passion for murder as broadly
meaningful as possible. Against the resistance of his friend Jane Newton to his
plan for killing off Bessie, Wright was adamant: "But I have to get rid of her. She
must die!" he insisted (Fabre). Killing Bessie was thus an act of self-liberation for
Wright as well as for Bigger. At the very least,

> Bigger's murder of Bessie marked a new stage in Wright's literary evolution: every-
> thing that he had learned from his naturalist models up to this point had prevented
> him from allowing his characters to give in to these demonic temptations, but now
> Bigger claimed his right to "create" in the existentialist meaning of the word, by reject-
> ing the accidental nature of his first murder with this further proof of his power to
> destroy.
>
> (Michel Fabre, *The Unfinished Quest of Richard Wright*)

But more than this, I think, can be ventured. Wright's conception of Bigger as
existential killer, forging out of the violence in his psyche a desperate and necessary identity, served also to manifest what Daniel Aaron calls "his hidden and perhaps repressed opposition to the Party." Wright's intense concern with Bigger's
psychological motives and existential plight were not the flowerings of his Marxist
perspective. Wright, as Aaron suggests, was leading a sort of intellectual double
life:

> One side of him—the Black Marxist, very likely a true believer in the Party's fight
> against its enemies at home and abroad—contributed useful articles and poems and sto-
> ries to the Party press. The other and private side tried to explain and define the mean-
> ing of being Black in white America, tried to discover his own identity and in effect, to
> create himself.

Wright's "private" perspective fostered his insistence on the personal, psychological dimensions of the black experience, and brought him, inevitably, into conflict
with the essentially pamphleteering approach of the American Communists.

In a letter to Mike Gold, written shortly after Gold's defense of *Native Son* in
the *Daily Worker* of April 29, 1940, Wright attacked the simplistic agitprop and
proletarian-heroes-vs.-capitalist-villains mentality of many in the Party:

> An assumption which says that a Communist writer must follow well established lines
> of perception and feeling, must deal with that which is readily recognizable and typical,

must depict reality only in terms of how it looks from a common and collective plane of reality . . . might seem sound. But I think those who put forward this reasoning forget the international framework in which we live and struggle today. . . . Are we Communist writers to be confined merely to the political and economic spheres of reality and leave the dark and hidden places of the human personality to the Hitlers and the Goebbels? I refuse to believe such. . . . Not to plunge into the complex jungle of human relationships and analyze them is to leave the field to the fascists and I won't and can't do that.

This vehement dissent from Party tradition, if not doctrine, was the beginning of Wright's dissociation from the Communists. He had found a supportive community amongst them, and through that community had found friends and a wife. But now the Party too had become a limiting and censoring authority in his life. His Communist readers were puzzled and displeased with his creation, Bigger Thomas. In the same letter to Gold, Fabre reports, "Wright complained that Bigger's humanity, so obvious to him, meant so little to them, and that Ben David [a prominent and powerful black Communist] thought Max should have pleaded 'not guilty.' "

Part of the fault is Wright's, for his long interpolation of Max's sociological appeal, while it puts across a necessary ideological interpretation of Bigger's situation, nevertheless serves to distract the reader's attention from Bigger's strategies for dealing with his final days. Kenneth Burke has attempted to justify Wright's handling of Max by arguing that the lawyer's long address is a "conceptual epitome" of the novel's emotional themes, "a culmination of the book in the sense that an essayist's last chapter might recapitulate in brief the argument of his whole book." In Burke's view, Wright, "after the symbolic committing of the offences through his imaginative identification with Bigger, had thus ritualistically 'transcended' the offences. . . . His role as Marxist critic transcended his role as Negro novelist." As indebted as I am to Burke in general, I must disagree with him in this particular. Book 3 of *Native Son* is not a capstone, some neatly trimmed and tailored conclusion of a case study, but rather an open-ended or suspended argument in which Wright is refusing to allow Bigger's individuality to be swallowed up or subsumed by Max's social analyses.

When Bigger's crime career ends, and he is captured and brought bumpily down to earth, dragged by his ankles into the cold, white, enshrouding snow, he is forced to set aside the sense of power that the murders had given him. The motive which has impelled his behavior throughout, however—his drive to find a viable sense of identity—is not cast aside. It is in fact now his only concern. In the face of his impending death he must come to terms with his life, find some way to accept it, if he is to be "at home" in the world before he leaves it forever. The release of his repressive tension in the acts of murder was not useless; as in a dream, Bigger's expression of his internalized, repressed aggression makes subconscious data available to his conscious mind. As Bigger considers his end, then, the complex social considerations of Max's argument do not figure in his thought. Max's elaborate analogies and metaphors are lost on Bigger. The materials of Bigger's final meditations are his own perceptions of the world around him, freed from stereotype and threat by his murderous acts. The structure of book 3 is provided by Bigger's efforts to realize out of these materials a vision of social relatedness, a sense of his being and belonging in the world. He asks:

> If he reached out his hands, and if his hands were electric wires, and if his heart were a battery giving life and fire to those hands, and if he reached out with his hands and touched other people, if he did that, would there be a reply, a shock?

And in seeking an answer Bigger rejects the alternatives his life had presented to him. As Robert Bone notes, "He rejects his family ('Go home, Ma.'); his fellow prisoners ('Are you the guy who pulled the Dalton job?'); the race leaders ('They almost like white folks when it comes to guys like me.') and religion." His spiritual victory, if he is to have one, must come from within, be composed entirely of the stuff of the self. "He was balanced on a hairline now, but there was no one to push him forward or backward, no one to make him feel that he had any value or worth—no one but himself."

Bigger comes through to a sense of identification with a human community at the very conclusion of his life and story. In his last conversation with Max, Bigger is calm and composed. Max has come "to offer compassion when Bigger seeks meaning," but "Bigger takes control of that final interview and 'comforts' Max" (Charles L. James). Max tries to give Bigger hope in a future collective human salvation, a Marxist vision of men reclaiming the world from their bosses. Bigger takes from what Max says confirmation of his new inner feeling, newly arrived at, that "at bottom all men lived as he had lived and felt as he had felt." Max tells him "the job in getting people to fight and have faith is in making them believe in what life has made them feel, making them feel that their feelings are as good as those of others." The feelings that Bigger accepts in himself are not, as so many critics have asserted, those of fear, shame, and hatred. But, Paul Siegel has recently noted, "it is hard to make men hear who will not listen. Seven times in the last page and a half of the novel Bigger cries out to Max, 'I'm all right,' the last time adding, 'For real, I am.' " Bigger is all right because, as he tries to tell Max, when he thinks about what Max has said he feels that he was right for wanting what he wanted—a sense of human integration, wholeness, identity.

> "They wouldn't let me live and I killed. Maybe it ain't fair to kill, and I reckon I really didn't want to kill. But when I think of why all the killing was, I begin to feel what I wanted, what I am. . . . I didn't want to kill! . . . But what I killed for, I *am*! It must've been pretty deep in me to make me kill! . . . What I killed for must've been good. . . . I didn't know I was really alive in this world until I felt things hard enough to kill for 'em."

Now Siegel is too busy defending Max to take note of the fact that Bigger is not defending his hate and shame but rather the motive that lay behind all the actions of his short life—the unsatisfied drive to reject the negative identity that the cultural stereotypes had forced on him and to discover an adequate, integral replacement. Max, for all his good will, has never really seen Bigger's individual humanity. As Donald Gibson notes, he "cannot accept the implications of Bigger's conclusions, nor indeed, can he fully understand the position that Bigger has finally arrived at." As he departs Max gropes for his hat, "like a blind man." At the last Bigger speaks as a free man and equal human being not to Max, who can not, finally, look him in the eye, but to Jan. Jan has paid his dues, suffered, and learned to see Bigger as a human being.

IV

At least implicitly, then, *Native Son* denies the notion of human salvation and integration through the medium of social process, even radical social process. Max, as spokesman for the political and social left, is unable either to give Bigger a satisfying ideological social vision or to measure the angle of vision from which Bigger views the world. Wright's separation from the Communist view of reality is foreshadowed here in the image of failed contact between Max and Bigger. If in Bigger's murderous rage Wright was elaborating personal as well as intellectual and social aggression, then in Bigger's rejection of Max's view of reality as inadequate Wright was repudiating the masked authority of the Party. Deep down, Wright felt a continuing and unbridgeable alienation from family and society, from religion, custom, and community. The Party had, for a time, given him the support he needed to articulate, albeit in symbolic terms, the elements of his situation. The symbolic outering of inner conflicts that reached back into personal and familial history reduced the pressure within and enabled him to marry and to carry on a career, but it also made clearer to him the essential loneliness incumbent on any person who, for whatever reason, must create a sense of values for himself.

The Dissociated Sensibility of
Bigger Thomas in Wright's *Native Son*

Louis Tremaine

Native Son is offensive to most readers of taste. Even critics sympathetic to Richard Wright's 1940 novel have generally stressed its historical and sociological importance while deploring many of its "literary failings."[1] And the offense has nothing to do with the "post-modernist" violence that has been done to fiction (or to the reader's expectations of it). Wright's book, rather, is an assault "from below." Its characters (apart from Bigger Thomas) are painfully transparent stereotypes; the plot is uniformly extravagant and improbable; the narrative perspective awkwardly straddles a gulf between the consciousness of an uneducated and unreflective protagonist and a third-person narrator who often conveys his character's motivation in the abstract jargon of a social scientist. In the last ten years, a flurry of studies have appeared defending (successfully for the most part) the composition of the final section of the novel with its lengthy, "propagandistic" courtroom oration by Bigger's lawyer.[2] But while these studies have restored a certain balance to the critical discussion of the work, they have done so at the cost of a piecemeal approach to the text.

It is time to put *Native Son* together again. What is most characteristic of the text, from first to last, and which therefore cannot be ignored, is precisely that which "offends" the reader's expectations of it as a serious work of fiction. By looking at, rather than away from, Wright's handling of character, plot, and narration, one discovers that these elements point directly to a dissociated sensibility

Reprinted from *Studies in American Fiction* 14 (1986): 63–76. By permission of *Studies in American Fiction*.

[1]Initial reviews of *Native Son* are collected in *Richard Wright: The Critical Reception*, ed. John M. Reilly (New York: Burt Franklin and Co., 1978). Of particular interest in the present context are those by Howard Mumford Jones, Peter Munro Jack, Margaret Marshall, and Burton Rascoe. Subsequent critical studies relevant to this point in the discussion include Robert Bone, *The Negro Novel in America* (New Haven: Yale Univ. Press, 1958); Irving Howe, "Black Boys and Native Sons" (1963), rpt. in *Critical Essays on Richard Wright*, ed. Yoshinobu Hakutani (Boston: G. K. Hall and Co., 1982), pp. 39–47; and Russell Carl Brignano, *Richard Wright: An Introduction to the Man and His Works* (Pittsburgh: Univ. of Pittsburgh Press, 1970).

[2]Among the most helpful of these studies are Phyllis R. Klotman, "Moral Distancing as a Rhetorical Technique in *Native Son*: A Note on 'Fate'," *CLAJ* 18 (1974): 284–85; Paul N. Siegel, "The Conclusion of Richard Wright's *Native Son*," *PMLA* 89 (1974): 519; and Jeffrey A. Sadler, "Split Consciousness in Richard Wright's *Native Son*," *SCR* 8, No. 2 (1976): 11–14.

lying at the heart of Bigger Thomas.[3] They are, in fact, the effective means by which the book as a whole functions as a formal projection of Bigger's struggle toward self-expression.

A number of critics have observed already that there exists a "split conscious-ness" in Bigger and have analyzed the various ethical and perceptual conflicts that plague him.[4] What needs further attention in order to understand the kind of dissociation that Bigger suffers, however, is the specific consequences of these conflicts for the character. In *Native Son,* these consequences are described repeatedly and forcefully and constitute a highly consistent pattern. Bigger's essential dilemma is not simply his ethical hesitation between social val-ues and self-interest, not simply his perceptual confusion of concrete reality and abstract symbol, but his inability, in his daily functioning, to express his emo-tional experience in ways that make its meaning accessible both to his own con-sciousness and to the consciousness of those around him. It is this dissociated sensibility, this conflict between experience and expression where there should be complementarity, that makes of Bigger a mass of unsatisfied urges, that cre-ates "the rhythms of his life: indifference and violence,"[5] that defines Bigger's very existence:

> There was something he *knew* and something he *felt*; something the *world* gave him and something he *himself* had; something spread out in *front* of him and something spread out in *back;* and never in all his life, with this black skin of his, had the two worlds, thought and feeling, will and mind, aspiration and satisfaction, been together; never had he felt a sense of wholeness (p. 225).

It is his longing somehow to bring these dissociated parts of himself together and thereby "explain" himself, create a true image of his feelings, that causes him to cling so desperately to life though condemned to certain death:

> He felt that he ought to be able to reach out with his bare hands and carve from naked space the concrete, solid reasons why he had murdered. He felt them that strongly. If he could do that, he would relax; he would sit and wait until they told him to walk to the chair; and he would walk (p. 323).

---

[3]The term "dissociation of sensibility" is, of course, T. S. Eliot's and was first used by him with ref-erence to writers in whom he sensed an emphasis on fine language to the detriment of genuine feel-ing. Eliot's particular judgments of Milton, Dryden, and others, in that instance, have since been often called into question, but the term itself has remained a serviceable one. It will be seen that, in the present case, the terms of the dissociation are reversed, for it is Bigger's intellectual and linguis-tic apparatus that is inadequate to express his very genuine emotional experience.

[4]See, for example, Sadler; Edward Kearns, "The 'Fate' Section of *Native Son,*" *ContL* 12, No. 2 (1971), 146–55; Sheldon Brivic, "Conflict of Values: Richard Wright's *Native Son,*" *Novel* 7 (1974); 231–45; Jerry H. Bryant, "The Violence of *Native Son,*" *SoR* 17, (1981), 303–19; and James Nagel, "Images of 'Vision' in *Native Son*" (1969), rpt. in *Critical Essays on Richard Wright,* ed. Yoshinobu Hakutani (Boston: G. K. Hall and Co., 1982), pp. 151–58.

[5]Richard Wright, *Native Son* (1940; rpt. New York: Harper and Row, 1966), p. 31. This is the Perennial Classic edition which contains Wright's introductory essay "How 'Bigger' Was Born" and the afterword by John Reilly. Subsequent page references will be to this edition.

This hunger for self-expression is due in part to socio-economic conditions that deny Bigger access to conventional modes of communication, to the tools of language and culture systematically reserved for the use of the dominant race and class. This is clear to most readers and is made explicit in Max's courtroom speech (pp. 365–66). But what Wright is most concerned with is the ways in which an individual's experience is distorted by these conditions. It is true that Bigger lacks words, audience, and forum, but the primary reason for his failure of self-expression is his fear of what he has to express, a characteristic and generalized fear that repeatedly blocks any efforts to integrate his own sensibility.

Partially responsible, of course, is a fear of whites, which not only motivates his fight with Gus but prevents him from understanding the nature of that motivation:

> His confused emotions had made him feel instinctively that it would be better to fight Gus than to confront a white man with a gun. But he kept this knowledge of his fear thrust firmly down in him; his courage to live depended upon how successfully his fear was hidden from his consciousness (p. 44).

But the willful suppression of awareness described in this passage operates in many other areas of his life as well and accounts for the imagery of barriers (walls, curtains, veils, and related images) which is so often commented on by critics. The first time such imagery appears is in the context of Bigger's efforts to shield himself from the wretched conditions of his existence and, more importantly, from his fear of *himself* as he faces those conditions:

> He hated his family because he knew that they were suffering and that he was powerless to help them. He knew that the moment he allowed himself to feel to its fullness how they lived, the shame and misery of their lives, he would be swept out of himself with fear and despair. So . . . he lived with them, but behind a wall, a curtain. . . . He knew that the moment he allowed what his life meant to enter fully into his consciousness, he would either kill himself or someone else (pp. 13–14).

A similar failure—or refusal—to delve into his own experience affects the operation of Bigger's consciousness with respect to religion as he knows it, to his marginal legal status, to the threat of betrayal in human relationships, and to other areas of Bigger's fear-ridden life from which he seeks instinctively to protect himself. Such situations are repeatedly presented in language that emphasizes this process of suppression: "Not once . . . had an image of what he had done come into his mind. He had thrust the whole thing back of him . . ." (p. 255); "there appeared before him . . . images which in turn aroused impulses long dormant, impulses that he had suppressed and sought to shunt from his life" (p. 263); "A strong counter-emotion waxed in him, warning him to leave this newly seen and newly felt thing alone" (p. 334). Bigger is thus caught between his deep need to make his own experience manifest to himself and his equally deep fear of doing so.

Bigger, in fact, yearns to make himself understood not only to himself but to those with whom he shares the world. He fears, however, that any attempt to establish such an understanding is futile and will only confirm his sense that he is different—different not only as a black but as Bigger. This longing for connectedness is at times directed toward "his people" (a term he fails to understand when it is spoken to him by the Daltons), "but that dream would fade when he looked at the other black people near him. Even though black like them, he felt there was too much difference between him and them to allow for a common binding and a common life" (p. 109). Later, as he awaits trial and execution, the yearning becomes more generalized:

> . . . And if he reached out with his hands and touched other people, . . . if he did that would there be a reply, a shock? . . . And in that touch, response of recognition, there would be union, identity; there would be a supporting oneness, a wholeness which had been denied him all his life (p. 335).

Such desires, though buried deep, are strong in Bigger and rise up confusingly as a result of his encounters with Mary, Jan, and Max, as well as of the existential crisis he faces as a condemned man.

His need is to communicate, and yet his instinct, an instinct he overcomes only with Max, is to dissemble. This becomes a recurring motif in Bigger's interactions with others throughout the book: he gauges how he is perceived, calculates what is expected of him, and then acts (in both senses of the word) to direct attention away from himself as he is and toward a more desirable image of himself. His fight with Gus, for example, is an effort to hide his fearful and irresolute nature from his poolroom friends and from Doc (p. 43). He puts on a different sort of act for Mr. Dalton:

> He stood with his knees slightly bent, his lips partly open, his shoulders stooped; and his eyes held a look that went only to the surface of things. There was an organic conviction in him that this was the way white folks wanted him to be in their presence . . . (p. 50).

With Peggy, he adjusts his table manners and tries to express the sympathy for the Daltons that he thinks she expects of him (pp. 56–58). He "distrusts" and "hates" Jan and Mary because he cannot read their expectations and act accordingly (p. 71). After the first murder, he is concerned with maintaining a pretense of normalcy with his mother: "He knew at once that he should not have acted frightened"; "He felt that his acting in this manner was a mistake"; "He had spoken in the wrong tone of voice; he had to be careful" (pp. 96–97). With Britten, he stands "with sleepy eyes and parted lips," even while hating him enough to want to kill him (p. 153). There is, in fact, no character in the book whose relations with Bigger are not explicitly conditioned by this need of Bigger's to mask his true feelings. Even with Max, he is initially wary and gradually makes his first ineffectual attempts to express himself to another only in response to a concerted—and professional—effort on Max's part to elicit Bigger's confidence. Max's repeated question "How do you feel, Bigger?" is no mere formulaic greeting.

Bigger yearns to understand his own feelings by expressing them both to himself and to others, but his fear both of himself and of others is an obstacle to such expression. Still, it might be asked whether he would be capable of such expression even if this barrier were removed. Certainly he lacks verbal talent and training. Bigger *is,* however, an image-maker. This particular expressive faculty comes into play at least three times in the novel and in all three cases is released under the impetus of strong sensation. The first two of these occur during the sexual act:

> . . . He floated on a wild tide, rising and sinking with the ebb and flow of her blood, being willingly dragged into a warm night sea to rise renewed to the surface to face a world he hated and wanted to blot out of existence, clinging close to a fountain whose warm waters washed and cleaned his senses . . . (p. 128).

> . . . He galloped a frenzied horse down a steep hill in the face of a resisting wind. . . . And then the wind became so strong that it lifted him high into the dark air, turning him, twisting him, hurling him . . . (pp. 219–20).

The third and most significant instance of extended mental image-making occurs in Bigger's cell, as he is "tired, sleepy, and feverish" but feels a "war raging in him." The narrator is explicit here about Bigger's struggle to integrate his sensibility: "Blind impulses welled up in his body, and his intelligence sought to make them plain to his understanding by supplying images that would explain them" (p. 334). Elaborate images of a "black sprawling prison" and a "strong blinding sun" follow, expressing hate and fear and a longing for wholeness respectively. It is at these rare moments in the book that Bigger is most at one with himself, that his feelings are most fully present to his consciousness.

His need remains, however, to externalize and project these feelings, either through direct communication or through other expressive behavior. A considerable case is made in the novel, and accepted by many critics, for the murder of Mary as Bigger's one successful expressive act. He insists to himself that the crime was no accident, that he "had killed many times before, only on those other times there had been no handy victim or circumstance to make visible or dramatic his will to kill," that in this act the "hidden meaning of his life . . . had spilled out" (p. 101). Even Max, in court, refers to the need of black people for self-expression and then characterizes Bigger's crime as "an act of creation" (p. 366). These remarks concern the killing of Mary in particular, but she and Bessie and the rat in Bigger's apartment are merely the most obvious, not the only, murder victims portrayed in the book. For in his mind, Bigger actively fantasizes killing Gus (p. 40), Mr. Dalton (p. 50), Jan and Mary (p. 70), Peggy (p. 111), Britten (p. 153), Jan again (p. 162), Bessie before her actual murder (p. 168), a reporter (p. 203), a black couple he overhears (p. 239), the men searching for him (pp. 242–43, 250), and all the people at the inquest (p. 307) and at the trial (p. 344). At several points, in fact, he includes himself as a victim in these fantasies: "He knew that the moment he allowed what his life meant to enter fully into his consciousness, he would seize some heavy object . . . and with one final blow blot it [Mary's car] out—with himself and them in it" (p. 70); "He would shoot when they were closer and he would save one bullet for himself" (p. 250); "There sprang up in him again the will to kill. But this time it was not directed outward toward people, but inward upon himself" (p. 255).

That is a lot of killing—but its function is not necessarily expressive. If one examines these killings, both real and imagined, in context one finds that each of them is in fact an instinctive response to fear, a means of escape from a physical or psychological threat, a survival strategy in the most direct sense. It is true that Bigger attempts to turn the killing of Mary to account after the fact, to attach expressive significance to the act in his memory. The act itself, however, is motivated by no such intention. In the page or so of text that recounts the first murder, Bigger and his feelings are described in the following terms: "hysterical terror," "fists clenched in fear," "afraid" (used twice), "fear," "frenzy," "frantically," and "intimidated to the core" (pp. 84–85). These or similar terms accompany each of the accounts of Bigger's killings, real or imagined. Killing, in other words, is not a consciously chosen form of self-expression for Bigger but rather an involuntary consequence of his failure to express his feelings, his failure to understand and communicate his own fear and thereby to disrupt "the rhythms of . . . indifference and violence" that rule his life.

The question still remains whether Bigger discovers any mode of expression capable of reunifying his dissociated sensibility and rendering him a whole human being. The answer is that the book itself, as a self-reflexive work of art, accomplishes that function. This success is a highly qualified one, however, for it is achieved only in the shadowy realm of virtual reality, of projected desire, and not in the realm actually inhabited by Bigger. As a human being, Bigger fails utterly to resolve the conflicting terms of his existence. What resolutions he achieves, he finds only by turning himself into a character and his life into art. This is not to imply that Bigger is somehow the author of the book—he emphatically is not. It is to say, rather, that the book is written in a manner consistent with an imaginative reality which Bigger struggles to create.

Irving Howe offers a useful observation in this regard in a 1963 essay which is often cited by critics, though generally for different reasons. Howe calls into question the conventional wisdom that classifies *Native Son* as a naturalistic novel in the tradition of Dreiser:

> *Native Son* is a work of assault rather than withdrawal; the author yields himself in part to a vision of nightmare. Bigger's cowering perception of the world becomes the most vivid and authentic component of the book. Naturalism pushed to an extreme turns here into something other than itself, a kind of expressionist outburst, no longer a replica of the familiar social world but a self-contained realm of grotesque emblems.[6]

Howe never follows up the logic of this insight (ignores it, in fact, in the next paragraph, which criticizes Wright's technique), but it is a logic which accommodates perfectly the central thematic concerns and which accounts at last for the book's excesses of characterization, plot, and narrative technique. It is, in effect, an expressionistic mode of composition which Wright describes in "How 'Bigger' Was Born" when he says,

---

[6]Howe, p. 43.

I restricted the novel to what Bigger saw and felt, to the limits of his feelings and thoughts, even when I was conveying *more* than that to the reader. I had the notion that such a manner of rendering made for a sharper effect, a more pointed sense of the character, his peculiar type of being and consciousness. Throughout there is but one point of view: Bigger's (p. xxxii).

Wright's practice is consistent with this stated intention: he gives the reader not the world Bigger lives in but the world Bigger lives. He presents the world as Bigger feels and experiences it. The writer's task here is not simply a problem in the logistics of point of view (describing what Bigger actually sees or what it means to him given what he already knows), nor is it an exercise in creative hallucination. Somewhere between the two lies a real and larger world, one seen through the distorting optic of fear. Bigger, again, is not the author of this book and there is much in it that he does not understand and could not have imagined independently, but its exaggerations, simplifications, and lack of proportion conform exactly to Bigger's "peculiar type of being and consciousness." It is the projection of this being and consciousness onto the world, and not what "really happens," that finally matters to Wright, to the reader, and especially to Bigger himself.

This technique of projection is most readily apparent in the depiction of characters. Wright acknowledges that he "gave no more reality to the other characters than that which Bigger himself saw" (p. xxxii), and Bigger sees only what his fear allows him to see. Bigger's interactions with others are conditioned by his efforts to meet expectations by conforming to type. He can do this only by first typing those for whom he must play his various roles. His visits to the movies may be seen in this light as research, and his playacting on the street with Gus as practice, in the serious business of human typology. The characters of the novel, apart from Bigger, are stereotypes because they are stereotypes for Bigger. They are individuals who have been reduced to what Bigger fears, needs, desires, and struggles to understand, and a different part of Bigger swings into action to meet the threat or, less often, the opportunity that each offers. Thus he is boastful with Buddy, tough with Gus, tender with Bessie, subservient with the Daltons, guarded with Jan, self-effacing with Britten, and so on. The reader sees what Bigger sees, a world full of typed characters even though some of them are types that Bigger has never met or identified before.

But all of this typing, both of self and of others, takes its toll. Bigger longs for genuine acceptance and understanding, though he continually frustrates this longing by the barriers he erects. His need to be something different to each is in tension with his need to be himself to all. This second and deeper need, long suppressed, eventually takes precedence, and the turning point depends upon a most improbable manipulation by the author: the scene in which a dozen characters all crowd into Bigger's jail cell. Wright himself comments on the implausibility of this scene in his introductory essay:

While writing that scene, I knew it was unlikely that so many people would ever be allowed to come into a murderer's cell. But I wanted those people in that cell to elicit a certain important emotional response from Bigger. And so the scene stood (p. xxxi).

What happens in that cell is that all of the distorted versions of Bigger represented by all of the characters in his life come together at once, and in the process a psychic critical mass is reached and exceeded. He must be several different Biggers at once, and he cannot do it:

> Desperately he cast about for something to say. Hate and shame boiled in him against the people behind his back; he tried to think of words that would defy them. . . . And at the same time he wanted those words to stop the tears of his mother and sister, to quiet and soothe the anger of his brother . . . (p. 275).

His solution is to assure his mother "I'll be out of this in no time" (p. 276), a statement which only shocks and embarrasses those whom it is intended to impress. Bigger is then forced to listen helplessly to a humiliating exchange among the characters in his life, the different parts of himself, that leaves him "weak and exhausted" (p. 281). He has seen that when all the separately maintained pieces of himself are brought together they make no sense and instead threaten to destroy him as an individual. After this scene, his conscious energy no longer focuses on maintaining his many outward guises but rather on the search for his own inner reality. His family returns once and he again lies to them, but he immediately rejects the lie, and the whole incident is reported briefly and indirectly. Otherwise, the little life that remains to him is devoted to his efforts to express a more authentic self-understanding.

The element of plot has the same function in the book as that of character, to project images that express Bigger's emotional experience. Plot, in part, supports character in this respect, for not only does it bring all the important surviving characters together in the crowded-cell scene, but it brings Bigger into contact in the first place, against all likelihood, with precisely those forces that he most fears and that most challenge his self-understanding, forces represented by the Daltons, Mary, Jan, Buckley, and Reverend Hammond. More importantly, it parallels the element of character in creating and arranging events which pose fundamental threats to Bigger at the same time that they serve his need to see his life as he really feels it. Like the characters, the events in the novel are "typed" events. They consist not of complex concatenations of forces and circumstances but of experience reduced to single emotions projected onto reality and objectified, haunting fantasies become real. The murder of Mary thereby becomes a concentrated, particular experience of fear, the disposal of her body one of dehumanization, the capture of Bigger on the water tower one of utter isolation and victimization, and so on. Bigger feels excluded from the conventional "picture of Creation" which, in his emotional core, he has "killed" and in its place "created a new world for himself" (p. 264). This "new world" is reflected in the book and its extravagant plot.

Not only do the events of the novel provide concrete images of Bigger's emotional experience, but they also work together to place him in a situation in which he is forced to contemplate them. As other critics have pointed out, in the "Fate" section Bigger has no choice but to shift from his customary active mode to an unwonted reflective one. And lest he turn away from his memory of these images, they are concretely reinforced, with all the emotional reality they embody, by new events, presented with the same expressionistic excess. He is, for example, taken from his cell to the Dalton home and told to re-enact his crime. Though he refuses to put on a show (which seems to be the only intention of his jailers), he does indeed re-enact, in his mind, his experience of *"that night,"* and on leaving is shown a burning cross, spat upon, and made to listen to a crowd howling for his death (pp. 310–13). And in court, despite Bigger's plea of guilty, he must sit and listen as some sixty witnesses recount his crime in detail and watch as Mary's charred bones are displayed, the furnace from the Dalton home is reassembled, and the disposal of the body acted out for the jury (pp. 350–52).

All of these self-images are, of course, painful to Bigger, and he shrinks from them and yet is irresistibly drawn to them as well, for he recognizes them as the products of his own emotional experience. This becomes clear in part through the often heavy-handed foreshadowing found in the first section. It has often been observed that the killing of the rat prepares both Bigger and the reader for later killings, but the foreshadowing hardly stops there. Shortly after, in Bigger's hearing, Vera asks her mother the question that lies at the heart of the entire novel: "How come Bigger acts that way?" Her answer: "He's just . . . plain dumb black crazy" (p. 12). Later, on the street, Bigger tells Gus that being black in a white world is "just like living in jail" and admits "sometimes I feel like something awful's going to happen to me" (p. 23), a feeling which he then reformulates: "It's like I was going to do something I can't help" (p. 24). In the movie theater, he tells Gus "Say, maybe I'll be working for folks like that if I take that relief job. Maybe I'll be driving 'em around" (p. 33). He then goes on to predict almost exactly the situation in which he will find himself that evening:

> Maybe Mr. Dalton was a millionaire. Maybe he had a daughter who was a hot kind of girl; maybe she spent lots of money; maybe she'd like to come to the South Side and see the sights sometimes. Or maybe she had a secret sweetheart and only he would know about it because he would have to drive her around; maybe she would give him money not to tell (p. 36).

Bigger has thus already imagined the general direction as well as many of the specific details of the plot that is to unfold. Once the murder is accomplished, he confirms his feeling that he "had been dreaming of something like this for a long time, and then, suddenly, it was true" (p. 88), and reconfirms it as he begins his flight from justice: "All his life he had been knowing that sooner or later something like this would come to him. And now, here it was" (p. 207).

Bigger recognizes these events as expressive of his own emotional reality and contemplates them in fascination, and he will not be denied the opportunity for self understanding that they represent. Repeatedly it occurs to Bigger that he had best escape, leave town, or at least shake down the ashes in the furnace in order to prevent Mary's remains from being discovered, and repeatedly he fails to do what he must to save himself from being caught. A blizzard at last conveniently seals off all exits from Chicago, and with them seals Bigger's fate. These "failures," however, are not the result of obtuseness on Bigger's part but of a compulsion to be a part of this plot until it plays itself out: "He was following a strange path into a strange land and his nerves were hungry to see where it led" (p. 107). In the Dalton house, before the discovery of Mary's body, "the thought that he had the chance to walk out of here and be clear of it all came to him, and again he brushed it aside. He was tensely eager to stay and see how it would all end, even if that end swallowed him in blackness" (p. 178). When Buckley suggests the possibility of an insanity plea to Bigger as a "way out," Bigger immediately responds, "I don't want no way out" (p. 287). Bigger seems, in fact, to be accepting and even hastening his own death. This impression is supported by Bigger's thoughts and fantasies of self-destruction as well as by other passages contributing to the same pattern: "He wished that they would shoot him so that he could be free of them forever" (p. 312); "An organic wish to cease to be, to stop living, seized him" (p. 319); Bigger's dream of his own severed head (p. 156). The significance that this pattern takes on in the context of Bigger's urge to self-expression is not simply that of a "death wish." Rather it is a recognition that the conditions of his life exclude the very thing that his being requires: the freedom to express his individual human needs without fear. The consequence of an attempt to re-weld his dissociated sensibility, despite this fundamental antithesis, is a kind of self-immolation. Bigger himself acknowledges the inevitability of this consequence: "It seems sort of natural-like, me being here facing that death chair. Now I come to think of it, it seems like something like this just had to be" (p. 331).

Like the characterization and plot, the narrative voice in *Native Son* serves as more than simply a technical support to a work of fiction. It too functions more particularly as an expressionistic projection of Bigger's sensibility. It not only expresses Bigger's dilemma, but in its particular mode of expression it concretely embodies that dilemma as well.

Broadly speaking, Bigger suffers from an inability to communicate a conscious understanding of his own emotional reality. In a narrower sense, Bigger lacks words and feels this lack as a potent form of alienation from others. James Nagel, commenting on "images of 'vision' in *Native Son*," suggests a similar insight, that only at the end does Bigger realize "that his real tragedy is not death; it is rather the fact of never having been clearly seen by anyone."[7] This is spelled out most clearly when Bigger attempts to express himself to Max, the one person who has come closest to understanding him:

> He could not talk. . . . Max was upon another planet, far off in space. Was there any way to break down this wall of isolation? Distractedly he gazed about the cell, trying to remember where he had heard words that would help him. He could recall none. He had lived outside of the lives of men. Their modes of communication, their symbols and images, had been denied him (p. 386).

The long-felt need to explain himself becomes at last, in the terms of the plot, a matter of physical survival, for he can finally do nothing to save himself but plead

[7]Nagel, p. 157.

his case to the court, and yet "he knew that the moment he tried to put his feelings into words, his tongue would not move" (p. 337). This premonition proves true when Bigger is given the opportunity to speak in court before being sentenced: "He tried to open his mouth to answer, but could not. Even if he had the power of speech, he did not know what he could have said" (p. 380).

If Bigger cannot speak for himself, however, others can and do speak for him and in the process take from him a large measure of control over his own destiny and over the satisfaction of his own needs. One notices this disparity, for example, when Bigger applies for a job and Mr. and Mrs. Dalton discuss his case in his presence but outside his comprehension: "The long strange words they used made no sense to him; it was another language" (p. 48). The press, often an important pressure impelling the plot forward, is another repository of the power of words, one which Bigger imagines that he has tapped by the power of his own actions:

> The papers ought to be full of him now. It did not seem strange that they should be, for all his life he had felt that things had been happening to him that should have gone into them. But only after he had acted upon feelings which he had had for years would the papers carry the story, *his* story (p. 208).

The power of the preacher to manipulate, through words, the images that hold meaning for Bigger's life has already been seen. But the most significant figure in this respect, of course, is the lawyer, Max, who promises Bigger, "I'll tell the judge all I can of how you feel and why" (p. 331), and who stands up in court before the assembled representatives of the world Bigger fears but needs, and announces, "*I shall witness for Bigger Thomas*" (p. 348). Max has been characterized by various readers as a mouthpiece for the Communist party. In fact, he is much more importantly a mouthpiece for Bigger, a fantasy come true: he possesses a vast audience, commands the language (words, imagery, frame of reference) of that audience, and stands in a privileged forum from which to address it. In every sense of the word, he *represents* Bigger to the world in a way that Bigger could never represent himself.

What Max is to Bigger's fictional life, the narrator is to the artistic image that is projected out of that life. The narrator's facility with words and propensity for extended abstract analysis and complex syntax compensate—indeed, *over*-compensate—for Bigger's stance of mute incomprehension before his own experience. As the novel proceeds, Bigger acts and feels while the narrator reasons aloud about these actions and feelings. The relationship is precisely the one described (by the narrator) between the two parts of Bigger as he lies in his cell awaiting trial: "Blind impulses welled up in his body, and his intelligence sought to make them plain to his understanding by supplying images that would explain them" (p. 334). The narrator speaks for Bigger just as Max does, supplying images to his impulses, mind to his body. Max's action is limited, however, and he does not succeed in his effort to explain Bigger. Because he lives in the same external world as Bigger, he faces the same barriers and threats. The "crazy" student in Bigger's cell is another example of someone who tries to express directly his understanding of reality and who suffers as a result (pp. 317–19). Bigger's only recourse, again, is to imagination, to art. Wright describes, in "How 'Bigger' Was Born," his intention to explain "everything only in terms of Bigger's life and, if possible, in the rhythms of Bigger's thought (even though the words would be mine)," acknowledging readily the range of technical and linguistic devices which contribute to this "explanation" (p. xxxi), a range which is utterly beyond Bigger's capabilities. And the narrator himself on occasion recognizes the differences between Bigger's voice and his own: "though he could not have put it into words, he felt that . . ." (p. 257). Because Bigger cannot "reach out with his bare hands and carve from naked space the concrete solid reasons" for his actions (p. 323), the narrator is created to carve those reasons from language, an equally resistant material for Bigger. There is nothing subtle about the narrator of *Native Son:* his comments are obtrusive, overwrought, and tendentious. He lacks sophistication. He is a literary cliché. And he is precisely the narrator Bigger would create, if he were able, to tell his story for him.

An enormous imaginative structure of characters, events, and narrative devices has been elaborated not merely to describe but to *express,* in the full sense of that word, the emotional experience of Bigger Thomas. The question which remains is whether this structure has been adequate either to repair or to circumvent Bigger's dissociated sensibility. There is a certain sense of failure implicit in any recourse to an expressionistic mode of writing, a despair at one's inability to make sense of experience that is fundamentally hostile to certain human needs or values. In *Native Son,* there seems to be a recognition of that failure or inadequacy built into the very terms of the work itself. In the first two sections, Bigger's persona expands to fill the world as he perceives it, and an extravagant sequence of characters, events, and commentaries provides him with images of his own experience. In the last section that sequence slows and eventually shuts itself off, leaving Bigger immobilized and forced—or free—to contemplate those images. Such contemplation is, in Bigger's terms, the function of the entire procedure. The original movement of expansion does not merely halt, however, but reverses itself as Bigger's persona collapses in on itself. As the trial plays itself out, Bigger's active experience becomes increasingly restricted and the *images* of his past experience take up exclusive and fixed residence inside his consciousness. His last hope for contact with others is cut off as Max backs away in terror from Bigger's dawning sense of "rightness" (p. 392). Gone too is any hope of escaping execution. All that is left in Bigger is a solipsistic acceptance of his own feelings, now beyond explanation or justification:

> What I killed for must've been good. . . . I can say it now, 'cause I'm going to die. I know what I'm saying real good and I know how it sounds. But I'm all right. I feel all right when I look at it that way . . . (p. 392).

Not only does Bigger have "the last word" over Max, as Irving Howe has so often been quoted to say,[8] but over the narrator as well, who drops away at last because

---

[8]Howe, p. 43.

Bigger "can say it now" and knows what he is saying "real good." This final pathetic utterance, so triumphant in Bigger's mind, isolates him forever and leaves him clinging with a kind of desperate joy to the fear and hate that have destroyed his life.

From St. Petersburg to Chicago:
Wright's *Crime and Punishment*

Tony Magistrale

Michel Fabre and Constance Webb, in their separate biographies of Richard Wright, document their subject's attraction to the fiction of Fyodor Dostoevski. When Wright gave advice to aspiring young writers or discussed his own literary inspirations, Dostoevski's novels were frequently mentioned.[1] Wright read *Crime and Punishment* for the first time in 1928, when he was twenty years old. The novel impressed him tremendously and he returned to it often, but not until the writing of *Native Son*, nearly two decades later, is there evidence of its influence exerting a definite shape over Wright's fiction. This topic has been suggested by Kenneth Reed,[2] but his sketchy treatment is much too brief and requires supplementary material and distinctions.

Crime and Punishment and *Native Son* share obvious similarities: both revolve around the theme of an impoverished youth who commits a double homicide and is subsequently captured and imprisoned. The victims in both novels are women; each of the youths is the product of a maternally based family; and to some degree both are influenced by morally conservative sisters while neither knows his father. The comparison between the two novels, however, extends beyond plot and character parallels. Dostoevski heightened Wright's awareness of the psychological dimensions of physical space, the sense of the city or a bedroom in possession of certain traits which influence human behavior. But even more important than this, was Dostoevski's model of the criminal mind—the motivations and consequences of antisocial behavior—and the antithetical struggle toward moral advancement and spiritual growth. Wright's personal experiences would have sufficed to enable the construction of a story about Bigger Thomas without knowledge of *Crime and Punishment*, but *Native Son* would have been a far less complex and engaging book had its author never been aware of Dostoevski. As Edward Margolies suggests, Wright's work is a psychological as well as sociologi-

Reprinted from *Comparative Literature Studies* 23.1 (1986): 59–70. By permission of *Comparative Literature Studies*, the Pennsylvania State University Press.

[1] See especially Constance Webb, *Richard Wright: A Biography* (New York: Putnam, 1968), 93, 145–6.

[2] Kenneth Reed, *"Native Son:* An American Crime and Punishment," *Studies in Black Literature* I (Summer 1970), 33–4.

cal novel, which not only shocks the reader's conscience, but also raises "questions regarding the ultimate nature of man."[3]

I

One of the most important aspects shared by *Crime and Punishment* and *Native Son* is an examination into the ways in which environmental conditions and society shape the individual personality. Dostoevski was strongly influenced by both the romantic and naturalistic schools of the eighteenth and nineteenth centuries. His vivid descriptions of room and city dwellings owe much to Poe, Balzac, Vidocq, and Dickens.[4] Unlike the fiction of his contemporaries in Russian literature—Tolstoy, Turgenev, Chekhov—*Crime and Punishment* does not take place behind the expansive backdrop of nature or the countryside. *Crime and Punishment,* like the urban *Native Son,* has a distinctive sense of confinement throughout and the major events invariably take place in the crowded city, among the heat and press of buildings and people. As Raskolnikov haunts the suffocating streets of St. Petersburg before and after his crime, so too does the hunted Bigger Thomas move within the condemned and stinking buildings of the Chicago ghetto. James A. Emanuel argues persuasively that Bigger's entire perception of the city—and, by extension, reality—is presented through images of restriction: urban closure, walls, curtains, and blurred vision.[5] In both *Crime and Punishment* and *Native Son,* the individual characters are confined by small apartments, narrow streets, and each other's presence. Compare, for example, these two environmental descriptions, the first from *Native Son:*

> He stretched his arms above his head and yawned; his eyes moistened. The sharp precision of the world of steel and stone dissolved into blurred waves. He blinked and the world grew hard again, mechanical, distinct.[6]

Raskolnikov, likewise, inhabits a similar cityscape:

> A terrible heat had settled upon the street; and then there was the closeness, the bustle of the crowd, plaster all around, scaffolding, bricks, dust, and that stench which is so peculiar to summer. The unbearable stench that was emitted from taverns, which were particularly numerous in that part of town, and the drunks, whom

---

[3]Edward Margolies, *Native Sons: A Critical Study of Twentieth-Century Negro American Authors* (Philadelphia: Lippincott, 1968), 82.

[4]For a more complete discussion of Dostoevski's relationship to these earlier writers, the reader should consult the following sources: for Dostoevski's relationship to Poe, Alfred Kazin, *An American Progression* (Vintage, 1985); for Dostoevski's relationship to Balzac, Leonid Grossman, *Balzac and Dostoevski* (Ardis, 1973); and for Dostoevski's connection to Dickens, Albert Guerard, *The Triumph of the Novel: Dickens, Dostoevski, Faulkner* (Oxford, 1976).

[5]James A. Emanuel, "Fever and Feeling: Notes on the Imagery in *Native Son,*" *Negro Digest* 18 (Dec. 1968), 16–24.

[6]Richard Wright, *Native Son* (New York: Harper and Row, 1966), 19. Further textual references will be cited parenthetically.

one encountered at every step, served to complete the picture's revolting and miserable tonality.[7]

Both Dostoevski and Wright lavish minute descriptions on the interiors of the living quarters occupied by their respective antiheroes. Raskolnikov's room in St. Petersburg is described as a "coffin," a "cupboard," a "tomb," where he sits "like a spider" in constant meditation. Similarly, Bigger's one room apartment must accommodate four people; their lack of privacy is a continual source of conflict and humiliation; and the family must cohabit this space with vermin the size of cats. The setting suffocates the characters by its tightness, noise, and filth; everything here, like Raskolnikov's garret, indicates a separation from nature. Both writers use the sordid cityscapes of *Crime and Punishment* and *Native Son* to create a world of chimera and illusion, where their antiheroes dissipate hours fluctuating between intense personal frustration and dreams of fantasy. Raskolnikov's gloomy room contributes to his depressed state and at one point he attributes to hunger his plan for murder. As the critic Konstantin Mochulsky points out, it would almost seem that the poisonous vapors that rise from the city's contaminated and feverish breath have penetrated the impoverished student's brain and there have helped give birth to his thoughts of murder.[8] Raskolnikov passes his life in thought; the exterior world, people, reality—these have ceased to exist.

Bigger Thomas's Chicago is as confining as Raskolnikov's St. Petersburg. Chicago's physical aspects—noisy, crowded, filled with a sense of power and fulfillment—make Bigger continually aware of the advantages available to whites, while simultaneously underscoring the impossibility of achievement for blacks. As Bigger acknowledges to his friend Gus early in the novel, " 'They don't let us do nothing. . . . Everytime I think about it, I feel like somebody's poking a red-hot iron down my throat' " (p. 20). Consequently, Bigger seeks escape from the frustrations that accompany a black man living in a white milieu, by losing himself in the fantasies of motion pictures. As Raskolnikov escapes from his St. Petersburg reality through dreams of wealth and power, so Bigger escapes to the narrow confines of his ghetto realm in a world where wealth and power are commonplace and where desires are magically fulfilled: "He wanted to see a movie; his senses hungered for it. In a movie he could dream without effort; all he had to do was lean back in a seat and keep his eyes open" (p. 17).

Bigger's interest in movie fantasies and Raskolnikov's turgid daydreams find further extension in their similar thoughts regarding world historic figures. On one level of being, *Crime and Punishment* and *Native Son* are novels which illustrate, for uniquely different reasons, the lure of power, and both Raskolnikov and Bigger are attracted to leaders who translate this desire into worldly conquests. Related to Raskolnikov's belief that the death of one human is justified when it alleviates the suffering of others and brings humanity a "new word," is Bigger's dream of a pow-

[7]Fyodor Dostoevski, *Crime and Punishment,* trans. Constance Garnett (New York: Random House, 1950), 169. Further textual references will be cited parenthetically.

[8]Konstantin Mochulsky, *Dostoevsky* (Princeton, New Jersey: Princeton University Press, 1967), 290–91.

erful individual who will come to rescue the oppressed black populace. Bigger is acutely aware of the fear and shame experienced by black people stemming from their treatment by the white world. He anticipates his own version of Raskolnikov's "extraordinary man" who will free blacks from the white force that has kept them separate and despairing: "He liked to hear how Japan was conquering China; of how Mussolini was invading Spain. He was not concerned with whether these acts were right or wrong; they simply appealed to him as possible avenues of escape. He felt that someday there would be a black man who would whip the black people into a tight band and together they would act to end fear and shame" (p. 110). Raskolnikov's initial justification for the pawnbroker's death emerges from a similar logic; it is the quest to end the life of a pernicious and cruel usurer in order to bring happiness to those who otherwise might perish. Early in the novel he says to Sonya, " 'By my very nature I cannot simply stand by and allow a miscreant to bring some poor defenseless being to ruin. I will interfere. Kill her, take her money and with the help of it devote oneself to the service of humanity and the good of all' " (p. 60).

Hegel's historic leaders—Alexander, Caesar, and Napoleon—become the basis for Raskolnikov's theory of the "extraordinary man" as an individual who possesses the right to circumvent conventional social ethics in order to become humanity's benefactor. While Bigger looks to contemporary political figures as illustrative of men who also exercised power to rise above the masses, it is important to note that he remains oblivious to Raskolnikov's larger issue of "the service of humanity and the good of all." This is less an indication of Bigger's insensitivity to the world or lack of a sophisticated intellect, than a reflection of the level of personal despair he must confront. Bigger simply does not share the comparative "leisure" of Raskolnikov's life; his awareness of power therefore exists only on the level of providing "possible avenues of escape."

While Bigger and Raskolnikov share similar environmental conditions and dreams of frustrated power, there exists an enormous difference between Raskolnikov's theoretical calculations and Bigger's existential bewilderment. In *Crime and Punishment* a good part of Raskolnikov's alienation proceeds from the interior sin of pride and deliberately cultivated speculation. In contrast, Bigger feels himself smothered by forces beyond his control. While environmental factors do play a major role in influencing Raskolnikov's personality, he, unlike Bigger, is able to exert his will upon circumstance. Raskolnikov *decides* to kill, he is not driven to do it.[9] Pinned between the grave of tomorrow and the racist barriers of yesterday, Bigger does not choose his choice; he lacks the initial freedom that allows Raskolnikov to construct his alternative superman theory: "He [Bigger] had been so conditioned in a cramped environment that hard words alone or kicks knocked

---

[9]Dostoevski purposely creates the character of Razumihin so that the latter might provide a mirror to Raskolnikov and the subject of determinism: Razumihin faces almost the same problems as Raskolnikov; nevertheless, he solves them differently. He gives lessons and translates articles to remain self-sufficient. Even Raskolnikov recognizes that he too could earn a living in the same manner. He says so to Sonya after the murder: " 'Razumihin works! But I turned sulky and wouldn't' " (p. 375).

him upright and made him capable of action—action that was futile because the world was too much for him" (p. 225).

The distinction between the two characters can also be extended to include their relationship to the crimes they commit. Raskolnikov's motives for the murders of the two women are as complex as the character himself. Dostoevski's notebooks are filled with various reasons, and at one point he has Raskolnikov murder in order to obtain money to aid his family. Bigger's crimes, by contrast, are nothing more than a desperate means of winning, through acts of spontaneous violence, the initial freedom denied him by the environment. Wright continually underscores the fact that Bigger is an impotent prisoner in a hostile land.[10] Since Mary Dalton is representative of all that the white world has traditionally held most sacred—aristocratic white womanhood—her murder brings Bigger his first real sense of power and identity. Consequently, a portion of the horror he experiences in committing the crime is alleviated by the knowledge that he, who is considered insignificant by whites, has actually killed a member of their race and outwitted them in their attempts to discover his identity. Essentially, Raskolnikov kills to test a self-will theory: the right of *l'homme superieur* to transgress the laws of morality.[11] Although *Native Son* does not attempt to condone the crime of murder, it does insist that only through that crime did Bigger manage to assert himself against those who had treated him as though he were merely a rat in a maze: "And, yet, out of it all, over and above all that had happened, impalpable but real, there remained to him a queer sense of power. He had done this. He had brought all this about. In all of his life these two murders were the most meaningful things that had ever happened to him" (pp. 224–25). Both Raskolnikov and Bigger kill out of the desire to attain freedom. However, the first understands freedom to mean the will to power; the second sees freedom as the legitimate claim of a human being.

In one sense, Bigger Thomas is a victim of his environment as Raskolnikov is a prisoner of his own self-willed theories. The crimes in both novels, then, stem directly from Raskolnikov's theory of a superior self and Bigger's contrasting inability to gain a satisfying concept of self. Neither Wright nor Dostoevski, however, draws a one-dimensional protagonist. Raskolnikov is more complex than merely another prefiguration of a Nietzschean *Übermensch*, while Bigger finally becomes a more complete character than most representatives of naturalist fiction. Although it may be argued that Raskolnikov and Bigger kill out of very different reasons, their crimes pave the way for similar moral awakenings. While Bigger

[10]Wright further establishes his attitude toward the influence of environment on the individual in the essay "How 'Bigger' Was Born": "I do say that I felt and still feel that environment supplies the instrumentalities through which the organism expresses itself, and if that environment is warped or tranquil, the mode and manner of behavior will be affected toward deadlocking tensions or orderly fulfillment and satisfaction" (p. xvi).

[11]Raskolnikov provides illumination into the actual motive behind his decision to murder in a conversation with Sonya (V, iv): " 'It wasn't to help my mother I did the murder—that's nonsense—I didn't do the murder to gain wealth and power and to become a benefactor of mankind. Nonsense! I did the murder for myself . . . I wanted to find out then and quickly whether I was a louse like everybody else or a man. Whether I can step over barriers or not . . .' " (p. 377).

and Raskolnikov experience a certain degree of "elation" in the commission of their respective murders, both men cannot escape the sense of guilt in reflecting upon their actions.

Despite Bigger's violent impulses and brutal reactions, there is in him none of the visceral delight in cruelty or perverse sexuality attributed by the Chicago newspapers and Buckley, the State's attorney. When he kills Bessie by hitting her with the brick, it is late at night, when she is asleep and the room is dark. Furthermore, the horror inherent in his disposal of Mary's corpse affects him so strongly that he has to force himself to go through each step of its dismemberment, fighting an omnipresent nausea and hallucinatory images. Indeed, Bigger is constantly beset by guilt and fear, from the haunting reappearance of the Dalton's white cat to the image of Mary's severed head, the dark curls wet with blood. He attempts to rationalize his actions by judging the white girl's behavior as foolish and conducive to a violent response, but eventually, as his dream subsequent to Mary's death effectively dramatizes, Bigger becomes aware that in performing the crime of murder he has also destroyed himself. In Bigger's dream, the streetlamp's light is the color of blood, and this "red glare of light" is associated with the first from the furnace he has used to burn Mary's corpse. The dream forces a connection between the street (Bigger's life) and the Dalton furnace (Mary) and continues this affiliation until Bigger finally exchanges places with his female victim:

> ... in a red glare of light like that which came from the furnace and he had a big package in his arms so wet and slippery and heavy that he could scarcely hold onto it and he wanted to know what was in the package and he stopped near an alley corner unwrapped it and the paper fell away and he saw—it was his own head—his own head lying with black face and closed eyes and lips parted with white teeth showing and hair wet with blood. . . . (p. 156).

It is possible that Wright borrowed from Dostoevski the use of dream symbolism as a method for revealing the criminal's repressed guilt and unconscious identification with his victim's suffering.[12] It is through the language of dreams that Wright and Dostoevski represent their protagonists' early stages of remorse. Similar to Bigger's nightmare, wherein he exchanges identities with the murdered Mary, Raskolnikov's dreams of Mikolka and the mare (I, iv) and the pawnbroker (III, vi) are warnings to the student that the old woman's death cannot be separated from his own life. In the dream of the beaten mare, Raskolnikov identifies with the little boy witnessing the brutal act, Mikolka performing it, and the mare itself who receives it. The dream of the pawnbroker comes after he has re-examined his "extraordinary man" theory and the crime

---

[12]As Andre Gide points out in his study *Dostoevsky* (New Directions, 1961), there is a fascinating narrative blend in Dostoevski's prose, combining both realistic and dream elements into a weave in which it is often impossible to distinguish one from the other: "Strange how Dostoevsky, when leading us through the strangest by-paths of psychology, ever must needs add the most precise and infinitesimal of realistic details, in order to make more secure an edifice which otherwise would appear the extreme expression of phantasy and imagination" (p. 122).

itself. In this dream Raskolnikov not only relinquishes his power in failing to kill the woman, but becomes the one tormented by her derisive gestures and "noiseless laughter":

> He stealthily took the axe from the noose and struck her one blow, then another on the skull. But strange to say she did not stir, as though she were made of wood. He was frightened, bent down nearer and tried to look at her; but she too bent her head lower. He bent right down to the ground and peeped up into her face from below, he peeped and turned cold with horror: the old woman was sitting and laughing, and shaking with noiseless laughter, doing her utmost that he should not hear it. (p. 250)

Both of these dreams reveal that Raskolnikov, like Bigger in his own dreamscape, is inextricably tied to the dual roles of the helpless victim and aggressive victimizer.

II

In relying on an axe as the instrument of murder in Raskolnikov's double homicide and Bigger's decapitation of Mary, the two men symbolically sever whatever bonds remain of their link to humanity as they split open the heads of their victims. The repulsive dreamscapes of *Crime and Punishment* and *Native Son* serve to introduce Bigger and Raskolnikov to the prison of self, incarcerating them both in spiritual isolation and torment. By themselves, neither man is capable of advancing beyond the acute awareness of his condition. Raskolnikov essentially acknowledges this after the death of the pawnbroker: "Did I murder the old woman? I murdered myself not her" (p. 297). In *Crime and Punishment* it is Sonya Marmeladov and Porfiry Petrovitch who lend relief to Raskolnikov by providing his suffering with moral direction. In *Native Son* the strength and concern of Jan Erlone and Boris Max convince Bigger that his life is important because it is linked to the fate of other people. Raskolnikov needs Sonya to forgive and love him and Porfiry to challenge his intellectual positions. Bigger's hostility is transformed into trust and love by the forgiveness of Jan and the sense of self-belief that Max helps him articulate at the end of the novel.

In Raskolnikov's acceptance of suffering as a way to salvation, Sonya becomes the only person capable of comforting him. She is the sainted whore whose abilities to express empathy give her the strength to accept Raskolnikov's cross. As is foreshadowed by the symbolic scene in which Raskolnikov and Sonya are united over the Biblical story of Lazarus (IV, iv), Raskolnikov, through the love of Sonya, comes to see and trust in the possibility of a "full resurrection to a new life, to a new and hitherto unknown future" (p. 492). Near the end of the book, when he leaves the police station unable to confess, it is Sonya's silent figure of suffering that makes Raskolnikov return and admit to the murders.

Just as Sonya comprehends and communicates her love to Raskolnikov, Jan Erlone forgives Bigger for killing the girl he loves and conveys to the black youth his first sense of a white man's humanity. When Jan first enters the room where

Bigger is held after his capture, Bigger's intitial thought is that Jan has come for revenge. Instead, Jan recounts his realization that if he were to kill Bigger, the dreadful cycle of violence would never stop, and asserts that his own suffering has led him to see deeper into Bigger's. By disassociating himself from hatred and revenge, Jan becomes the impetus to Bigger's change in perception:

> . . . a particle of white rock had detached itself from that looming mountain of white hate and had rolled down the slope, stopping still at his feet. The word had become flesh. For the first time in his life a white man became a human being to him; and the reality of Jan's humanity came in a stab of remorse: he had killed what this man loved and had hurt him. He saw Jan as though someone had performed an operation upon his eyes, or as though someone had snatched a deforming mask from Jan's face. (p. 268)

Sonya and Jan serve as the embodiments of the deeply human qualities Bigger and Raskolnikov desperately need—acceptance of other people's differences, compassion, and selfless love. Sonya and Jan struggle not through ideas and sermons, but by deeds and example. They do not intellectualize and do not moralize, but trust and love. " 'One can be great even in humility,' " says Sonya, and Jan's image in *Native Son* corresponds with few modifications.

In *Crime and Punishment* reasonings about life and about the meaning of spiritual suffering pass from Sonya to Porfiry Petrovitch. A corresponding movement can be traced in *Native Son* with the introduction of Boris Max. Max, in his capacity as Bigger's lawyer, is able to elicit from his client a comprehension of his hopes and dreams, his frustrations and rages. In his courtroom arguments, Max shows a clear understanding of how Bigger's crimes were both destructive and liberating, in the sense that they furnished Bigger with his first real identity. Although it is too late for Bigger to join the others who, like Max, support principles of human worth and dignity, the lawyer continues to embellish Bigger's evolving commitment to other human beings: "He had lived outside the lives of men. Their modes of communication, their symbols and images, had been denied him. Yet Max had given him the faith that at bottom all men lived and felt as he felt. And of all the men he had met, surely Max knew what he was trying to say" (p. 386).

Like the version of Boris Max we find in *Native Son*, Porfiry Petrovitch in *Crime and Punishment* understands both the situation and context for Raskolnikov's crimes. Unlike Poe's Dupin or Hugo's Javert, the literary models Dostoevski initially may have had in mind in the development of his own magistrate, Porfiry is a new type of "super-cultured" administrator, straight-forward and sympathetic; he is aware of the struggle for man's soul—for the inspector assumes he has one—the contest for the individual psyche as it is pulled between two abysses, good and evil. It is for this reason that he does not simply arrest Raskolnikov. Porfiry seeks more than merely the apprehension and punishment of a law breaker; he is interested in Raskolnikov's moral regeneration. Porfiry understands that the student's soul requires "fresh air, fresh air" (p. 412). Siberia is literally that fresh air, which Raskolnikov breathes after he is transplanted from the polluted depths of St. Petersburg. Thus, Porfiry's role is similar to Boris Max's: they exist to inspire Raskolnikov and Bigger to continue the process of self evaluation, and from this struggle to attain insight into moral development.

The influence of Sonya and Porfiry as well as the personal struggles of good and evil that tear at his soul, give Raskolnikov at least the possibility of a resurrection and a future life with Sonya. Dostoevski leaves his young student invested with the ability to distinguish good from evil and the capacity for exerting his moral will. Through the assistance of Porfiry and Sonya, Raskolnikov comes to acknowledge the principle of equipoise: that the evil in one's nature must be balanced through love, understanding, and suffering.[13]

In *Native Son* Bigger Thomas is not provided the chance for a new life in Siberia, and American society, as represented by a Chicago courtroom, once again forfeits the opportunity to liberate itself. But Bigger, like Raskolnikov, achieves his own freedom before his execution takes place. Although he is condemned to die as a violator of society's laws, his death is really a final triumph over forces that have controlled his life since birth. While society fails to change in its attitude toward Bigger, ironically his attitude toward society is transformed. His blind resentment toward the limitations of his family develops into a comprehension of the cause and compassion for their suffering; his violent outbursts against Gus, G. H., and Jack evolve into an awareness that they, too, are victims of prejudice and rejection; and his universal fear and distrust of white people are replaced by respect and love for Jan and Max.

Richard Wright's use of parallel characters, atmospheric effects, and a similar belief in the power of the human spirit to transform itself bear a marked resemblance to *Crime and Punishment*. The confluence between the two works, however, is never literal: it is not a matter of direct quotations or plagiarism,[14] but of a relationship in situations, motives, effects, and procedures. *Crime and Punishment* represented a reservoir from which Wright drew deeply—recasting characters and reshaping themes—in order to produce material relevant to his own purposes. It may be argued, for example, that Dostoevski's identification with a Christian

---

[13]The duality of Raskolnikov's personality, which presents a moral conflict throughout the novel, ultimately provides the reader with a final aesthetic question at the conclusion of *Crime and Punishment*: namely, how credible is Raskolnikov's spiritual and religious reawakening? Many critics, especially Edward Wasiolek in his book *Dostoevsky* (M.I.T. Press, 1964), have felt that the Epilogue is superimposed on the novel's overall structure and that Raskolnikov's rebirth is unjustified when examined in light of his prior behavior and strategies. Any conclusion about the novel must deal with the fact that there are always two Raskolnikovs: the lover of life and humanity, and the murderer, who is "further than ever from seeing that what [he] did was a crime" (*CP*, p. 466). As Ernest J. Simmons argues in *Dostoevsky* (Vintage, 1940), it is impossible for Raskolnikov to accept either route as an absolute salvation: the path of blood and crime to power or the road of submission and suffering to a Christ-like salvation (p. 151). On the other hand, it must also be argued that in a final analysis the influence of the other characters mixed with the personal torment that Raskolnikov undergoes, provides at least the promise of resurrection and credibility toward a personal renascence.

[14]Even in parallel passages such as the symbolic "soft and gentle eyes" of Raskolnikov's victim, Lizaveta (p. 249), reappearing in the piercing accusations of Bigger's victim, Bessie: "Suppose when he turned on the flashlight, he would see her lying there staring at him with those round large black eyes. . ." (p. 223).

vision of life finds a parallel in Wright's secular humanism. While Sonya guides Raskolnikov toward the philosophy of atonement as a method for counterbalancing evil, Bigger's life is given new priorities through contact with men who embody Marxist principles. Wright's interest is not in religion itself (although there are certainly a number of references to Bigger as a Christ-figure), but in its social excrescences: racism, ignorance, hypocrisy. Even as the central themes of *Crime and Punishment* and *Native Son* are filtered through each writer's personal affiliation with Christianity or radical politics, their protagonists are left invested with a similar commitment to other people and the capacity for moral growth. Unlike the naturalist tradition which influenced both novelists, *Native Son* and *Crime and Punishment* are not pessimistic evaluations of human destiny. In fact, quite the opposite is true, since both Bigger and Raskolnikov are finally victorious over the brutal facts of their personal histories. The differences between the two characters reveal much about cultural opportunities; their similarities address those elements universal to humankind: a deathless faith in the potential for self-improvement and the dream of a final reconciliation among all men.

Papa Dick and Sister-Woman: Reflections on Women in the Fiction of Richard Wright

Sherley Anne Williams

Lulu Mann, wife of the hero, Brother Mann, in Richard Wright's story, "Down by the Riverside,"[1] is a metaphor of the general representation of women in Wright's work. Lulu suffers quietly and dies as mutely as she has lived; she speaks nary a word in the story. To be sure, much of the heroic and tragic action of the story is occasioned by Lulu's sex and role: she is in the midst of a long and difficult childbirth and her husband makes a superhuman effort to get her to the hospital during a flood, rowing Lulu, their young son, and Lulu's mother across a flooded landscape against a treacherous current. "What if the levee break?" runs like a refrain through the first part of the story, reminding us that nature can be worked with, even manipulated, but is ultimately beyond human control. And Brother Mann must also brave fear-crazed white civilians and carelessly racist troops: " '. . . in times like these they'll shoota nigger down jus like a dog . . .' "

We infer something of the quality of Lulu's and Mann's relationship from his dogged and willing attempts to get her to the hospital. The only transportation available is a rowboat stolen from an especially racist white man. In order to get Lulu help, Mann must brave not only the hostile environment but the wrath of a white man and, possibly, the white man's law. His problem is compounded when he is forced, in self-defense, to kill the owner of the boat: to get Lulu to the hospital now almost certainly means his own death. Still, Mann persists in his efforts to save his wife's life. "He could not turn back now for the [safety of] the hills, not with Lulu in this boat. Not with Lulu in the fix she was in." It is this very selflessness that proves his undoing for even as he makes this decision, Lulu is already dead. All that he has willingly suffered on her behalf is for nothing. He continues to pay.

Reprinted from *American Novelists Revisited: Essays in Feminist Criticism*, ed. Fritz Fleischmann (Boston: G.K. Hall, 1982), pp. 394–415. By permission of Sherley Anne Williams.

[1] Richard Wright, *Uncle Tom's Children: Five Long Stories* (New York: Harper & Row, 1940). Originally published in 1938 by Harper's, the first edition included "Big Boy Leaves Home," "Down by the Riverside," "Long Black Song," and "Fire and Cloud." "The Ethics of Living Jim Crow," an autobiographical sketch (parts of which were later incorporated in *Black Boy*, the story of Wright's childhood and adolescence in the South), and "Bright and Morning Star" were added to the 1940 edition. All quotes are from the 1940 version of the collection.

Mann is conscripted to work on the levee and when the levee breaks, he goes with another black man to rescue a last family from the rapidly approaching flood waters. We are not surprised that the family is that of the racist Mann has killed: Wright was first a naturalist, at his best depicting the relentless momentum with which chance can catch one. This incident is, in addition, yet another instance in which Mann, unlike Wright's later heroes—indeed, the heroes of many naturalist novels—makes the human and selfless choice. He is unable, because of his own humanity, to escape the consequences of the actions set in motion by nature, on the one hand, and the inhuman racial system, on the other. He can neither kill nor abandon the racist's family. And, predictably, once safe in the hill camp for flood victims, the dead man's wife and son denounce our Mann. He is seized, but he chooses to die escaping rather than at the hand of the unjust justice (" 'Did he bother you, Mrs. Heartfield?' " the white men ask. " 'The little girl?' " whipping themselves up for a lynching: " 'Did he bother you, *then*, Mrs. Heartfield?' ") that he knows awaits him at the hands of the white legal system.

It is a classic story of black male heroism, much in keeping, as are all of Wright's short stories and his autobiographical narratives, with the sense of heroism in Afro-American traditions.[2] That sense of heroism is basically to fight, by whatever means are available, against the racism and exploitation that continues to victimize black and other ethnic groups in America. Wright's hero begins his struggle toward self-definition through his attempt to save his wife's life, but this attempt is pushed to the background as Mann's struggle with the environment, with the system and the white man are portrayed. The background is the classic place of women and male-female relationships in much of the tradition. Neither women characters nor "women's questions" figure centrally in Wright's fiction; when they appear at all, they are subsumed under larger political or philosophical themes. Lulu is not an identifiable personality but an occasion for the hero to demonstrate soul, his persistence and grace under pressure.[3]

The only physical description we are given of any of the black characters in the story is Lulu's. She is "a small woman with large shining eyes." Despite, perhaps because of, these few details, she remains anonymous behind her "thin black face." Though she herself is silent, women do in fact speak in the story. These are older women, but their voices seem to stand, at least in part, for the younger Lulu. Sister Jefferson suggests the prototypical strong-black-woman who goads others to action no matter how futile or self-destructive. She poses the central question of the story, " 'Whutcha gonna do, Brother Mann?' " In her insistence that " 'Yuh gotta do something, Brother Mann,' " she stands for generations of black women who have demanded that their men make a way for them in a racist society out of no way at all. Brother Mann rises to the occasion, responds to the demand, only to

[2]*Eight Men*, a short-story collection (Cleveland and New York: World Publishing Co., 1961); and *Black Boy* (New York: Harper & Row, 1945) and *American Hunger* (New York: Harper & Row, 1977), the autobiographical narratives.

[3]I have adapted this definition of *soul* from Eleanor Traylor, who in turn adapted it from Ernest Hemingway's definition of courage.

be cheated of success by the weakness of his wife's flesh, the narrow hips that will not allow his child to pass.

Grannie, Lulu's mother, attempts, in the name of Jesus Christ or his surrogate on earth, the white folks, to suppress any actions but the most conventional and acceptable to the white powers that be. She refuses, at first, to get into the boat that is their only hope of getting to safety because it was stolen from a white man. And though she does finally accompany Mann, it is obvious that the white folks are more terrifying to her than a mere flood could ever be.

I have felt at liberty to give "Down by the Riverside" this rather exaggerated reading because Lulu, Sister Jefferson, and Grannie, lightly sketched though they are, foreshadow black female characterizations in Wright's later work. The distinguishing characteristics of Granny and Sister Jeff, religion-haunted racial timidity and domineering strength, come to define Wright's view of the black matriarch— the most prevalent female character type in Afro-American literature. Lulu's condition and her silence suggest something of the link Wright is later to make between black women and a mindless sexuality that almost as much as racism is the bane of the black man's existence. This latter view is, of course, troubling, and Wright's handling of the matriarch figure, even at its most illuminating and provocative, is not without its problems. Rather than being merely another instance of the general male chauvinism pervasive in both Afro- and Anglo-American literature, Wright's female portraits are a part of a systematic presentation in the landscape he paints as backdrop for the actions of his heroes. His portraits of black women, often no more than cameos or vignettes, are some of the most compelling and complex in the literature and place him at the extreme edge of the tradition in a position that is both extremely sexist and racist. The claim here is not that Wright did not know black women, which in some very real sense he clearly did—after all, his mamma was one. Rather, Wright seldom loved his black female characters and never liked them, nor could he imagine a constructive role for them in the black man's struggle for freedom. Moreover, his fictional portrayals of black women justify, by implication, the hunger of his black heroes for that forbidden American fruit, the white woman, and the validity of his own use of the white woman as the ultimate symbol of the black man's freedom.

Richard Wright is the father of modern Afro-American literature. His most famous novel, *Native Son* (1940), is seen in some quarters as "the model"[4] for contemporary black novelists, his autobiographical narrative, *Black Boy* (1945), as the text that authenticates "the extraordinary articulate self that lies behind"[5] this most famous novel of black privation and rage. *Native Son* began an era of new realism in Afro-American fiction, as black writers, inspired by the thrilling example of Wright, exposed the filth, corruption, and depravity of urban slums that, together with American racism, stunted and deformed the blacks forced to live in them. In

[4]Addison Gayle, Jr., *The Way of the New World* (Garden City, N.Y.: Anchor–Doubleday, 1975), 209.

[5]Robert B. Stepto, *From Behind the Veil* (Urbana: University of Illinois Press, 1979), 129.

his nonfiction work, *Twelve Million Black Voices* (1941), *Black Power* (1954), and *White Man Listen!* (1957), Wright documented the social and psychological effects on and reactions of black and other Third World peoples forced to live under the oppression of internal and external colonialism. In doing so, he took upon himself the task of being spokesman for some twelve million black people in America. And if his art suffered, as some critics have charged, because of this political spokesmanship, he at least made it possible to admit, explore, and thus move beyond the almost elemental expression of rage that drives *Native Son* to its powerful climax. But Wright also fathered a bastard line, racist misogyny—the denigration of black women as justification for glorifying the symbolic white woman—and male narcissism—the assumption that racism is a crime against the black man's sexual expression rather than an economic, political, and psychological crime against black people—that was to flower in the fiction of black writers in the late sixties and early seventies.

Women are only supporting players with bit parts in Wright's fiction. The women in *Native Son*, for example, are all cardboard figures: the white woman, Mary Dalton, whom Bigger Thomas accidentally kills, was never meant to transcend the symbolism of American fruit forbidden the black man; and Bigger's girlfriend, Bessie, whom he murders with malice aforethought, represents nothingness, a meaningless void that Bigger's killings allow him to rise above. Bigger's mother and his sister represent modern versions of toming and accommodation. We excuse these characterizations within the context of the novel because of the power of Wright's psychological portrait of Bigger; this is Bigger's story, and not even the introduction of an articulate white male character, Bigger's lawyer Max who, in a twenty-page speech, attempts to summarize something of what Wright had rendered (often brilliantly and beautifully) in the preceding two hundred and fifty pages, can diminish Bigger's presence in the novel. Because the characterization of women in Wright's novels is so limited, one must turn to Wright's stories in order to understand both the range and the issues involved in these portrayals. Wright never, in his published work, moves beyond these early characterizations of black women.[6]

I

The only published works in which women characters are protagonists, "Long Black Song" and "Bright and Morning Star," appear in *Uncle Tom's Children*, the short-story collection written while Wright was a member of the Communist party. In this first collection, Wright set out to explore the question, "What quality

[6]Wright completed a novel "entitled *Little Sister* and then *Maud* (unpublished) . . . intended as a social commentary on the role of women in American society." Constance Webb, *Richard Wright* (New York: Putnam's, 1968) 408. I did not have access to this manuscript, but given Webb's description of the heroine—she "whitened her skin by taking arsenic waters orally"—I cannot think that it would change substantially the cumulative portrayal of women in Wright's work.

of will must a Negro possess to live and die with dignity in a country that denies his humanity?" The epigraphs at the beginning of the book tell us more about the context in which Wright tries to answer this question. The first is a definition of an Uncle Tom, "the cringing type of [freedman] who knew his place before white folk," a household word among post-Civil War Negroes that Wright states unequivocally "has been supplanted by a new [one] from another generation which says Uncle Tom is dead!" The lyrics from a popular song "Is It True What They Say about Dixie?" make up the second epigraph. "Does the sun really shine all the time?/Do sweet magnolias blossom at everybody's door?. . .Do they laugh, do they love like they say in ev'ry song? . . ./If it's true that's where I belong." The stories, then, are at once political and mythic in the sense that Wright is trying to establish images that will have as much currency and resonance as the sentimental and superficial ones that color white society's present views of the South and the Negro. In each of the five stories, a black man is called upon to defend himself, his family, his community against a hostile and racist environment. The heroes in the first three stories are forced by events beyond their control into essentially private rebellions against southern racism. Their acts of heroism, often nihilistic and Pyrrhic, are also the means through which they achieve a measure of authentic self-consciousness—which of course the racist system must deny or destroy. In the final two stories, "Fire and Cloud" and "Bright and Morning Star," Wright is able to assimilate Marxist ideology into fiction and create characters whose struggles are symbolic of the entire community's and affirm the validity of collective action.

The central characters display an increasing level of political consciousness. Big Boy, the adolescent hero of "Big Boy Leaves Home," the first story in the collection, is an apolitical innocent upon whom consciousness, of a sort, is forced. Johnny Boy, in "Bright and Morning Star," the last story in the collection, is an organizer for the Communist party in rural Mississippi. The characterizations of women follow a similar pattern; in the early stories their condition initiates some action that significantly affects the life course of the protagonist. Once that course has been influenced, however, these female characters no longer figure in the story—consider the white woman who sees the naked Negro boys in "Big Boy" and thus precipitates murder and flight, or Lulu. Women characters have a more central role in later stories in the collection.

"Bright and Morning Star" is one of the most deft and moving renderings of a black woman's experience in the canon of American literature. Writing while he was still a staunch believer in communism as the hope of the world's oppressed, Wright was able to achieve in this story a synthesis of ideology and literary expression that he was only occasionally able to equal in later, longer works. The mute Lulu, the childish wanton Sarah in "Long Black Song," May, the stereotyped and scary wife of the hero in "Fire and Cloud": these characterizations of black women are somewhat redeemed in the character of Aunt Sue. Yet, paradoxically, Wright's loving characterization also reinforces the image of the black woman as a symbol of the reactionary aspects in Afro-American tradition implicit in the preceding three stories.

Aunt Sue is a blend of the mother of Afro-American ideal and the mammy of American experience. She takes in washing for a living, carrying the hundred-pound baskets on her head; her most characteristic pose—when she is not iron-ing—standing with her "gnarled black hands folded over her stomach," is one of familiar humbleness. This pose later helps her to hide a gun and so is akin to the minstrel mask and the vaudeville grin as one of the disguises forced upon black people and made "renegade" through sly acts of self-assertion.[7] Sue is, to use the jargon of the day, a "single" parent (I have often wondered what a double or triple parent looks like), a widow who has raised her sons, Sug and Johnny Boy, to man-hood alone. She has struggled against being engulfed in poverty and racism, aided by her wits and, more importantly, an abiding faith in Jesus Christ as Lord of Heaven and Savior of the world. Personal service on whites, endurance, a neces-sary self-effacement, a truncated family structure—these factors so characterize our conception of the so-called matriarch that they have in the aggregate almost the quality of archetype. Certainly the character of Aunt Sue approaches the ideal. Yet Sue is also a dynamic character who in Wright's treatment rises above the social definition of *mammy.*

When Sug and Johnny Boy enter manhood and "walk forth demanding their lives," Sue has the strength to let them go. Her heart follows them as they become organizers, for she loves, as a mother must, but she loves without smothering. Her love for her sons leads Sue to embrace the work of the Party; the wrongs and suf-ferings of black men "take the place of Him nailed to the Cross as the focus of her feelings," giving meaning to her life of toil as Christianity had before. In the party, Sue becomes aware of a kind of personal strength and pride that no one, least of all herself, thought a "black woman . . . could have": the will to work against the racist power structure. We understand, of course, that Aunt Sue has willingly sub-sumed her own aspirations, her own personality under first one man, Jesus Christ, then another, the wronged heroic Black Man, that she would consider the wrongs done to her as a black woman negligible compared to what black men suffer. She believes that righting the wrongs of black men will automatically eliminate her own exploitation. This elementary conception of black liberation does not trouble us unduly; Wright subtly implies his own deeper understanding of the political sit-uation of women when he explains why it is natural for Reva, a young white woman comrade, to trudge through a downpour to deliver an urgent message— "Being a woman, Reva was not suspect; she would have to go." He probably takes a devilish delight in portraying that symbol of deadly femininity, the white woman, using her privileged position to strike at his white male oppressors.

Yet, despite the changes wrought in her attitude by the new light shed by the party, Sue never quite accepts its dictum that she " 'not see white n [she] not see

---

[7]The mask is one of the most ubiquitous symbols in Afro-American literature; see, for example, the Paul Laurence Dunbar poem, "We Wear the Mask," in *The Complete Poems of Paul Laurence Dunbar* (New York: Dodd Mead & Co., 1913); W. E. B. DuBois, *The Souls of Black Folk* (New York: New American Library, 1969); LeRoi Jones, "A Poem for Willie Best," in *The Dead Lecturer* (New York: Grove Press, 1964) 18–27.

black.' " She cannot entirely discard the teachings of her experience: " 'You can't trust ever white man yuh meet.' " Johnny Boy's position, " 'Yuh can't judge folks by how yuh feel bout em n by how long yuh don knowed em,' " is, of course, the correct party line. And though in this instance, Sue proves correct (the informer is one of the newly recruited white party members), Sue's insistence upon "pitting her feelings against the hard necessity of his [Johnny boy's] thinking" symbolizes the hold that the old life and the old ways still have over her.

A white man posing as a friend of the little band of party members tricks her into revealing the names of the local group, even as Johnny Boy is captured by the sheriff's posse. Carrying a sheet for his burial, Aunt Sue gains access to the place where Johnny Boy is held captive, the place to which the informer must return to lay his information before the sheriff. Sue is forced to watch while Johnny Boy is tortured. She considers killing him to spare him pain, but chooses to wait and kill the informer and so save the lives of all the other comrades. She succeeds in killing the informer and is herself killed. She dies with a defiant cry, " 'You didn't git what you wanted!' " on her lips.

That defiant cry is ironic for these are the words of defiance that precipitated the crisis in the first place. They reinforce the quality of noble hubris that is an important part of her characterization. " 'Ah just want them white folks t try t make me tell *who* is *in* the party n who *ain*!... Ahll show em something they never thought a black woman could have,' " she tells Johnny Boy early on in the story. And she is given a chance to show that something. The sheriff and his men come looking for Johnny Boy and refuse to leave when she orders them out of her house. Despite her uppitiness, the sheriff seeks to be conciliating: " 'Now Anty . . .' " he begins, only to be brought up short by Sue's retort, " 'White man don yuh *Anty* me!' " She rejects the bogus conciliation and the counterfeit respect the title implies; and rejects also the *place* in which that title puts her. In the ensuing exchange of words with the white men, she further demonstrates her pride and courage: " 'Twenty of yuh runnin over one ol woman! Now ain yuh white men glad yuh so brave?' " The sheriff slaps her, for she is not to him a woman, but a nigger woman, a beast of burden to be beaten when it proves recalcitrant. As Aunt Sue does: She refuses to tell them anything about Johnny Boy. Balked, the sheriff and his men start to leave. Sue, wanting to drive home her victory for she has shown that there is nothing they could do to her that she could not take, taunts them as they go out her door. " 'Yuh didn't git wht yuh wanted! N yuh ain gonna nevah git it!' " This so enrages the sheriff that he beats her senseless.

While Sue is dazed from the assault, Booker, whom she suspects of being an informer, seduces her into telling the names of her comrades (" 'Is yuh scared a me cause Ahm *white*?' " he demands indignantly; then, cleverly invoking her son's name, " 'Johnny Boy ain like tha.' ") Later, after Reva has confirmed her suspicions that Booker is the informer, Sue reflects, pinpointing her moment of transcendent strength as the moment of her blind fall. "She put her finger upon the moment when she had shouted her defiance to the sheriff, when she had shouted to feel her strength . . . If she had not shouted at the sheriff, she would have been strong enough to resist Booker; she would have been able to tell the comrades herself," instead of entrusting the task to the traitor.

But hubris is only the superficial flaw. The "fit of fear" that had come upon her when she regained consciousness and discovered herself looking into a white face was "a part of her life she thought she had done away with forever." But that part of her life, "the days when she had not hoped for anything on this earth," had been evoked through her singing of the old sorrow songs, the spirituals that she " 'can't seem to fergit,' " in the first part of the story. And in singing, she has opened herself to both the tragic expression of pride and that old-timey fear. She sang for the traditional reason, "to ease the anxiety [about Johnny Boy's safety] that was swelling in her heart." She had thought that it meant no more than this when she sang now. But the events of the evening reveal that the songs are not, even now, an empty symbol. She has almost, without knowing it, called on Jesus; and He had not answered. This is the "deeper horror": the fight for black men's freedom had not truly replaced Christ in her heart. This realization mires her temporarily between two worlds, neither of which she seems able to abandon or live in.

In succumbing to the fit of fear induced by Booker's presence, Sue has in her own mind reverted to type, to the stereotypical image of the servile, cringing slave. And she is ashamed of herself and even more "shamed whenever the thought of Reva's love crossed her mind." In the white girl's trust and acceptance of her, Sue has found her first feelings of humanity, and Reva's love draws her toward a re-integration and reaffirmation with the peoples of the earth. Reva's relationship to Aunt Sue is a re-reading of the conventional one between mammy and mistress. It represents the ideal solidarity possible between black and white workers and the sisterhood between women workers. Moreover, the black mother and the white girl are bound together by their love for Johnny Boy. Reva's love for Sue, her faith in the old black woman, represent for Sue the promise of the party made real in a genuine human relationship. That love is likened to the light from the airport beacon in far-off Memphis that in the story becomes a metaphor for the new day that communism will bring.

Sue's pride before the white girl causes her to shield Reva from any knowledge of the mistake she has made, and this is consistent with the literal, denotative level of the story. Sue has already lost one son, Sug, to "the black man's struggle." He is in jail. Johnny Boy, she realizes during the sheriff's visit, is as good as gone; he will either be jailed, killed, or forced to flee because of his work with the party. Reva "was all she had left." Thus, when the young white girl comes to her house, after the sheriff and Booker have left, she cannot bring herself to reveal the full extent of her weakness. Reva's confidence (" 'An Sue! Yuh always been brave. Itll be awright!' ") seems to mock her. It also goads her into thinking of a way to rectify her mistake. Ironically, this deception recalls the outline of the old mammy-mistress relationship, for one of the unacknowledged but understood tasks of the old family retainers—whether "Aunty" or "Uncle"—was to guide their young charges through the shoals of adolescence, shielding them from as much unpleas-antness as possible and ministering to their hurts when it was not possible to keep them from pain. This latent aspect of Sue's love for Reva is reinforced by the suggestion of Reva as a sleeping beauty at the end of Section V of the story. Reva has come to spend the night with Sue in case there is trouble. She stays, even though the trouble has already come. Sue, resolved upon a course of action, gets Johnny Boy's gun and a sheet. Reva is in the room "sleeping; the darkness was filled with her quiet breathing . . . [Sue] stole to the bedside and watched Reva. Lawd, hep her!" Sue then steals away on her deadly errand, leaving Reva asleep, Reva's trust in black people intact, her world unshaken.

Concomitant with re-reading the relationship between mammy and mistress is the explicit sanctioning of romantic love between black men and white women as a symbol of racial equality and economic justice. Long before Sue gives Johnny Boy up to physical death in the service of the party, she gives him up to Reva. "The brightest glow her heart had ever known was when she had learned that Reva loved Johnny Boy"—this despite the fact that she knows the two of them "'couldna been together in this here south,' " to put it mildly. (We cannot help but remember the fate of Big Boy and his friends, the mob in "Down by the Riverside"—" 'Did he *bother* you Mrs. Heartfield? The little girl? Did he *bother* you *then?*' ") Yet Sue's approval of the match is used consistently to demonstrate that Sue has broken with her old outlook and embraced a new one, that she has broken with her old allies and found new ones. Sue never draws back from her approval of the match, whereas she early shows that she cannot accept all of the party tenets without reservation and her "Lawd hep" 's are a kind of subconscious refrain through much of the story. Sue's last thought as she starts out with her winding sheet is of Reva: "Lawd hep her! But maybe she was better off . . . she wont nevah know. Reva's trust would never be shaken." And as Sue starts across the fields holding the gun and the sheet against her stomach, " 'po Reva . . . Po critter . . . Shes fast ersleep.' "

Reva is fast asleep to Johnny Boy's fate, to Sue's frailty, Sue's humanity, to the dark realities and hardships of black life. Despite the exigencies of life in the party, nothing has happened to disturb Reva's faith in human nature, the party, her belief in the perfectibility of the world. And it is as much to keep this white world intact as it is to redeem her own self-esteem that Aunt Sue sets out to hunt down the informer.

In "Bright and Morning Star," Wright articulates a dream of rapprochement between the old and the new Negro, between the generations spawned in the bloody reprisals of Reconstruction and the generation nurtured on radical ideology in the new century, between black woman and white. He uses "the most beloved and familiar character"[8] in American experience, the mammy, to inveigh against adherence not only to the substance but to the form of the folk culture, to urge a complete break with the old-fogeyish past. The hope implicit in the story—if this old woman can change, anyone can—is never realized in portrayals of younger black women. Indeed, an episode from *American Hunger* (1977), the posthu-

[8]Webb, *Richard Wright*, p. 165.

mously published sequel to *Black Boy,* illustrates how completely Wright came to equate black women and black culture with the reactionary and regressive.

Wright worked as a publicity agent for the Federal Negro Theatre in Chicago during the early thirties. His attempts to bring "adult" drama to Chicago audiences met with resistance from the black actors and actresses in the company. Wright recalls that he had "the skinny white woman who directed" the company replaced by "Charles DeSheim, a talented Jew," and the company's repertoire of "ordinary plays all of which had been revamped to 'Negro style' with jungle scenes, spirituals and all," exchanged for "serious" dramatic works. A controversy erupted over the company's repertoire. The blacks reject the "grim, poetical, powerful, one-acter dealing with chain gang conditions in the south," written by a white man[9] because they think it "indecent." As one actor in Wright's recollection put it, " 'I lived in the south and I never saw any chain gangs.' " We share Wright's surprise and disappointment at this appallingly disingenuous statement, yet we also recognize in the actors' stammered responses to this opportunity to act out something of the painful realities of black experience a similarity to Richard's own response, earlier in the narrative, when the inpenetrable wall of racism opened suddenly and so unexpectedly that he could not believe the light when he saw it. In that earlier episode, he was immobilized by the responses that racism had forced him to internalize and so missed an opportunity for human interaction, human communication across the color line.

The stultifying, inhibiting effects of racism are a dominant theme in Wright's work, and we understand that racism has stunted the aspirations of these black performers. There is more than a hint of heroism in the young writer's challenging the former vaudevilleans to become actors and actresses. There is also an awful and poignant irony in the climax to the angry meeting that follows: Richard is denounced as an Uncle Tom by a black girl. Wright *has* played the "Uncle Tom" in a literal sense; he did tell the white director that the actors had started a petition demanding his removal. But Wright, of course, told DeSheim of the petition, not as an informing lackey, but out of a sense of loyalty to a fellow artist: Wright had suggested the play that caused the controversy just as he had suggested that DeSheim be hired. Wright has also tomed in a more subtle and more important sense: he had implied the superiority of a white writer's version of black life over that of numerous black playwrights who were then struggling against enormous odds to get their works produced. But the company, in rejecting an opportunity to engage audiences in serious considerations of Afro-American experience and Anglo-American racism, had implicitly endorsed a continuation of the self-parodies, the black-face burlesques of Shakespeare and Molière that had been their staple fare. Moreover, they accepted these burlesques as their "place before white folk" in the theater. One feels a kind of absolute truth in Wright's statement that the blacks "were scared spitless at the prospect" of being allowed out of that place. The actors were in fact able to rise above some, at least, of their fears for, as

---

[9]*Hymn to the Rising Sun* by Paul Green.

Constance Webb tells us in her official biography of Wright, "most of the difficulties were eventually smoothed over and the play went into rehearsal." And, when the play was banned as too "controversial," the actors and actresses continued to demand that they be allowed to perform it—though to no avail.[10] This is not, however, how the episode recorded in *American Hunger* ends.

After the angry meeting, a "huge" "fat" "black" woman, a *blues* singer, "found an excuse to pass [Richard] as often as possible and she hissed under her breath in a menacing singsong: 'Lawd, Ah sho hates a white man's nigger.' " This is more than a vernacular restatement of the tragicomic tensions of the first denouncement, for this worrying of the line poses the issues at another level. The politics of encounter and confrontation—represented by Richard, the writer—challenge the politics of accommodation and acceptance—represented by the anonymous "folk" singer. Though literature is routed, it is obvious that Wright, even in his apparent defeat, does not expect the blues to live. "I telephoned my white friends in the Works Progress Administration," he states blandly. " 'Transfer me to another job,' " he tells them, giving us to understand that if he is a white man's nigger, he at least is nigger to a white man with clout: "Within twenty-four hours DeSheim and I were given our papers. We shook hands and went our separate ways." The exclusion, the actual suppression of factual information is obvious and, we must assume, deliberate. Wright, the rising young black intellectual, joins the progressive, creative white man, leaving the Negro actors (one almost wants to say "masses") to their childish and backward ways.

Wright did make some attempt to retrieve this implicit and surprising alliance. "I felt—but only temporarily—that perhaps the whites were right, that Negroes were children and would never grow up." Yet the image of the fat, black, blues-singing woman, hissing the hero (who, after all, is only championing what *ought* to be her own desire for adult Negro dramatics), threatening and intimidating young Richard to the point that he felt in danger of his life, leaves an indelible mark. This image of the black woman hissing down progressive ideas is twin to the one of Sue, standing at her ironing board, unconsciously singing the old sorrow songs, opening the door to the past that the new day ought to have closed.

Wright never again creates so complex and dynamic a female character as Aunt Sue, nor does a strong black woman again figure so centrally in a piece of Wright's fiction. Strength in black women is seen increasingly as emanating from a kind of religious hysteria—Cross Damon's mother in *The Outsider* (1953),[11] for example, or Richard's grandmother in *Black Boy*. Religion does not ennoble these later characters as it had Sue. Whether they come to religion, as did Sue, because life was hard and the white man was hard with it (as Bigger's mother does in *Native Son*) or because they have been sexually betrayed by some black man, as Cross's mother does, these religious strong women are portrayed as ineffectual in the face

---

[10]Webb, *Richard Wright*, p. 113.
[11]Richard Wright, *The Outsider* (New York: Harper & Row, 1953). All quotations are from this edition unless otherwise noted.

of the poverty and racism of their lives and as unacknowledged allies of the society in keeping black men in their place. These are primarily older women, for power, even in such a limited form, is seldom a quality Wright associates with younger black women.

Sue is intuitively political rather than consciously so; the only other black female character who approaches Sue's level of political involvement is Sarah, wife of a communist organizer in *The Outsider*. She urges her husband to fight the party's decision that he stop organizing among the men on his job. The incident is meant to illustrate the brutal capriciousness of the party, the way it tramples over individual and small-group interests in the name of some vague, generalized "higher good." But the strident tones in which Sarah challenges her husband— " 'What in hell did I marry, a Marxist or a mouse? Listen, nigger, you're going to *organize,* you hear?' "—identify her as a closet ball-breaker who, under the guise of supporting and encouraging the black man in his struggle to maintain his dignity, constantly forces him into situations where that dignity will be trampled, his life put in danger. The incident illustrates, too, the kind of perverted strength that, at best, characterizes Wright's women. Sarah, like Sister Jefferson, nags, goads a man into action because her status as a woman prevents her from acting on her own behalf. " 'Men made themselves,' " a male character observes in the same novel, " 'and women were made through men.' " Wright seems incapable of creating strong black women who are independent of the crutch of religion. Sarah, the militant communist, crushed by the deportation of her husband, the suicide of her best friend, announces "I'm going to confession." We, like Cross, did not even know she was Catholic. It is significant that what Sarah really wants, as she reveals under Cross's questioning, is a man. But she is "thirty-five years old," "pretty old for that," and "fat now." "[She's] no confidence in herself anymore." Confession, the church, represent a yearning to submit to a master, to be relieved of responsibility for her life. Sarah was, evidently, Wright's final word on the strong-black-woman, for such a character does not again appear in his fiction.

It is interesting that Sarah, like Sue, approves, at least at first, of Cross's love affair with the white woman, Eva Blount. When she withdraws her approval, it is because Cross has been revealed as an amoral killer, not because of race. Sarah's approval is not made much of, it is actually pooh-poohed, put down to her matchmaking instinct. This casual attitude toward the affair merely becomes another element in the bizarre world in which the hero moves.

White women in Wright are never more than cardboard characters. One can divide them into "red necks" who cry rape and cause the death of black men (seen most clearly in Mrs. Carlson in *The Long Dream*), and "sweet little girls" who symbolize a freedom beyond a black woman's wildest imaginings. Wright makes it clear in *The Long Dream* that he understands the historical basis and the present pathology of this fatal fascination:

> . . . that white world had guaranteed [the black man's] worth in the most brutal and dramatic manner. Most surely he was something, somebody in the eyes of the white world or it would not threaten him [with castration and death]. He knew deep in his heart that

there would be no peace in his blood until he had defiantly violated the line [touching a white woman] that the white world had dared him to cross under the threat of death.

Now, one has no quarrel with this rationale; it is as good as any, and Wright does correctly identify the black man's image of the white woman as an indication of the black man's "forced," "abnormal" development.[12] What does madden one is the way Wright uses these unflattering images of black women to justify the black man's surrender to this pathology.

II

Sarah,[13] "a simple peasant woman" in the soberly lyrical story "Long Black Song," betrays her hard-working husband with a white gramophone salesman. Sarah's husband, Silas, discovers her infidelity, kills the white man, and is himself killed by a white lynch mob. The sensationalism of the story line is tempered by a spare lyrical style rarely effected in Wright's later work. There is something in its somber lyricism that calls to mind "Blood Burning Moon," Jean Toomer's tale of an interracial triangle.[14] The similarities go beyond style. The black men in both stories are responsible and independent: " 'An next year,' " Tom Burwell boasts to Louisa in his wooing speech, " 'I'll have a farm. My own' " (p. 57). Silas boasts upon his return from town after selling his cotton for a good price: " 'Ah bought ten mo acres o lan. Ahma have to git a man to hep me nex spring . . .' " They are also proud of their ability to act as (white) men, despite the obstacles in their way. " 'My bales,' " Tom continues, " 'will buy yo what y gets from white folks now. Silk stockings an purple dresses— . . .' " (p. 57). And Silas continues, " 'Ain't tha the way the white folks do? Ef yuhs gonna git anywhere yuhs gotta do jus like they do.' " Both men meet fiery ends because they will not allow white men to trample on their pride by exploiting their women sexually. This view, that the rape of a black woman is not so much an attack upon her person, an assault upon her honor as an affront to the masculinity of black men, is in keeping with the patriarchal tenets of the tradition. Wright, as we shall see, is an extreme case, even within the general paternalism of the tradition.

Rather than the lurid, gothic landscape of Toomer's south—"Up from the dusk the full moon came, blowing like a fired pine knot, it illumined the great door and shadowed the Negro shanties . . . the full moon in the great door was an omen. Negro women improvised songs against its spell" (p. 51)—Wright's southern landscapes, where they appear at all, are usually straightforwardly hostile, or less often, as in "Long Black Song," sentimentally suggestive: "Sarah saw green

---

[12]Ellen Wright and Michel Fabre, eds., *Richard Wright Reader* (New York: Harper & Row, 1978) 738.

[13]Wright seems to have been particularly fond of three feminine names, "Sarah": the name of characters in "Long Black Song" and *The Outsider*; "Bess" or "Bessie": in *Black Boy* and *Native Son*, respectively; and "Gladys": Cross Damon's wife in *The Outsider*, and the name of the hero's girlfriend in *The Long Dream*.

[14]Jean Toomer, *Cane* (New York: Harper & Row, 1969), 51–70.

fields wrapped in the thickening gloom . . . The after-glow lingered, red, dying, somehow tenderly sad. And far away, earth and sky met in a soft swoon of shadow." More important is the contrast between the two women who stand at the apex of the triangles. Louisa is a woman, both sexually and racially aware: "To meet Bob [Stone, the younger son of the white family for whom she works] in the canebrake as she was going to do in an hour or so was nothing new." On the other hand, in her womanliness, Louisa *feels*, correctly, that Tom's proposal is on the way. And she genuinely cares for both men: "By measure of that warm glow which came into her mind at the thought of [Stone] he had won her" (p.51). Yet Tom Burwell "held her to the factory town more firmly than he thought . . . His black balanced and pulled against the white of Stone when she thought of them" (p. 52). Tom declares himself and makes it clear to her that she cannot have both Stone and himself. Given this kind of choice, Louisa's decision to have Tom carries all the more weight and Stone's refusal to accept her decision is all the more reprehensible.

Compared to Louisa, Sarah seems almost infantile in her behavior. She continually misreads the signs implicit in the white man's presence: "She looked at him; she saw he was looking at her breasts. He's just like a lil boy. Acks like he can't understand *nothin!*" She cannot see the economic trap posed by the installment plan the white salesman proposes for the purchase of the gramophone clock: " 'It only costs fifty dollars' " [fully one-fifth of all that Silas has earned for the year's cotton crop!] " '. . . just five dollars down and five dollars a month,' " the white man urges. Sarah smiles, "the white man was just like a little boy. 'Jus like a chile.' " "Jus like a lil boy, jus like a chile" runs through Sarah's encounter with the white man. And she is, in some literal sense, correct. He is a college student working at a summer job.

Yet it is clear from the beginning of this encounter that the salesman represents something more than the stereotypically lusting white boy-man. His presence is heralded by a throb that Sarah at first thinks is an airplane. It turns out to be the throbbing engine of a car. These two ubiquitous symbols of the twentieth century usually spell trouble in the backwater world of southern Negroes and poor whites. And so it proves. The white man sells both time and timelessness—a gramophone with a clock built into it. We are, of course, aware, as perhaps Wright was only dimly so, that the gramophone made possible the preservation and perpetuation of Afro-American musical culture in the face of the fragmentation caused by industrialization and urbanization in the first half of the twentieth century. Indeed, music was one of the chief apolitical elements in the tradition holding blacks together as a group.

The clock and the gramophone are an intriguing symbol in this regard for what the white man sells Sarah is a kind of carrot-and-stick initiation into the twentieth century: a means of participating in the collective culture, and the instrument that has helped to alienate people from natural time and made them vulnerable to mechanization. And Sarah is enthralled by the music. She is totally puzzled, however, about the need for a clock. She and Silas " 'git erlong widout time.' " They know when to get up because they " 'git up wid the sun.' " They tell when it's night (a rather stupid question on the white man's part) because it gets dark when the sun goes down.

The discrepancy between Sarah's world and the world represented by the white man is further underscored by Baby Ruth who beats on an old discarded clock; the bang! bang! bang! of her destruction of the old timepiece punctuates the initial dialogue, almost as though the baby is trying to recall Sarah to a consciousness of her marriage and family. Wright uses this echo as an ironic sound effect to climax the sexual act between Sarah and the white man. "She rode on the curve of the white bright days and dark black nights . . . till a high red wave of whiteness drowned her . . . and boiled her flesh *bangbangbang*," fusing the romantic long-ings that have dominated Sarah's thoughts, the climax of the sex act, and the real-ity of Sarah's marriage in a cold and literal image that foreshadows how Sarah's world ends.

In the seduction scene itself, Sarah is clearly torn between her own aroused desires: "Where his hands held her breast the flesh seemed to knot . . . she felt his lips touching her throat and where he kissed it burned," and the racial implications of her act: "But he's a *white* man, a *white* man," she thinks. He's a white man, a white man is a minor, a very minor refrain, meant obviously (But he's . . . Naw Naw) to conjure up centuries of oppression and physical violation as a protection against the present weakness of the flesh. The spell does not work for Sarah. Or perhaps another spell is at work.

Wright has been careful to show that Sarah can control her sexual impulses. She has demonstrated sexual reserve prior to her marriage with Tom, a former suitor (thoughts of whom come to her mind throughout the story): "She had held Tom up and he had held her up; they had held each other up to keep from slipping to the ground there in the corn field." Or again: "She had closed her eyes and . . . gone weak in his arms and had felt that she could not breathe any more and had torn away and run run run home." A look at the response of Aunt Sue ("Bright and Morning Star") to the physical presence of a white man provides further insight into Sarah's ambiguous response to the white man's advances.

Aunt Sue, beaten senseless by a mob of white men, regained consciousness and saw a white face that for a moment she could not recognize. In her dazed condition, she felt "somehow that she existed only by the mercy of the white face . . ." The face had for her the fear of "all the white faces she had ever seen in her life . . . She stood stone still" (as Sarah is still when the white man's arms tighten around her). Sue accepted the white man's "presence because she felt she had to . . . It seemed that the white man towered over her as a challenge to her right to exist upon the earth." And finally—"She was speaking even though she did not want to; the fear of the white man had hold of her, compelled her . . ." as Sarah is compelled "to straighten" her body against the white man's and so rub against his length as he holds her, "or die." Implicit here is the idea that black women have been conditioned by the threat of physical force to an almost unconscious submissiveness in the presence of white men, and it is this threat that helps to make "seduction," rather than rape, possible between Sarah and the white man.[15]

This, perhaps, explains the actual seduction. It cannot account for Sarah's reaction after the seduction: she lies in bed, "conscious of herself all over, full of a vast peace." We will, for the moment anyway, take the fact that Sarah leaves incriminating evidence—the white man's hat, his soiled handkerchief—lying about for Silas to find, that she spends no time reflecting on her actions or planning, however crudely, what she will tell Silas about the gramophone, as hasty plotting, undercharacterization. This is, after all, one of Wright's early stories. But we must note that only Silas's almost casual threat of violence galvanizes Sarah to some sort of defense. Nor can Sarah understand, at least initially, the enormity of her betrayal. "She wanted to tell Silas," after he has discovered the hat and the handkerchief, put one and one together, and chased her from the house, "that there was nothing to be angry about, that what she had done did not matter; that she was sorry; that after all she was his wife and still loved him."

Sarah does eventually come to acknowledge and understand something of the consequences of her action. Her maturation makes "Long Black Song" the story of Sarah's initiation into black adult/woman-hood. As she hides in the darkness waiting for what the morning will bring, Sarah realizes that Silas is a good man, as good to her "as any black man could be to a black woman." In betraying him, she has betrayed a rare personage in early Afro-American experience, a black man who has succeeded in acquiring the legitimate economic means to care for his family almost as well as the average white man. And most significantly, she has betrayed the collective dream, the idea that given a decent chance at economic stability and upward mobility black people could build stable families and viable communities.

Sarah gains also an increased and, one hopes, more functional racial consciousness: "Silas would never forgive her for something like [her infidelity]. If it were anybody but a white man it would be different." And she begins to assume responsibility for her actions: "She should not have done that last night [had sex with the white man]. This was all her fault, 'Lawd if anything happens t im its mah blame.'" Her maturity comes too late. The white man, even as she acknowledges her guilt, has returned to collect the down payment on the gramophone, and Silas is about to confront him.

The growth of Sarah's character, however, is overshadowed by the greater development in the character of Silas. There is some suggestion of the petty bourgeoisie, the thrift and accommodationist rhetoric of Booker T. Washington, in the way he talks of his land and his emulation of the white man's economic practices. Economic security may have driven Sarah into his arms. Certainly her thoughts when he returns from town are not of her own actions but of what he

---

[15]Much the same sort of rationale is offered by a white character in Ernest Gaines, *The Autobiography of Miss Jane Pittman* (New York: Dial Press, 1972), pp. 193–94. Miss Jane, an old exslave, greets this theory with incredulity: " '. . . ain't this specalatin?' " Certainly the theory is far more plausible in the case of Sarah and Aunt Sue than it is in Miss Jane's autobiography.

might have brought her—the red calico she had asked for, it turns out, and a pair of high top shoes as a surprise. Yet under the goading of Sarah's infidelity, Silas grows before our eyes, not so much taking over the story from Sarah as shining her down. For in her descent into worldly knowledge, Sarah is only able to traverse so far: " 'Lawd,' " she asks as she watches from afar while Silas awaits the white mob he knows will come to avenge the death of the white man he has killed, " 'how could Silas want to stay there like tha [and fight it out with the mob]?' " She has no understanding of Silas's heroic vision.

Silas dies in "eager plumes of red." But Sarah's is the last action: "She turned and ran . . . blindly across the fields crying" and the last words, " 'Naw Gawd!' " We are left with a final image of a black man flung into a bloody and violent conflict with the racist society by the thoughtless action of his helpmate; our final image of the black woman is that of a flighty wanton who has carelessly tossed away her own honor and that of her husband—perhaps without even realizing that there is such a thing as racial or sexual honor—whose grasp of her husband's heroism, even though she has seen it in action, is still and at best, minimal. The message of the story, simply put, is that the black man must combat racist oppression without and treachery from the black woman within.

Wright later shows some understanding of the sexual harassment to which black women are often subjected by white men in "Man of All Work,"(*Eight Men*, 1962), in which a black man poses as a woman in order to get a job and support his wife and family. But the coupling of a peasant mentality with an overriding sexuality as dominant characteristics of black women in the flower of their productive years appears again and again in his works.

There is Bess Moss, the daughter of Wright's landlady in *Black Boy*, who is "astoundingly simple yet vital in a way that [he] had never known." Young Richard is both attracted and repelled by her. "What could I do with a girl like this? Was I dumb or was she dumb? I felt that it would be easy to have sex relations with her and I was tempted." But, he wonders, "could I even talk to her about what I felt, hoped? Could she even understand my life? What had I above sex to share with her, and what had she? But I knew that such questions did not bother her." Even so, "he kissed her and petted her. She was eager, childish, pliable . . ." Or the "nameless and illiterate black child with a baby" whose father she does not know in *American Hunger*: "She was not calculating; if she liked a man she just liked him. Sex relations were the only relations she had ever had; no others were possible, so limited was her intelligence." This time, young Richard is more repelled than attracted. "I wondered just what a life like hers meant in the scheme of things and I came to the conclusion that it meant absolutely nothing." But unlike the preceding episode, these reflections do not keep him from engaging in sex with the young woman.

Dot, Cross Damon's young mistress in *The Outsider*, while more complex, is still recognizable as the wanton. She is described as "a passionate child achingly hungry for emotional experience . . . He would try to talk to her and as he talked he could tell that she was not listening; she was pulling off her dress, slipping down her nylon stockings, stepping out of her nylon slip and panties." Though she is a passionate child, Dot has little of that "terrible simplicity" that characterized Bess Moss and the nameless illiterate of Wright's early days in Chicago. During their first meeting, a secret erotic link springs up between Dot and Cross, but to admit this, Dot must also acknowledge that she allowed Cross, then a stranger, to fondle her breasts in public. She balances her moral notions with her emotional hungers by denying that she was aware of Cross's touch—this despite the fact that Cross has felt the proof of her arousal. And beneath her ardent denials, behind the shame and indignation whenever he mentioned the incident, "there was a furtive sense of erotic pleasure." There is too in this characterization a certain mindless self-absorption that makes communication impossible: "He came at last to believe that she accepted the kind of talk in which he indulged as a mysterious part of a man's equipment, along with his sex organs."

Cross does not see that Dot's response to "his emptying out of his soul the dammed up waters of reflections and brooding thoughts" is very similar to that of Gladys, his wife, in the early stages of their relationship when "he told her something important": "Her feminine instinct placed him at once in the role of a strong and reliable man and encouraged him to play it." Both women appear vulnerable at first. Gladys had simply clung to him, making no demands, imposing no condition, setting no limits. Dot is a younger version of Gladys just as she is a younger version of Cross's mother. The three are linked together by their common betrayer, Cross, the black man, a link that Wright makes explicit when Cross's mother upbraids him about Dot's pregnancy. Cross knows that as his mother speaks, she is "reliving her own experience, grieving over her thwarted hopes that had driven her into the arms of religion for the sake of her sanity." And Dot's vulnerability, as was Gladys's, is deceptively double-edged. Dot is not the nonentity that her name implies, rather she is "Miss Dorothy Powers," underage victim of his statutory rape.

Wright's description of Gladys makes clear why it is impossible for Cross ever really to relate to the three women. "When she spoke at all on general topics it was about how good it was to have someone to be with when the whole world was white and she was colored." Cross, inspired by an almost missionary zeal, "hungered for her as a woman of his own color who was longing to conquer the shame imposed upon her by her native land because of her social and racial origins." Gladys is crippled by color consciousness, a fact that in time Cross "grew to accept along with her womanness." Because she is crippled, she is incapable of ever understanding anything about him. When she denies him at the end of the novel, she is being quite literally correct for she has never known Cross.

What disturbs here is not so much the portraits themselves, for one cannot, *ought not,* deny the psychological ravages of racism or the tortured moral positions that the double standard imposes upon black women. Rather, the disturbing element is the implication that sex and sexuality somehow preclude black women's ever acquiring a deep understanding of the situation of black men. This implication is made explicit in *The Long Dream* (1958). Fish Tucker, the young hero of the novel, is attracted to Gladys because she looks like a white woman. Yet, even the almost white Gladys is afflicted with the black woman's lack of comprehension: "Didn't she know that black men were killed for riding in cars side by side with women of her color," Fish wonders as he drives her around their small southern community. "Or did she regard it all as a childish game? It was plain that he would have to educate her, tell her what the racial score was." Fish realizes that Gladys does not possess enough imagination to see herself or the life she lived in terms that white people saw black people. True to the heroic ideal, Fish himself "hotly rejected the terms in which white people weighed or saw him for those terms made him feel agonizingly inferior . . . he was astounded that Gladys could feel or sense none of this." Finally he concludes, "In a certain way she was mentally *blacker* than he was, though she looked whiter."

In *The Outsider,* Wright goes on to develop in the character of Eva Blount a soul mate for Cross Damon who is an outsider, not because he "was born black and poor, but because he had thought [his] way through the many veils of illusion." That Cross's soul mate is a white woman is supposed to be beside the point, for what stands between Cross and Eva is "a wall not of race but of mutual guilt, blood and false identity." And maybe for Cross, Eva's race is incidental. Certainly there seems to be only simple chauvinism and egomania in his acceptance of her: "Her soul was reaching toward him for protection, for solace. Cross smiled, feeling that he was listening to her words as perhaps God listens to prayers. . . . A wave of hot pride flooded him. She was laying her life at his feet. With a gesture of his hand he could own her, shield her from the party, from fear, from her own sense of guilt." Yet Eva's white skin seems to be all that distinguishes her from the other women whom Cross has fled. Like Cross's mother, his wife, and his mistress, "Eva would never be able to comprehend that he was a lost soul spinning like a stray atom far beyond the ken of her mind. . . . She did not understand who or what he was or what he had done, could not believe it when she heard it." Rather than arousing contempt, her ignorance excites Cross's desire, ". . . he turned to her and took her in his arms and had her so slowly and so intensely and with a mounting frenzy of sensual greed . . ." The irony is that Cross finds Eva only to lose her. His deeds are so dark and terrible that even "this sweet girl" clinging to him could not absolve him of his guilt.

The loss of Eva underscores the central theme of the novel, that modern man, having thought himself through the many veils of illusion, stands forever outside the possibility of human fellowship. Eva is the classic white woman, beautiful, delicate, helpless, a character seen fairly often in Afro-American fiction of the fifties and sixties, particularly in novels by black men. Invariably, the white woman's beauty, her sensitivity, her *whiteness* symbolize ultimate liberation and justify the denigration of the black woman.

One feels less churlish now than ten years ago in pointing out that there is something at least ironic, if not downright contradictory, in calling the murderer of a black woman a rebel of the ghetto as critics persist in doing with Bigger Thomas in *Native Son*. It is not simply that Bigger's murder of his girlfriend, Bessie (because she *might* tell the police about his murder of the white woman, Mary Dalton), compromises his claim to heroic status, but that murder—literally or figuratively—seems to be the only means that Wright has of dealing with black women in his work—when he can bring himself to deal with them at all. We know, of course, that black women are more than, other than, the weak mothers and whores portrayed in his work; know also that neither the imagery nor the author's stance is unique in the tradition. This discussion of an important subtext in Wright's work can even be seen as casting a deeper and truer light over his reputation, rather than diminishing it, for his place in the tradition does not depend upon these often scandalous portraits of black women. Yet, we must also acknowledge that insofar as Wright refused, by rehashing the old stereotypes, to engage with black women, he stunted his own artistic growth. His treatment of black women blinded him to the strengths of Afro-American traditions, the folk culture he thought could not survive outside the South, that even as he began his career as a writer was already being transformed in urban ghettos in the north and west. Only toward the end of his life did he awaken to the value of Afro-American popular music as something more than setting.

Having said all this, one is still left with the question, What does one do with a brother who don't love you, who even when he is "loving" you ain't liking you? In part we are answered by the works of black women writers—Ann Petry, Dorothy West, Gwendolyn Brooks, Paule Marshall, Lorraine Hansberry—who in the two decades following the publication of *Native Son* explored much the same urban landscape as Wright. The effects of racism are portrayed clearly and movingly, yet none of these writers sees black life so exclusively in terms of deprivation as Wright, nor do they carry on in their works the kind of covert sexism that is endemic to Wright's fiction. In part we are answered by the work of black feminist critics—Barbara Smith, Mary Helen Washington, Maria K. Mootry, and others—who are forcing the reevaluation and reinterpretation of the entire canon of Afro-American literature so that it more accurately reflects the presence and role of women. And finally, and perhaps most effectively, we are answered by the silent sister-woman in our own hearts: Papa Dick is an example, chile, not a model for making a constructive start.

I Do Believe Him Though I Know
He Lies: Lying as Genre and Metaphor
in Richard Wright's *Black Boy*

Timothy Dow Adams

Since the publication of *Black Boy* in 1945, reactions to its authenticity have been curiously contradictory, often mutually exclusive. For many readers the book is particularly honest, sincere, open, convincing and accurate. But for others *Black Boy* leaves a feeling of inauthenticity, a sense that the story or its author is not to be trusted. These conflicting reactions are best illustrated by the following representative observations by Ralph White and W.E.B. DuBois. White, a psychologist, identified "ruthless honesty" as "the outstanding quality which made the book not only moving but also intellectually satisfying."[1] But DuBois noted that while "nothing that Richard Wright says is in itself unbelievable or impossible; it is the total picture that is not convincing."[2] Attempting to reconcile these opposing views, I wish to argue that both sides are correct, that the book is one of the most truthful accounts of the black experience in America, even though the protagonist's story often does not ring true, and that this inability to tell the truth is Wright's major metaphor of self. A repeated pattern of misrepresentation becomes the author's way of making us believe that his personality, his family, his race—his whole childhood and youth—conspired to prevent him from hearing the truth, speaking the truth, or even being believed unless he lied.

In terms of truth, we expect from an autobiography obedience to the conventions of the genre which hold that the story being presented is a significant part of a person's life, written in retrospect by the subject of the story, who purports to believe that he or she is telling a truthful version of the past. The reader expects, even enjoys, detecting misrepresentations, odd emphasis, telling omissions, and over and under determination, and will willingly overlook factual errors, but for most readers an autobiography is dishonest if the author does not seem to be try-

Reprinted from *Prose Studies* 8.2 (1985): 172–187. By permission of Timothy Dow Adams and Frank Cass and Co. Ltd.

[1]Ralph K. White, "*Black Boy*: A Value Analysis," *Journal of Abnormal and Social Psychology* 42 (1947), 442–3.

[2]W.E.B. DuBois, "Richard Wright Looks Back," *New York Herald Tribune Weekly Book Review*, 4 March, 1945, p. 2; rpt. in *Richard Wright: The Critical Reception*, ed. by John M. Reilly (New York: Burt Franklin, 1978), 133.

ing to tell the overall truth. I agree with A.O.J. Cockshut's assertion that "the simple truth of accurate record of facts is clearly important; but as a rule this is overshadowed by other kinds. At the same time we are judging the autobiographer's central idea" which must have "its own momentous dignity" and must be "truly felt as working through the contingent and everyday."[3] For most contemporary readers worries about *Black Boy's* trustworthiness stemmed from questions of genre: although the book was clearly not called "The Autobiography of Richard Wright," its subtitle—"A Record of Childhood and Youth"—did suggest autobiography. The following descriptions of *Black Boy* reflect the confusion of readers: biography, autobiographical story, fictionalized biography, a masterpiece of romanced facts, a sort-of-autobiography, pseudo-autobiography, part fiction/part truth, autobiography with the quality of fiction, and case history.[4]

Some of these generic confusions were generated by Wright's statements about his creation; he meant the work to be collective autobiography, a personalized record of countless black Americans growing up with a personal history of hunger, deprivation, and constant racism. He also remarked that he decided to write his life story after giving an autobiographical talk to a racially mixed audience at Fisk University in Nashville in 1943. After the talk, he noted that he "had accidentally blundered into the secret black, hidden core of race relations in the United States. That core is this: nobody is ever expected to speak honestly about the problem. . . . And I learned that when the truth was plowed up in their faces, they shook and trembled and didn't know what to do."[5] A year later, Wright used the same metaphor when he wrote "the hardest truth to me to plow up was in my own life."[6] But speaking honestly about a racism endemic throughout America was more complicated, both for author and for reader, than Wright could have known, and, for many, a more delicate instrument than a plow was needed for harvesting the past. Using truthfulness as his watchword, Wright began *Black Boy* as an attempt to set the record straight, including his personal one, which already consisted of a number of "biographies of the author" or "notes on contributors" written by himself in the third person, sometimes with exaggerated accounts of his youth. In several interviews, as well as in "The Ethics of Living Jim Crow," an autobiographical sketch published originally in *American Stuff: WPA Writers' Anthology* in 1937, Wright had already given an incorrect birth date, and begun to establish a history overemphasizing the negative aspects of his early life.[7]

Most revelatory about the conflict between his intentions and the actual writing of his personal narrative is the following observation from a newspaper article called "The Birth of Black Boy":

[3]A.O.J. Cockshut, *The Art of Autobiography in 19th & 20th Century England* (New Haven: Yale Univ. Press, 1984), 216.

[4]For these terms see, in Reilly, the following: Gottlieb, Creighton, DuBois, Garlington, Bentley, Richter, and Hamilton, 122–76.

[5]Quoted in Michel Fabre, *The Unfinished Quest of Richard Wright*, trans. by Isabel Barzun (New York: William Morrow, 1973), 578.

[6]Fabre, *Unfinished Quest*, 578.

[7]Fabre, *Unfinished Quest*, 250.

The real hard terror of writing like this came when I found that writing of one's life was vastly different from speaking of it. I was rendering a close and emotionally connected account of my experience and the ease I had had in speaking from notes at Fisk would not come again. I found that to tell the truth is the hardest thing on earth, harder than fighting in a war, harder than taking part in a revolution. If you try it, you will find that at times sweat will break upon you. You will find that even if you succeed in discounting the attitudes of others to you and your life, you must wrestle with yourself most of all, fight with yourself; for there will surge up in you a strong desire to alter facts, to dress up your feelings. You'll find that there are many things that you don't want to admit about yourself and others. As your record shapes itself an awed wonder haunts you. And yet there is no more exciting an adventure than trying to be honest in this way. The clean, strong feeling that sweeps you when you've done it makes you know that.[8]

Although Wright seemed unsure of his book's generic identity, he never referred to *Black Boy* as an autobiography. His original title, "American Hunger," later used for his life story after leaving Memphis for Chicago, came after he had rejected *The Empty Box, Days of Famine, The Empty Houses, The Assassin, Bread and Water,* and *Black Confession,* all of which sound like titles for novels.[9] When his literary agent suggested the subtitle "The Biography of a Courageous Negro," Wright responded with "The Biography of An American Negro," then with eight other possibilities including "Coming of Age in the Black South," "A Record in Anguish," "A Study in Anguish," and "A Chronicle of Anxiety," which indicate his feeling that the book he had written was less personal, more documentary—a study, a record, a chronicle or even a biography—than autobiography.[10] Constance Webb reports that Wright was uneasy with the word *autobiography,* both because of "an inner distaste for revealing in first person instead of through a fictitious character the dread and fear and anguished self-questioning of his life" and because he realized he would write his story using "portions of his own childhood, stories told him by friends, things he had observed happening to others" and fictional techniques.[11]

Although some readers see Wright as unsuccessful in his struggle neither "to alter facts" nor to "dress up feelings," the book's tendency to intermix fiction and fact is clearly part of both Wright's personal literary history and the Afro-American literary tradition in which he was writing. The form of *Black Boy* partly imitates the traditional slave narrative, a literary type which allowed for a high degree of fictionality in the cause of abolition.[12] A number of major works of literature by

[8]Quoted in Fabre, "Afterward," to *American Hunger* (New York: Harper & Row, 1977), 138.

[9]Alternate titles cited in Constance Webb, *Richard Wright: A Biography* (New York: G.P. Putnam's Sons, 1968), 206–7 and in Charles T. Davis and Michel Fabre, *Richard Wright: A Primary Bibliography* (Boston: G.K. Hall, 1982), 56.

[10]Fabre, *Unfinished Quest,* 254 and 578.

[11]Webb, 198 and 207–8.

[12]For a discussion of *Black Boy* and slave narratives see Robert B. Stepto, *From Behind the Veil: A Study of Afro-American Narrative* (Urbana: U. of Illinois Press, 1979); Sidonie Smith, *Where I'm Bound: Patterns of Slavery and Freedom in Black Autobiography* (Westport, Conn.: Greenwood Press, 1974); and Stephen Butterfield, *Black Autobiography in America* (Amherst: U. of Massachusetts Press, 1974).

black Americans, such as DuBois' *The Souls of Black Folks,* Toomer's *Cane,* and Johnson's *The Autobiography of an Ex-Coloured Man,* featured mixtures of genres, and Wright, simultaneously a poet, novelist, essayist, journalist, playwright, and actor, often used the same material in different genres. For example, "The Ethics of Living Jim Crow," first an essay, later appeared attached to the stories of *Uncle Tom's Children,* one of which, "Bright and Morning Star," is told in *Black Boy* as a tale which held the protagonist in thrall, even though he "did not know if the story was factually true or not."[13] When "black boy" says that the story is emotionally true, he reflects exactly the kind of truth he wants his readers to respond to in *Black Boy.* Several episodes recounted in "The Ethics of Living Jim Crow" are told in significantly different ways in *Black Boy,* and portions of *Eight Men* were once planned as part of that book. Some of the characters in *Black Boy* have been given fictional names, while Bigger Thomas, the central character in *Native Son,* was the real name of one of Wright's acquaintances.[14] That he used real names in fiction and fictional names in non-fiction is typical of Richard Wright who further confounded the usual distinctions between author and persona by playing the role of Bigger Thomas in the film version of *Native Son.*

Richard Wright makes clear that *Black Boy* is not meant as a traditional autobiography by presenting much of the story in the form of dialogue marked with quotation marks, which suggests the unusual degree of fiction within his factual story. Although critics often point to Wright's first novel, *Native Son* (1940), as the other half of *Black Boy,* another model for this autobiographical work was his just-completed *Twelve Million Black Voices: A Folk History of the American Negro in The United States* (1941). Writing *Black Boy* in the spirit of folk history seemed a reasonable thing to do, and Wright apparently saw no hypocrisy in omitting personal details which did not contribute to what he was simultaneously thinking of as his own story and the story of millions of others. Wright's claim to be composing the autobiography of a generic black child is reinforced by the narrator's particular reaction to racism: "The things that influenced my conduct as a Negro did not have to happen to me directly; I needed but to hear of them to feel their full effects in the deepest layers of my consciousness" (190).

Roy Pascal is correct in asserting that "where a lie is the result of a calculated intention to appear right or important, danger is done to autobiographical truth" and that "the most frequent cause of failure in autobiography is an untruthfulness which arises from the desire to appear admirable."[15] However, most of the omission in *Black Boy* is designed not to make the persona appear admirable, but to make Richard Wright into "black boy," to underplay his own family's middle-class ways and more positive values. He does not mention that his mother was a successful school teacher and that many of his friends were children of college faculty

[13]Richard Wright, *Black Boy: A Record of Childhood and Youth* (1945; rpt. New York: Harper & Row Perennial Classic, 1966), 83. Parenthetical references within the text are to this edition.
[14]See Webb 402 and Richard Wright, "How 'Bigger' was Born," Foreword to *Native Son* (1940; rpt. New York: Harper Perennial Classic, 1969).
[15]Roy Pascal, *Design and Truth in Autobiography* (Cambridge: Harvard U.P., 1960), 63 and 82.

members; he omits most of his father's family background, and his own sexual experiences. Reactions from sensitive Southern whites are mainly left out, including those of the Wall family to whom, we learn from Michel Fabre's biography, "he sometimes submitted his problems and plans . . . and soon considered their house a second home where he met with more understanding than from his own family."[16]

In addition to omissions, name changes, poetic interludes, and extensive dialogue, *Black Boy* is replete with questionable events that biographical research has revealed to be exaggerated, inaccurate, mistaken, or invented. Fabre's section dealing with the *Black Boy* years is characterized by constant disclaimers about the factuality of the story. Some omissions can be explained because the urbane ex-Communist who began *Black Boy* "wanted to see himself as a child of the proletariat" though "in reality he attached greater importance to the honorable position of his grandparents in their town than he did to his peasant background."[17] While these distortions are acceptable to many, especially in light of Wright's intention of using his life to show the effects of racism, there are numerous other manipulations less acceptable because more self-serving.

Most of these incidents are relatively minor, and so doubts seem unimportant; however, the misrepresentations in two of the book's most important episodes— the high school graduation speech and the story of Uncle Hoskins and the Mississippi River—might be less acceptable. "Black boy's" refusal to deliver the principal's graduation speech rather than his own is apparently based on truth, but the version in *Black Boy* leaves out the important fact that Wright rewrote his speech, cutting out more volatile passages as a compromise.[18] The story of Uncle Hoskins does not ring true, for how could a boy whose life had been to that point so violent, be scared of his uncle's relatively harmless trick? One reason the tale feels false is that the story, complete with revelations about Uncle Hoskins such as "I never trusted him after that. Whenever I saw his face the memory of my terror upon the river would come back, vivid and strong, and it stood as a barrier between us," actually happened to Ralph Ellison who told it to Wright.[19]

For many critics, including Edward Margolies, these deliberate manipulations reduce *Black Boy's* authenticity as autobiography because they set up doubts about everything, the same doubts that resonate through the remarks of black writers from DuBois to Baldwin to David Bradley, all of whom have persisted in taking *Black Boy's* protagonist to be Richard Wright.[20] But "Richard Wright is not the same person as the hero of that book, not the same as 'I' or 'Richard' or the 'Black boy', not by several light years," argues James Olney, who refers to the book's chief character as "black boy," explaining that "by means of an encompassing and creative memory, Richard Wright imagines it all, and he is

[16]Fabre, *Unfinished Quest*, 47.
[17]Fabre, *Unfinished Quest*, 6.
[18]Fabre, *Unfinished Quest*, 54.
[19]Webb, 419.
[20]Edward Margolies, *The Art of Richard Wright* (Carbondale: Southern Illinois U.P., 1969), 16.

as much the creator of the figure that he calls 'Richard' as he is of the figure that, in *Native Son,* he calls 'Bigger.' "[21] Olney's idea that the central figure be treated as a single person referred to as "black boy," a literary character representing both the actual author as a child and the adult author—the famous writer imagining himself as representative of inarticulate black children—is finally convincing. That seems to be what Richard Wright meant to do, said he had done, and what he did.

Of course he was working in what we now see as dangerous areas, as recent literary history has shown. Black journalist Janet Cooke was labelled a liar, fired from the *Washington Post,* and relieved of her Pulitzer Prize for inventing a black boy in a series of articles on drug use; Clifford Irving was imprisoned for writing what he presented as Howard Hughes's autobiography; and Alastair Reid has recently been castigated for "cleaning up quotations," condensing, inventing personae and locations, and in general using new journalistic techniques in *The New Yorker.* But Wright's accomplishment in *Black Boy* is different, first because he announces his intentions—in authorial statements external to the text, and by title, quotation marks, use of symbolic and imagistic description, and well-organized plot—and second because he is manipulating his own story, not someone else's. Ellison's review–essay on *Black Boy,* "Richard Wright's Blues," begins with the refrain, "If anybody ask you/ who sing this song,/ Say it was ole [Black Boy]/ done been here and gone,"[22] a blues singer's signature formula that clarifies two important facts about the book. First, the protagonist is a literary character named "Black Boy" who bears the same similarity to Richard Wright as the character Leadbelly, for example, does to the blues singer Huddie Ledbetter who sang about himself so often. Second, Ellison's refrain forewarned that the identity of the protagonist would be called into question by critics who would wonder who the elusive hero was and where he went. Unlike Ellison, who sees *Black Boy* as a talking blues, it is for me a be-bop jazz performance in which Wright uses his life as the melody on which he could improvise.

Part of the complication about lying in *Black Boy*—who is lying and to whom—derives from the interplay between audiences, the resonances between the actual audience, the authorial audience, and the narrative audience, to use Peter Rabinowitz's terms.[23] The actual audience is the group of real humans holding *Black Boy* in their hands as they read. The authorial audience is the group Wright imagined himself addressing. The narrative audience, which Gerald Prince calls the narratee (*narrataire*), is the group of people to whom the narrator is speaking.[24] Sorting out these audiences is particularly confusing

[21]James Olney, "The Ontology of Autobiography," in *Autobiography: Essays Theoretical and Critical,* ed. by James Olney (Princeton: Princeton Univ. Press, 1980), 244–5.

[22]Ralph Ellison, "Richard Wright's Blues," *Shadow and Act* (New York: New American Library, 1966), 89.

[23]Peter J. Rabinowitz, "Assertion and Assumption: Fictional Patterns and the External World," *PMLA* 96 (1981), 408–19.

[24]Gerald Prince, "Introduction à l'étude du narrataire," *Poétique* 14 (1973), 178–96.

but interesting in *Black Boy* because the book is autobiographical and therefore the relation between author and narrator is more complicated than in much fiction, and because both author and narrator are black. The important questions about the race, sex, and assumptions of the reader in the text are difficult to answer absolutely, but it seems clear that Richard Wright relates to the authorial audience as "black boy" does to the narrative audience. Because Wright's actual audience at Fisk University was racially mixed, and because he cited his speaking there as the specific impetus for writing the book, it is logical to assume that the authorial audience is composed of both black and white members. Because the book is dedicated to "ELLEN and JULIA," Wright's white wife and interracial daughter, it seems reasonable to assume that he thought of his authorial audience as being both male and female, black girls as well as black boys.

The question of the narrative audience is more complex, but I believe that the readers inscribed in and by the text, the audience to whom "black boy" is speaking, is also racially mixed, This audience is in one sense made up of all of the people described in the book, black and white, who failed to understand the narrator during his lifetime. At other times the narrator is addressing himself only to a white audience, as in the following presentation of schoolboy boasting, glossed for the white reader:

"Man, you reckon these white folks is ever gonna change?" Timid, questioning hope.

"Hell, no! They just born that way." Rejecting hope for fear that it could never come true.

"Shucks, man. I'm going north when I get grown." Rebelling against futile hope and embracing flight.

"A colored man's all right up north." Justifying flight. (90)

Although the authorial audience includes males and females, the narrative audience seems limited to males, as the narrator makes plain in such statements as "It was degrading to play with girls and in our talk we relegated them to a remote island of life" (90).

These distinctions between audiences are important because the actual reader's attempt to react to the book properly, that is in the right spirit, is somewhat like the narrator's attempts to react properly to the different values in the black and white worlds. Lying to white people is one thing, lying to blacks another. And, as Wright discovered after his speech in Nashville, telling the truth to a mixed audience is more dangerous than separating the truth into white and black versions. When *Black Boy's* authorial and narrative audiences converge, the reader is the least likely to question the authenticity of the story. As the two audiences move apart, the reader begins to feel uneasy, partly because of trying to decide which audience to join.

Many critical objections to *Black Boy's* methods of getting at the truth come from those who instinctly feel something strange about the work, not so much in its generic confusions, as in its tone and in what Albert Stone senses when he writes that "a proud and secret self presides over the text, covertly revealing itself

through event, style, and metaphor."[25] When confronted with *Black Boy's* devia-
tions from absolute biographical truth, less sophisticated readers, such as students,
are seldom bothered. They sense that discrepancies uncovered by reading other
texts have little bearing on the truth of the text at hand. Nevertheless, the same
students often respond unfavourably to what they perceive as inauthenticity arising from within *Black Boy*. And part of their dislike of and distrust for "black boy"
grows from the sense of the times that "narrative past. . . has lost its authenticating
power," as Lionel Trilling observes. "Far from being an authenticating agent,
indeed, it has become the very type of inauthenticity."[26] Caring little about the
crossing of generic boundaries, students are disturbed by the idea that "life is sus-
ceptible of comprehension and thus of management," as Trilling further remarks.[27]
In short, they are uncomfortable with *Black Boy*, not because it is not true, but
because for them it does not ring true. They experience what Barrett Mandel calls
"dis-ease with the autobiography. It seems as if the author is lying (not, please,
writing fiction), although readers cannot always easily put their finger on the lie."[28]

The lying they sense centres on these three concerns: "black boy" is never
wrong, is falsely naive, and is melodramatic, three characteristics of what Mandel
refers to as autobiography in which "the ratification is negative—the light of now
shines on the illusion the ego puts forth and reveals it as false."[29] Mandel believes
that most autobiographers are basically honest, but those who are not give themselves away through tone: "Since the ego is in conflict with the truth, the reader
very often gets that message. The author has created an illusion of an illusion. . . .
The tone is forever slipping away from the content, giving itself away."[30] While
Mandel does not include *Black Boy* in the category of dishonest autobiographies,
instead citing it as a typical reworking of the past, many critics have echoed my students' concerns. For example, Robert Stepto finds fault with two early incidents in
which "black boy" insists on the literal meaning of words: when he pretends to
believe his father's injunction to kill a noisy kitten, and when he refuses ninety-
seven cents for his dog because he wants a dollar. "The fact remains that *Black
Boy* requires its readers to admire Wright's persona's remarkable and unassailable
innocence in certain major episodes, and to condone his exploitation of that innocence in others," writes Stepto. "This, I think, is a poorly tailored seam, if not precisely a flaw, in *Black Boy's* narrative strategy."[31] Rather than seeing these
episodes, and others like them, as examples of bad faith or as rough edges in the
narrative fabric, I see them as deliberate renderings of the terrible dilemma of
black boys, and their need to dissemble about everything, especially about the

---

[25]Albert E. Stone, *Autobiographical Occasions and Original Acts* (Philadelphia: Univ. of
Pennsylvania Press, 1982), 124.
[26]Lionel Trilling, *Sincerity and Authenticity* (Cambridge: Harvard Univ. Press, 1972), 139.
[27]Trilling, 135.
[28]Barrett J. Mandel, "Full of Life Now," in Olney, *Autobiography: Essays Theoretical and Critical*, 65.
[29]Mandel, 65.
[30]Mandel, 66.
[31]Stepto, 143.

nature of their naiveté. Wright's persona is confessing, not boasting. His family life and his difficulty with hypocrisy made lying at once a constant requirement for survival, and a nearly impossible performance, especially for a poor liar whose tone gives him away.

The inability to lie properly, exhibited in countless scenes, is "black boy's" major problem in adjusting to black/white relations in his youth. Asked by a potential white employer if he steals, "black boy" is incredulous: "Lady, if I was a thief, I'd never tell anybody" (160), he replies. *Black Boy* is filled with episodes in which its hero is unable to lie, forced to lie, caught between conflicting lies, not believed unless he lies. Poorly constructed lies are appropriate metaphors to portray a boy whose efforts to set the record straight are as frustrated as his grandfather's attempts to claim a Navy pension, which is thwarted by bureaucratic error for his whole life. Falsehoods are an apt metaphor for the speech of a boy who distrusts everyone, himself included.

Black Boy's opening, in which Wright describes how his four-year-old self burnt his grandmother's house out of boredom and experimentation, is cited by virtually every commentator as an allegory for the fear, rebellion, anxiety, and need for freedom of the hero, as well as for the motifs of fire, hunger, and underground retreat. After the fire, which destroys more than half of the house, the child delivers this recollection:

> I was lashed so hard and long that I lost consciousness. I was beaten out of my senses and later I found myself in bed, screaming, determined to run away. . . . I was lost in a fog of fear. A doctor was called—I was afterward told—and he ordered that I be kept abed, that I be kept quiet, that my very life depended upon it. . . . Whenever I tried to sleep I would see huge wobbly white bags, like the full udders of cows, suspended from the ceiling above me. Later, as I grew worse, I could see the bags in the daytime with my eyes open and I was gripped by the fear that they were going to fall and drench me with some horrible liquid. . . . Time finally bore me away from the dangerous bags and I got well. But for a long time I was chastened whenever I remembered that my mother had come close to killing me. (13)

Albert Stone perceptively notes that the last line of this passage represents "a striking reversal." "Where the reader expects a confession that the boy has tried (although inadvertently or unconsciously) to attack his own family, one finds the opposite. Such heavy rationalization clearly demands examination."[32] The adult autobiographer is not justifying setting houses on fire; rather he is trying to show graphically and suddenly how distrustful a child of four had already become. The episode does not ring true because it is not necessarily literally true. In fact Wright used a contradictory description in "The Ethics of Living Jim Crow," written eight years earlier. Describing a cinder fight between white and black children, he claims he was cut by a broken milk bottle, rushed to the hospital by a kind neighbour, and later beaten by his mother until he "had a fever of one hundred and two. . . . All that night I was delirious and could not sleep. Each time I closed my eyes I

[32]Stone, 126.

saw monstrous white faces suspended from the ceiling, leering at me."[33] The cinder fight is retold in a later section of *Black Boy*, though in this version the hero's mother takes him to the doctor, and beats him less severely.

Like Nate Shaw in Theodore Rosengarten's National Book Award winning *All God's Dangers*, who distinguishes between stories "told for truth" and those "told to entertain," or the old time musician, Lily May Ledford, in Ellesa Clay High's *Past Titan Rock: Journeys Into An Appalachian Valley*, who says "I never tell a story the same way twice, but I tell the truth," Richard Wright has borrowed the rhetoric of the oral historian in consciously fictionalizing the story of the burning house and his subsequent punishment, while sending the reader signals that he has done so. He wants the reader to feel that there is something not quite right about the whole scene. That the three-year-old brother can see the folly of playing with fire when the four-year-old "black boy" cannot, that the reasons for setting the fire are as spurious as the explanation—"I had just wanted to see how the curtains would look when they burned" (11)—that the nightmarish description of white bags filled with foul liquid are obviously meant to be symbolic, and finally that the boy is chastened, not by his actions, but by the thought that his mother had come close to killing him—all these signals are meant to paint a truthful picture of a boy who later came to hold "a conviction that the meaning of living came only when one was struggling to wring a meaning out of meaningless suffering" (112). The opening scene suggests the whole atmosphere of the book, a desperate fear of meaningless visitations of violence without context, a life of deliberate misrepresentations of the truth and complete distrust of all people, a world in which "each event spoke with a cryptic tongue" (14). Throughout *Black Boy* Wright presents a lonely figure whose life does not ring true because "that's the way things were between whites and blacks in the South; many of the most important things were never openly said; they were understated and left to seep through to one" (188), so that all actions are tempered by a sub-text, though obvious to everyone, a strategy which the author claimed to have discovered when he delivered his Fisk University oration.

Whenever the narrator questions his mother about racial relationships, she is defensive and evasive. "I knew there was something my mother was holding back," he notes. "She was not concealing facts, but feelings, attitudes, convictions which she did not want me to know" (58), a misrepresentation which disturbs "black boy" who later says "my personality was lopsided; my knowledge of feeling was far greater than my knowledge of fact" (136). While he holds back or conceals facts, he is usually straightforward about emotional feelings, even though he can say "the safety of my life in the South depended upon how well I concealed from all whites what I felt" (255). Worrying less about factual truth, Wright was determined to stress the emotional truth of Southern life to counteract the stereotypical myths shown in the song which prefaced *Uncle Tom's Children*: "Is it true what they say about Dixie? Does the sun really shine all the time?"

[33]Richard Wright, "The Ethics of Living Jim Crow," in *Uncle Tom's Children* (1938; rpt. New York: Harper Perennial Library, 1965), 4–5.

One of the particular ironies of *Black Boy* is that the narrator's constant lying is emblematic of the truth that all black boys were required not only to lie, but to lie about their lying. In the boxing match between "black boy" and a co-worker, this pattern is played out almost mathematically. The two black boys are coerced into a fight they both know is false, based on lies that are obvious to all. Much of the shamefulness of the whole situation is that they are forced to pretend that they are neither aware that the situation is false, nor that they know the whites know they know. These paradoxes are clearly analyzed in Roger Rosenblatt's essay "Black Autobiography: Life as the Death Weapon":

> They had been goaded into a false and illogical act that somehow became logical and true. At the end of their fight, Wright and Harrison *did* hold a grudge against each other, just as their white supervisors had initially contended. The madness of the situation did not reside in the hysteria of the onlookers, nor even in the confusion of defeat and victory or of power and impotency on the parts of the boxers. It resided in the fact that a lie became the truth and that two people who had thought they had known what the truth was wound up living the lie.[34]

Although personal and institutional racism was everywhere evident, Southern whites generally maintained that they treated blacks more humanely than did Northern whites, that they understood blacks and knew how to deal with them, and that they were friendly with blacks (as evidenced by their calling them by their first names), all of which blacks were supposed to pretend they believed. Whites deliberately set up situations where blacks were forced to steal, and not only did they like to be stolen from, they forced blacks to lie by repeatedly asking them if they were thieves. "Whites placed a premium upon black deceit; they encouraged irresponsibility; and their rewards were bestowed upon us blacks in the degree that we could make them feel safe and superior" (219), notes the narrator. When "black boy" forgets to call a white co-worker named Pease "Mister," he is caught in a trap from which the usual escape is "a nervous cryptic smile" (208). The boy's attempt to lie his way out of the situation fails, despite his ingenuity in turning the false accusation into an ambiguous apology:

> If I had said: No, sir, Mr. Pease, I never called you *Pease,* I would by inference have been calling Reynolds a liar; and if I had said: Yes, sir, Mr. Pease, I called you *Pease,* I would have been pleading guilty to the worst insult that a Negro can offer to a southern white man. I stood trying to think of a neutral course that would resolve this quickly risen nightmare. . . .
>
> "I don't remember calling you *Pease,* Mr. Pease," I said cautiously, "And if I did, I sure didn't mean . . ."
>
> "You black sonofabitch! You called me *Pease,* then!" he spat, rising and slapping me till I bent sideways over a bench. (209)

---

[34]Roger Rosenblatt, "Black Autobiography: Life as the Death Weapon," in Olney, *Autobiography: Essays Theoretical and Critical,* 173.

Episodes like this make clear that inability to tell the truth does not make black boys into liars. Instead the frequent descriptions of the protagonist as a prevaricator reveal to white readers the way blacks used lies to express truths, used, for example, the word "nigger" to mean one thing to white listeners, another to black. The elaborate system of signifying, of using words exactly the opposite of white usage (bad for good/ cool for hot), of wearing the mask to cover emotions, of the lies behind black children's game of dozens—all of these are behind the motif of lying in *Black Boy*. Wright's metaphoric use of lying is made more complex by his awareness that a history of misrepresentation of true feelings made it difficult for black people to be certain when they were merely dissembling for protection, when they were lying to each other, or to themselves. "There are some elusive, profound, recondite things that men find hard to say to other men," muses "black boy," "but with the Negro it is the little things of life that become hard to say, for these tiny items shape his destiny" (254). What sets him apart from his contemporaries is his difficulty with the lying they find so easy: "In my dealing with whites I was conscious of the entirety of my relations with them, and they were conscious only of what was happening at a given moment. I had to keep remembering what others took for granted; I had to think out what others felt" (215).

The actual audience must narrow the gap between the narrative and authorial audience; the reader of *Black Boy* must strive to be like the narrator of *Black Boy*, must keep what is happening at a particular moment and the entire history of black/white relations—the content and the context—together in his or her mind. Wright's context includes the need to speak simultaneously as an adult and as a child, to remove everything from his story that, even if it happened to be true, would allow white readers to maintain their distorted stereotype of Southern blacks. He was searching for a way to confess his personal history of lying, forced on him by his childhood, while still demonstrating that he could be trusted by both black and white. His solution is what Maya Angelou calls "African-bush secretiveness":

> "If you ask a Negro where he's been, he'll tell you where he's going." To understand this important information, it is necessary to know who uses this tactic and on whom it works. If an unaware person is told a part of the truth (it is imperative that the answer embody truth), he is satisfied that his query has been answered. If an aware person (one who himself uses the stratagem) is given an answer which is truthful but bears only slightly if at all on the question, he knows that the information he seeks is of a private nature and will not be handed to him willingly.[35]

What makes *Black Boy* compelling is its ability to remain autobiography despite its obvious subordination of historicity. Although a reader may not be aware of the complexities of "black boy's" "African-bush" slanting of truth, or know about the book's fictionalizing, there is, nevertheless, something unmistakably autobiographical about *Black Boy* that convinces even the unaware. What makes this true is the

---

[35]Maya Angelou, *I Know Why The Caged Bird Sings* (1970; rpt. New York: Bantam, 1971), 164.

way the author signifies his lying through rhetoric, appeals in writing to both black and white, as he was unable to do in his speech at Nashville. One of the patterns of the book's lies involves just such a distinction between speaking and writing.

Wright's claim to be speaking for the millions of inarticulate children of the South is in an ironic way reinforced by the constant difficulty the narrator has with the spoken as opposed to the printed word. Although it is a love of literature that saves "black boy," he is constantly threatened by speaking. Often out of synchronization, he speaks when he should be quiet, or is unable to utter a word when questioned; his words slip unaware from his mouth, flow out against his will. But just as often he is totally paralyzed, unable to produce a phrase. In answer to his early questioning—"What on earth was the matter with me . . . every word and gesture I made seemed to provoke hostility?" (158)—the narrator answers, toward the end of the book, "I knew what was wrong with me but I could not correct it. The words and actions of white people were baffling signs to me" (215).

The problem with the spoken word begins with the narrator's killing the kitten because of the pretence of not reading his father's command as figurative, and continues with the melodramatic description of himself begging drinks as a six-year-old child, memorizing obscenities taught to him in a bar. Later he learns "all the four-letter words describing physiological and sex functions" (32), and yet claims to be astonished, while being bathed by his grandmother, at her reaction to his command: " 'When you get through, kiss back there,' I said, the words rolling softy but unpremeditatedly" (49). Wishing to recall those words, though only vaguely understanding why he is once again being punished so severely, "black boy" says "none of the obscene words I had learned at school in Memphis had dealt with perversions of any sort, although I might have learned the words while loitering drunkenly in saloons" (53). This explanation is weak and unconvincing, given his earlier description of himself and other children stationing themselves for hours at the bottom of a series of outdoor toilets, observing the anatomies of their neighbours.

Forced to declare his belief in God by his family of Seventh Day Adventists, "black boy" mis-speaks again and again. " 'I don't want to hurt God's feelings either,' I said, the words slipping irreverently from my lips before I was aware of their full meaning" (126). Trying to keep his grandmother from questioning him about religion, he hits upon the strategy of likening himself to Jacob, arguing that he would believe in God if he ever saw an angel. Although this plan was imagined with the purpose of "salving . . . Granny's frustrated feelings toward him" (128), the result is that his words are misconstrued. His grandmother thinks he *has* seen an angel, and "black boy" once again has "unwittingly committed an obscene act" (131). His explanation is another example of his difficulty in speaking as others did: "I must have spoken more loudly and harshly than was called for" (131).

Called before a teacher to explain a schoolyard fight with two bullies, the protagonist says, "You're lying!," which causes the teacher to reply, "Don't use that language in here" (137), even though he is right. Once again daydreaming, the narrator interrupts his family's "arguing some obscure point of religious doctrine"

(147) with a remark which he says "must have sounded reekingly blasphemous" (137). This time his grandmother is in bed for six weeks, her back wrenched in attempting to slap her grandson for his statements. Again "black boy" is an innocent victim, beaten for not allowing his grandmother to slap him—his physical, like his verbal skills, out of rhythm with his family. He is slapped for asking his grandmother, on a later occasion, what his dying grandfather's last words were, and for replying to the question "What time have you?" with "If it's a little slow or fast, it's not far wrong" (173). "Black boy's" poor sense of timing makes him feel unreal, as if he "had been slapped out of the human race" (210), makes him resemble Ellison's invisible man who believes that his condition "gives one a slightly different sense of time, you're never quite on the beat. Sometimes you're ahead and sometimes behind. Instead of the swift and imperceptible flowing of time, you are aware of its nodes, those points where time stands still or from which it leaps ahead."[36] Ellison's words, which are also suggestive of the sense of time essential to jazz, describe the narrator who is out of phase with everyone until he can control the timing of his life through the syncopated rhythms of *Black Boy*.

In light of the repeated pattern—swift physical reprisal delivered to the totally astonished narrator for speaking out of turn—it is surprising to read the following justification for his resorting to threatening his Aunt with a knife: "I had often been painfully beaten, but almost always I had felt that the beatings were somehow right and sensible, that I was in the wrong" (118). This confession sounds false because "black boy" never seems to admit that he is blameworthy for anything. "Nowhere in the book are Wright's actions and thoughts reprehensible," objects Edward Margolies, echoing a number of others.[37] Robert Felgar makes a similar point when he remarks that "the reader does tire of his persistent self-pity and self-aggrandizement."[38] An early reviewer argues that "the simple law of averages would prevent any one boy from getting into as many situations as we have related in this story, and one senses with regret, that it is hard to know where biography leaves off and fiction begins."[39] What these critics see as foolish self-pity is most apparent in the heavily melodramatic description of the familiar playground game of crack-the-whip, which the narrator describes in life or death terms: "They played a wildcat game called popping-the-whip, a seemingly innocent diversion whose excitement came only in spurts, but spurts that could hurl one to the edge of death itself. . . . The whip grew taut as human flesh and bone could bear and I felt that my arm was being torn from its socket" (122).

Here the author is depicting a children's game using the kind of rhetoric usually reserved for a slave narrative—a cruel overseer whipping a runaway slave "to the edge of death." Wright's words are not self-pitying; instead he is presenting a naive youth who was never good at lying or exaggerating. The misrepresentation is so obvious that only a particularly inept liar would attempt it, a child who did not

---

[36]Ralph Ellison, *Invisible Man* (1952; rpt. New York: Vintage, 1972), 8.
[37]Margolies, 19.
[38]Robert Felgar, *Richard Wright* (Boston: Twayne Publishers, 1980), 46.
[39]Patsy Graves, *Opportunity* 23 (July 1945), rpt. Reilly, 173.

want to be good at lying. Only an outsider such as "black boy" to the established systems of lying by both races, a representative of the many black adolescents then coming of age—what Wright hoped would be a new generation of the children of Uncle Tom, no longer willing to accept the old lie that the best way to fight racism was to lie through both omission and commission—could fail to distinguish between melodrama and genuine oppression, and to be surprised at the power of his words.

Black Boy should not be read as historical truth which strives to report those incontrovertible facts that can be somehow corroborated, but as narrative truth, which psychiatrist Donald Spence defines as "the criterion we use to decide when a certain experience has been captured to our satisfaction; it depends on continuity and closure and the extent to which the fit of the pieces takes on an aesthetic finality."[40] The story that Richard Wright creates in *Black Boy,* whatever its value as an exact historical record, is important both in telling us how the author remembers life in the pre-Depression South and in showing us what kind of person the author was to have written his story as he did. Although he is often deliberately false to historical truth, he seldom deviates from narrative truth. "Consistent misrepresentation of oneself is not easy," writes Roy Pascal, and in *Black Boy* Wright has made both the horrifying dramatic and the ordinary events of his life fit into a pattern, shaped by a consistent, metaphoric use of lying.[41] "Interpretations are persuasive," argues Donald Spence, "not because of their evidential value but because of their rhetorical appeal; conviction emerges because the fit is good, not because we have necessarily made contact with the past."[42]

In *Black Boy* Wright creates a version of himself whose metaphor for survival and for sustenance is falsehood. But the multiple lies of the narrator, like the fibs of children trying to avoid what they see as irrational punishment, are palpably obvious. They are not meant to deceive; they are deliberately embarrassing in their transparency. For the protagonist, whose home life was so warped that only when he lied could he be believed, Alfred Kazin's dictum—"One writes to make a home for oneself, on paper"—is particularly true.[43] The author's manipulations of genre and his metaphoric lies produced a book about which DuBois's assessment was, in my judgment, exactly backward: although much of what Wright wrote is not literally true, the total picture is ultimately convincing, taken in context. For all his lying, "black boy's" essential drive is for truth, and his constant revelation of how often he was forced to lie should be judged according to the standard set forth by Marcel Eck in *Lies and Truth*: "We will be judged not on whether we possess or do not possess the truth but on whether or not we sought and loved it."[44]

[40]Donald Spence, *Narrative Truth and Historical Truth: Meaning and Interpretation in Psychoanalysis* (New York: W.W. Norton, 1982), 31.

[41]Pascal, 189.

[42]Spence, 32.

[43]Alfred Kazin, "The Self as History: Reflections on Autobiography," in *Telling Lives: The Biographer's Art,* ed. Marc Pachter (Washington, D.C.: New Republic Books, 1979), 89.

[44]Marcel Eck, *Lies and Truth,* trans. by Bernard Murchland (New York: Macmillan, 1970), 160.

Call and Response: Intertextuality in Two Autobiographical Works by Richard Wright and Maya Angelou

Keneth Kinnamon

In his provocative account of Afro-American literary criticism from the 1940s to the present, Houston A. Baker, Jr. traces three stages of development: integrationism, the "Black Aesthetic," and the "Reconstruction of Instruction." As his major representative of the first stage, "the dominant critical perspective on Afro-American literature during the late 1950s and early 1960s," Baker makes a strange choice—Richard Wright, in the 1957 version of "The Literature of the Negro in the United States." According to Baker, Wright, sanguine because of the Supreme Court school desegregation decision of 1954, believed that the leveling of racial barriers in American society would lead to a homogenous American literature in which minority writers would be absorbed into the mainstream of cultural expression. Even the verbal and musical folk forms of the black masses would eventually disappear with the inevitable triumph of democratic pluralism in the social order.[1] Actually, Wright's essay is not basically an optimistic statement of integrationist poetics. It is, rather, a document in the proletarian-protest stage of Afro-American literature and literary criticism that dominated the Thirties and Forties, constituting the stage immediately preceding Baker's first stage.[2] The proletarian-protest stage anticipates elements of all three of Baker's stages. Like the integrationist stage it postulates a fundamental unity of human experience transcending racial and national (but not economic) boundaries. Its commitment to an engaged literature is as fierce as that of the Black Aestheticians. And in "Blueprint for Negro

Reprinted from *Studies in Black American Literature, Vol. II: Belief vs. Theory in Black American Literary Criticism*, eds. Joe Weixlmann and Chester J. Fontenot, pp. 121–134. By permission of Keneth Kinnamon and Penkevill Publishing Company.

[1]"Generational Shifts and the Recent Criticism of Afro-American Literature," *Black American Literature Forum* 15 (1981), 3-4.

[2]Baker seems unaware that "The Literature of the Negro in the United States" in its first version was a lecture Wright delivered in 1945, closer in time and temper to "Blueprint for Negro Writing" (1937) than to the late Fifties. The concluding pages of the essay in Wright's *White Man, Listen!* (Garden City, New York: Doubleday, 1957), 105-150, mentioning the Supreme Court decision, are an addendum for the benefit of European audiences to the lecture first published as "Littérature noire américaine," *Les Temps Modernes*, No. 35 (August, 1948), pp. 193-220. Baker's treatment of Wright here contains other examples of chronological and interpretive confusion.

Writing,"[3] at least, it advocates a sophisticated modern literary sensibility, as does the Stepto-Gates school. What it does not do is examine the special perspective of black women writers, a failing shared by the following three stages. This deficiency seems particularly conspicuous now that good women writers are so abundant and female critics are beginning to assess their achievement in relation to the total Afro-American literary tradition.

Despite its unfortunate effort at social disengagement, to my mind the most illuminating effort to provide a theoretical framework for the interpretation of Afro-American literature is Robert B. Stepto's *From Behind the Veil: A Study of Afro-American Narrative* (Urbana: University of Illinois Press, 1979). In this seminal work Stepto argues that the central myth of black culture in America is "the quest for freedom and literacy." Shaped by the historical circumstances of slavery and enforced illiteracy, this myth exists in the culture prior to any literary expression of it. Once this "pregeneric myth" is consciously articulated, it begins to take generic shape, especially as autobiography or fiction. The resulting narrative texts interact with each other in complex ways that constitute a specifically Afro-American literary tradition and history. In his book Stepto explores this intertextual tradition, dividing it into what he designates "The Call" and "The Response." In "The Call," he treats four slave narratives (by Bibb, Northup, Douglass, and Brown), *Up From Slavery*, and *The Souls of Black Folk*. To this call he discusses the twentieth century response of *The Autobiography of an Ex-Coloured Man, Black Boy,* and *Invisible Man*. All would agree that, of these nine works, those by Douglass, Washington, Du Bois, Johnson, Wright, and Ellison are classics of Afro-American literature, but notice that all of these authors are not only men, but race men, spokesmen, political activists. By way of complementing Stepto's somewhat narrow if sharp focus, I propose here to examine some intertextual elements in *Black Boy* and *I Know Why the Caged Bird Sings* to ascertain how gender may affect genre in these two autobiographical quests for freedom and literacy and, in Angelou's case, community as well.

In many ways these two accounts of mainly Southern childhoods are strikingly similar. Both narratives cover a period of fourteen years from earliest childhood memories to late adolescence: 1913 to 1927 (age four to eighteen) in Wright's case, 1931 to 1945 (age three to seventeen) in Angelou's case. Both Wright and Marguerite Johnson (Angelou's given name) are products of broken homes, children passed back and forth among parents and other relatives. Both have unpleasant confrontations with their fathers' mistresses. Both spend part of their childhoods in urban ghettoes (Memphis and St. Louis) as well as Southern small towns. Both suffer physical mistreatment by relatives. Both are humiliated by white employers. Lethal white violence comes close to both while they are living in Arkansas. Each child is subjected by a domineering grandmother to rigorous religious indoctrination, but each maintains a skeptical independence of spirit. From

---

[3]Richard Wright, "Blueprint for Negro Writing," *New Challenge* 2 (Fall, 1937), 53-65.

the trauma or tedium of their surroundings, both turn to reading as an escape. Both excel in school, Wright graduating as valedictorian from the eighth grade of Smith-Robinson School in Jackson, Mississippi, and Johnson as salutatorian of Lafayette County Training School in Stamps, Arkansas, fifteen years later.

In addition to these general similarities, some highly specific resemblances suggest more than mere coincidence or common cultural background. In *Black Boy* Wright recalls an incident in Memphis involving a preacher invited to Sunday dinner, the main course being "a huge platter of golden-brown fried chicken." Before the boy can finish his soup the preacher is picking out "choice pieces": "My growing hate of the preacher finally became more important than God or religion and I could no longer contain myself. I leaped up from the table, knowing that I should be ashamed of what I was doing, but unable to stop, and screamed, running blindly from the room. 'That preacher's going to eat *all* the chicken!' I bawled."[4] The gluttonous preacher's counterpart in *I Know Why the Caged Bird Sings* is Reverend Howard Thomas, whose "crime that tipped the scale and made our hate not only just but imperative was his actions at the dinner table. He ate the biggest, brownest and best parts of the chicken at every Sunday meal."[5] Wright's literary imagination was first kindled by the story of Bluebeard. As a child Angelou also learned of Bluebeard. A later common literary interest was Horatio Alger, who nurtured Wright's dreams of opportunities denied in the South. To Marguerite Johnson, however, Alger was a reminder that one of her dreams would be permanently deferred: "I read more than ever, and wished my soul that I had been born a boy. Horatio Alger was the greatest writer in the world. His heroes were always good, always won, and were always boys. I could have developed the first two virtues, but becoming a boy was sure to be difficult, if not impossible" (p. 74). One is tempted to think that Angelou had Wright specifically in mind in this passage, but even if she did not, her text provides an instructive gloss on Wright's, pointing out that sexism as well as racism circumscribes opportunity.

Other parallel passages provide additional intertextual clues to a basic difference in perspective on childhood experiences. One of the numerous relatives with whom young Richard could not get along was Aunt Addie, his teacher in a Seventh-Day Adventist school in Jackson. After a bitter confrontation in which the twelve-year-old boy threatens his aunt with a knife, she finds occasion for revenge:

> I continued at the church school, despite Aunt Addie's never calling upon me to recite or go to the blackboard. Consequently I stopped studying. I spent my time playing with the boys and found that the only games they knew were brutal ones. Baseball, marbles, boxing, running were tabooed recreations, the Devil's work; instead they played a wildcat game called popping-the-whip, a seemingly innocent diversion whose excitement came only in spurts, but spurts that could hurl one to the edge of death itself. Whenever

[4]*Black Boy* (New York: Harper, 1945), p. 23. Subsequent parenthetical page citations in the text are to this edition.

[5]Maya Angelou, *I Know Why the Caged Bird Sings* (New York: Random House, 1969), 33–34. Subsequent parenthetical page citations in the text are to this edition.

we were discovered standing idle on the school grounds, Aunt Addie would suggest that we pop-the-whip. It would have been safer for our bodies and saner for our souls had she urged us to shoot craps.

One day at noon Aunt Addie ordered us to pop-the-whip. I had never played the game before and I fell in with good faith. We formed a long line, each boy taking hold of another boy's hand until we were stretched out like a long string of human beads. Although I did not know it, I was on the tip end of the human whip. The leading boy, the handle of the whip, started off at a trot, weaving to the left and to the right, increasing speed until the whip of flesh was curving at breakneck gallop. I clutched the hand of the boy next to me with all the strength I had, sensing that if I did not hold on I would be tossed off. The whip grew taut as human flesh and bone could bear and I felt that my arm was being torn from its socket. Suddenly my breath left me. I was swung in a small, sharp arc. The whip was now being popped and I could hold on no more; the momentum of the whip flung me off my feet into the air, like a bit of leather being flicked off a horsewhip, and I hurtled headlong through space and landed in a ditch. I rolled over, stunned, head bruised and bleeding. Aunt Addie was laughing, the first and only time I ever saw her laugh on God's holy ground. (pp. 96-97)

In Stamps pop-the-whip was considerably less dangerous: "And when he [Maya's brother Bailey] was on the tail of the pop the whip, he would twirl off the end like a top, spinning, falling, laughing, finally stopping just before my heart beat its last, and then he was back in the game, still laughing" (p. 23). Now pop-the-whip is not among the gentlest of childhood activities, but surely it is less potentially deadly than Wright makes it out, surely it is closer to Angelou's exciting but essentially joyous pastime. With his unremittingly bleak view of black community in the South, Wright presents the game as sadistic punishment inflicted by a hateful aunt. In Angelou's corrective it becomes a ritual of ebullient youthful bravado by her "pretty Black brother" who was also her "unshakable God" and her "Kingdom Come" (p. 23).

Another pair of passages shows the same difference. Both Wright's Grandmother Wilson and Johnson's Grandmother Henderson ranked cleanliness close to godliness. On one occasion Wright remembers his grandmother bathing him:

I went to her, walking sheepishly and nakedly across the floor. She snatched the towel from my hand and began to scrub my ears, my face, my neck.

"Bend over," she ordered.

I stooped and she scrubbed my anus. My mind was in a sort of daze, midway between daydreaming and thinking. Then, before I knew it, words—words whose meaning I did not fully know—had slipped out of my mouth.

"When you get through, kiss back there," I said, the words rolling softly but un-premeditatedly. (p. 36)

Naturally the response to this call is a severe beating. Angelou treats a similar situation with humor:

"Thou shall not be dirty" and "Thou shall not be impudent" were the two commandments of Grandmother Henderson upon which hung our total salvation.

> Each night in the bitterest winter we were forced to wash faces, arms, necks, legs and feet before going to bed. She used to add, with a smirk that unprofane people can't control when venturing into profanity, "and wash as far as possible, then wash possible." (p. 26)

No children like to scrub or be scrubbed, but Wright uses the occasion to dramatize hostility between himself and his family, while Angelou's purpose is to portray cleanliness as a bonding ritual in black culture: "Everyone I knew respected these customary laws, except for the powhitetrash children" (p. 27).

In *Black Boy* the autobiographical persona defines himself *against* his environment, as much against his family and the surrounding black culture as against the overt hostility of white racism. Like the fictional persona Bigger Thomas, the protagonist of *Black Boy* is an archetypal rebel who rejects all social norms. In the opening scene he sets his family's house on fire, eliciting a traumatically severe whipping from his mother. His father "was always a stranger to me, always alien and remote" (p. 9). Young Richard subverts his paternal authority by a disingenuous literalism in the cat-killing episode. At the end of the first chapter he recalls his last meeting with his father in 1940, providing an exaggerated geriatric description complete with toothless mouth, white hair, bent body, glazed eyes, gnarled hands.[6] His father was a brutalized "black peasant," "a creature of the earth" without loyalty, sentiment, tradition, joy, or despair—all in contrast to his son, who lives "on a vastly different plane of reality," who speaks a different language, and who has traveled to "undreamed-of shores of knowing" (pp. 30, 31). Wright's symbolic effort to bury his father corresponds to a persistent attempt to come into his own by opposing or ignoring all members of his family, who consistently try to stifle his articulation of his individuality, to inhibit his quest for freedom. Shouting joyously at the sight of a free-flying bird outside his window, Richard is rebuked in the opening scene by his younger brother with the words " 'You better hush.' " His mother immediately steps in to reinforce the message: " 'You stop that yelling, you hear?' " (p. 3). These are the first words spoken to Richard in *Black Boy*, but they reverberate in other mouths throughout the work. His brother plays an exceedingly minor role before being sent to Detroit to live with an aunt. His mother is presented more sympathetically than are other members of the family, but even she functions as a harsh disciplinarian striving to suppress her son's dangerous individualism. His grandmother and other relatives join this effort, leading often to violent arguments in which Richard threatens them with knife or razor blade.

Outside the family the boy's relations to other black children are marked by fights on the street and in the schoolyard described with the same hyperbolic violence employed in the pop-the-whip episode. In the classroom he has to struggle

---

[6]The extent of the exaggeration is evident from the photographs Wright took of his father at the time, which reveal an erect, black-haired, rather youthful appearance for a man in his early sixties. See Constance Webb, *Richard Wright: A Biography* (New York: Putnam, 1968), following p. 128, and Michel Fabre, *The Unfinished Quest of Richard Wright* (New York: Morrow, 1973), 19, 205. Wright's "description" of his father actually corresponds much more closely to a photograph of a sharecropper in Wright's *12 Million Black Voices* (New York: Viking, 1941), 23.

against a paralyzing shyness that renders him almost mute and unable to write his own name: "I sat with my ears and neck burning, hearing the pupils whisper about me, hating myself, hating them; I sat still as stone and a storm of emotion surged through me" (p. 67). In describing his contacts with the general black community Wright emphasizes brutalization and degradation, as in his account of saloons in Memphis or in this paragraph on life in West Helena:

> We rented one half of a double corner house in front of which ran a stagnant ditch carrying sewage. The neighborhood swarmed with rats, cats, dogs, fortunetellers, cripples, blind men, whores, salesmen, rent collectors, and children. In front of our flat was a huge roundhouse where locomotives were cleaned and repaired. There was an eternal hissing of steam, the deep grunting of steel engines, and the tolling of bells. Smoke obscured the vision and cinders drifted into the house, into our beds, into our kitchen, into our food; and a tarlike smell was always in the air. (p. 52)

Richard learns about sex voyeuristically by peeping at the whores at work in the other half of the duplex in the Arkansas town, as he had earlier watched the exposed rears of privies in Memphis. When he does manage to establish some degree of rapport with other boys, "the touchstone of fraternity was my feeling toward white people, how much hostility I held toward them, what degrees of value and honor I assigned to race" (p. 68). But as the reader of "Big Boy Leaves Home," *The Long Dream,* or biographies of Wright knows, in *Black Boy* the author minimizes the important role his friendship with peers actually played in his adolescent life. Religion is also rejected, whether the peripheral Seventh-Day Adventism of his grandmother or the mainstream black Methodism of his mother. So estranged and isolated from the nurturing matrices of black culture, an estrangement as much willed from within as imposed from without, Wright was able to utter this famous indictment:

> (After I had outlived the shocks of childhood, after the habit of reflection had been born in me, I used to mull over the strange absence of real kindness in Negroes, how unstable was our tenderness, how lacking in genuine passion we were, how void of great hope, how timid our joy, how bare our traditions, how hollow our memories, how lacking we were in those intangible sentiments that bind man to man, and how shallow was even our despair. After I had learned other ways of life I used to brood upon the unconscious irony of those who felt that Negroes led so passional an existence! I saw that what had been taken for our emotional strength was our negative confusions, our flights, our fears, our frenzy under pressure.
>
> (Whenever I thought of the essential bleakness of black life in America, I knew that Negroes had never been allowed to catch the full spirit of Western civilization, that they lived somehow in it but not of it. And when I brooded upon the cultural barrenness of black life, I wondered if clean, positive tenderness, love, honor, loyalty, and the capacity to remember were native with man. I asked myself if these human qualities were not fostered, won, struggled and suffered for, preserved in ritual form from one generation to another.) (p. 33)

In part this passage attempts to shame whites by showing them what their racism has wrought, but in a more crucial way it defines Wright's individualistic alienation from all sense of community, that permanent spiritual malaise that is both the key biographical fact and the ideological center of his art.

With Maya Angelou the case is quite otherwise. If she never experienced the physical hunger that characterized much of Wright's childhood, he was not raped at the age of eight. Yet here youthful response to rejection and outrage is to embrace community, not to seek alienation. *I Know Why the Caged Bird Sings* is a celebration of black culture, by no means uncritical, but essentially a celebration. Toward her family, young Marguerite is depicted as loving, whether or not her love is merited. She idolizes her slightly older brother Bailey. Her Grandmother Henderson is presented not only as the matrifocal center of her family but as the leader of the black community in Stamps, strong, competent, religious, skilled in her ability to coexist with Jim Crow while maintaining her personal dignity. She is a repository of racial values, and her store is the secular center of her community. Crippled Uncle Willie could have been presented as a Sherwood Anderson grotesque, but Angelou recalls feeling close to him even if he was, like Grandmother Henderson, a stern disciplinarian. Angelou would seem to have every reason to share Wright's bitterness about parental neglect, but she does not. When her father shows up in Stamps she is impressed by his appearance, his proper speech, and his city ways. Her mother beggars description: "To describe my mother would be to write about a hurricane in its perfect power. Or the climbing, falling colors of a rainbow. . . . My mother's beauty literally assailed me" (p. 58). Absorbed in their own separate lives, her parents neglect or reject her repeatedly, but she is more awed by their persons and their personalities than she is resentful. Her maternal family in St. Louis is also impressive in its worldly way, so different in its emphasis on pleasure and politics from the religious rectitude of the paternal family in Stamps.[7] Even Mr. Freeman, her mother's live-in boyfriend who first abuses and then rapes the child, is presented with more compassion than rancor.

Afflicted with guilt after Freeman is killed by her uncles, Marguerite lapses into an almost catatonic silence, providing an excuse to her mother to send her back to Stamps. Southern passivity provides a good therapeutic environment for the child, especially when she is taken under the wing of an elegant, intelligent black woman named Mrs. Bertha Flowers, who treats her to cookies, Dickens, and good advice. Better dressed and better read than anyone else in the community, she nevertheless maintains good relations with all and urges Marguerite not to neglect the wisdom of the folk as she pursues literary interests: "She said that I must always be intolerant of ignorance but understanding of illiteracy. That some people, unable to go to school, were more educated and even more intelligent than college professors. She encouraged me to listen carefully to what country people called mother wit. That in those homely sayings was couched the collective wisdom of generations" (p. 97). In contrast to Wright's grandmother, who banished from her house the schoolteacher Ella for telling the story of Bluebeard to Richard,

---

[7]George E. Kent discusses this contrast with his customary acuity in "Maya Angelou's *I Know Why the Caged Bird Sings* and Black Autobiographical Tradition," *Kansas Quarterly* 7, No. 3 (1975), 72-78.

Grandmother Henderson is quite friendly with "Sister" Flowers, both women secure in their sense of self and their mutual respect.

Angelou also recalls favorably the larger rituals of black community. Religious exercises, whether in a church or in a tent revival meeting, provide a festive atmosphere for Marguerite and Bailey. Racial euphoria pervades the black quarter of Stamps after a Joe Louis victory in a prizefight broadcast on Uncle Willie's radio to a crowd crammed into the store.[8] A summer fish fry, the delicious feeling of terror while listening to ghost stories, the excitement of pre-graduation activities—these are some of the pleasures of growing up black so amply present in *I Know Why the Caged Bird Sings* and so conspicuously absent in *Black Boy*.

A comparison of the graduation exercises in the two works is particularly instructive. Marguerite is showered with affectionate attention and gifts, and not only from her family and immediate circle of friends: "Uncle Willie and Momma [her Grandmother Henderson] had sent away for a Mickey Mouse watch like Bailey's. Louise gave me four embroidered handkerchiefs. (I gave her three crocheted doilies.) Mrs. Sneed, the minister's wife, made me an undershirt to wear for graduation, and nearly every customer gave me a nickel or maybe even a dime with the instruction 'Keep on moving to higher ground,' or some such encouragement" (p. 169). Richard feels more and more isolated as graduation nears: "My loneliness became organic. I felt walled in and I grew irritable. I associated less and less with my classmates" (p. 152). Refusing to use a speech prepared for him by the school principal, he resists peer and family pressure, as well as the implicit promise of a teaching job, in order to maintain his sense of individual integrity. Giving his own speech, he rejects utterly the communal ceremony implicit in the occasion:

> On the night of graduation I was nervous and tense; I rose and faced the audience and my speech rolled out. When my voice stopped there was some applause. I did not care if they liked it or not; I was through. Immediately, even before I left the platform, I tried to shunt all memory of the event from me. A few of my classmates managed to shake my hand as I pushed toward the door, seeking the street. Somebody invited me to a party and I did not accept. I did not want to see any of them again. I walked home, saying to myself: The hell with it! With almost seventeen years of baffled living behind me, I faced the world in 1925. (p. 156)

The valedictorian of Marguerite's class accepts the help of a teacher in writing his speech, but before he mounts the podium a white politician delivers the Washingtonian message that "we were maids and farmers, handymen and washerwomen, and anything higher that we aspired to was farcical and presumptuous" (pp. 175-176). But this ritual of racial humiliation is immediately followed by a ritual of racial survival and solidarity. After giving his speech, the valedictorian improvises by singing "Lift Ev'ry Voice and Sing" with renewed meaning, joined

---

[8]Wright did share the racial pride in Joe Louis. See "Joe Louis Uncovers Dynamite," *New Masses* 18 (8 October, 1935), 18-19; "High Tide in Harlem," *New Masses* 28 (5 July 1938) 18-20; *Lawd Today* (New York: Walker, 1963), 52; and "King Joe," *Letters* 38 (1971), 42-45.

by all present, the white man having left. From shame the collective emotion is transformed by the song of a black poet to pride: "We were on top again. As always, again. We survived. The depths had been icy and dark, but now a bright sun spoke to our souls. I was no longer simply a member of the proud graduating class of 1940; I was a proud member of the wonderful, beautiful Negro race" (p. 179). Unlike Wright, Angelou stresses the intimate relation of the black creator to the black audience. Gathering his material from the stuff of the black experience, with its suffering and its survival, James Weldon Johnson transmutes the experience into art, giving it back to the people to aid them to travel the stony road, to fortify their spirit by reminding them of their capacity to endure. The episode is a paradigm of Angelou's own artistic endeavor in *I Know Why the Caged Bird Sings*.

It is important to recognize that Angelou's Southern environment is as grievously afflicted by white racism as Wright's. Just as young Richard is tormented by whites, so is Marguerite by her employer Mrs. Cullinan, who calls her out of her name, or by Dentist Lincoln, who owes Grandmother Henderson money but will not treat the child's toothache because " '. . . my policy is I'd rather stick my hand in a dog's mouth than in a nigger's' " (p. 184). White violence comes dangerously close to both Uncle Willie and Bailey. Indeed, the town is quintessentially Southern in its racial attitudes, comparable to Wright's Elaine or West Helena or Jackson: "Stamps, Arkansas, was Chitlin' Switch, Georgia; Hang 'Em High, Alabama; Don't Let the Sun Set on You Here, Nigger, Mississippi; or any other name just as descriptive. People in Stamps used to say that the whites in our town were so prejudiced that a Negro couldn't buy vanilla ice cream. Except on July Fourth. Other days he had to be satisfied with chocolate" (p. 47). It is not that Angelou de-emphasizes the racist assault on Black personality and community; it is just that she shows with respect if not always agreement the defensive and compensatory cultural patterns developed to survive in such an environment. This is Maya Angelou's response in *I Know Why the Caged Bird Sings* to the call of *Black Boy*.

One hesitates to generalize on the basis of a single book by one woman writer, but a quick recall of such writers as Linda Brent, Zora Neale Hurston, Gwendolyn Brooks, Margaret Walker, Paule Marshall, Sonia Sanchez, Toni Morrison, Sherley Anne Williams, Nikki Giovanni, Carolyn M. Rodgers, Ntozake Shange, Alice Walker, Gayl Jones, and numerous others suggests that, more than male writers, women are concerned with such themes as community, sexism (especially sexual exploitation), and relations with family and friends. They seem correspondingly less interested in individual rebellion, alienation, and success against the odds. A theory which can encompass both visions, adding community to the myth of freedom and literacy, accommodating *I Know Why the Caged Bird Sings* as easily as *Black Boy*, may follow the stages delineated by Houston Baker and become the primary contribution of the present decade to Afro-American literary criticism.

Negating the Negation as a Form of Affirmation in Minority Discourse: The Construction of Richard Wright as Subject

Abdul R. JanMohamed

> This battle with Mr. Covey was the turning point in my career as a slave. . . . I now resolved that, however long I might remain a slave in form, the day had passed forever when I could be a slave in fact. I did not hesitate to let it be known of me, that the white man who expected to succeed in whipping, must also succeed in killing me.
>
> In learning to read, I owe almost as much to the bitter opposition of my master, as to the kindly aid of my mistress. I acknowledge the benefit of both.
>
> —Frederick Douglass, *Narrative of the Life of Frederick Douglass*

I

Writing and death stand as the two determining parameters of Douglass's as of Richard Wright's life and career, and the twin imperative of the former can be used to elucidate the latter's self-representation. In light of Douglass's experience and Orlando Patterson's definition of "social death" as a mode of oppression through which slaves, and by extension those who grew up under the control of Jim Crow society, are coerced and controlled, Richard Wright's first autobiographical work, *Black Boy*, can be seen as a complex exploration of his successful attempt to survive the rigors of a racist Southern hegemony and to escape from that confinement through writing. The content of *Black Boy* describes how Wright managed to resist Jim Crow society's attempt to limit his development to that of a "black boy," a sub-human creature devoid of initiative and entirely compliant to the will of white supremacy, whereas the very existence of *Black Boy* as an articulate and penetrating discursive text demonstrates his ability to overcome that drastically limiting formation. In short, *Black Boy* is a testament to the struggle over the formation of black subjectivity in a racist society.

As I hope to demonstrate in this paper, Wright's autobiography illustrates the value of a sustained negation of the attempted hegemonic/ideological forma-

Reprinted from *Cultural Critique* 7 (Fall 1987): 245-266. © Oxford University Press. Used with Permission.

tion—a negation that seems to me paradigmatic of all negation that lies at the center of minority discourse. According to Gilles Deleuze and Félix Guattari the three salient characteristics of minority literature are: 1) the deterritorialization of the dominant or major language by the minor literature that uses that language as a vehicle, 2) the fundamentally political nature of all minor literature, and 3) its tendency to represent collective values. This description, though limited by the fact that it is based on the study of one European writer, Kafka, is quite accurate.[1] Yet it seems to me that Deleuze and Guattari do not trace the genealogy of minority discourse all the way back to its phenomenological source in the relations of domination that constitute the antagonism between dominant and minority groups. I would argue that the three characteristics are based on the minority's prior will to negate the hegemony. Such a will takes precedence because the hegemonic formation of minorities is itself based on an attempt to negate them—to prevent them from realizing their full potential as human beings and to exclude them from full and equal participation in civil and political society—and because minorities cannot take part in the dominant culture until this hegemonic negation is itself negated. The most crucial aspect of resisting the hegemony consists in struggling against its attempt to form one's subjectivity, for it is through the construction of the minority subject that the dominant culture can elicit the individual's own help in his/her oppression. One of the most powerful weapons in the hands of the oppressor is the mind of the oppressed; without control of the latter's mind the dominant culture can enforce compliance only through the constant use of brute force.

Wright's major tactic in resisting hegemonic formation consisted of establishing a specular relation with society's attempt to negate him; he turned himself into a mirror that reflected the negation back at the hegemony: "in what other way had the South allowed me to be natural, to be real, to be myself," he asks rhetorically, "except in rejection, rebellion, and aggression."[2] In a paradox that typifies his life, Wright thrived on resisting all attempts to coerce or break him—his stubbornness gained strength from opposition, and he managed to find virtue in negation. Yet in defining the positive value of literature, the cultural formation that provided him with the only possibility of escape from racist confinement, Wright was partially blind to the relation between the negative and positive components of his subjective formation. Toward the end of his autobiography Wright ponders how he, a young man in many respects as ordinary as hundreds of other black boys in the South, had managed not to succumb to the racist hegemony—why had he retained, indeed cultivated, a consciousness of open possibilities, of larger horizons, of freedom while the white *and* black people surrounding him had "demanded submission." His unequivocal answer points to redeeming the value of literature:

---

[1]Gilles Deleuze and Félix Guattari, *Kafka: Toward a Minor Literature*, tr. Dana Polan (Minneapolis: University of Minnesota Press, 1986): see particularly Chapter Three.

[2]Richard Wright, *Black Boy* (New York: Harper and Row, 1945), 284. All further references to this autobiography will be included in the text.

It had been only through books—at best, no more than a vicarious cultural transfusion—that I had managed to keep myself alive in a negatively vital way. Whenever my environment had failed to support or nourish me, I had clutched at books. (*BB*, 282)

While there is no doubt, judging from the evidence he furnishes, that literature did simultaneously provide him with information about the external world and with an inner, symbolic space wherein he could keep alive the hope of a less constrained life, his endorsement of literature begs the question. Why was he, out of all the other black boys, predisposed to this influence of literature? Why did he find it valuable while others did not and why did he approach it in such a way that it did not become simply a realm of escapist fantasy for him but rather a combative political and aesthetic tool, one that he later used in order to investigate the ideological world of an oppressive society? As he himself admits, and as I shall show later, literature initially played a negative function for him; he had clutched at it more from desperation than from an abiding sense of its intrinsic, independent value. But even this negativity, part of a much larger, sustained negativity, does not provide a sufficient explanation of his unique ability to survive the overwhelming restrictions of racist confinement. No doubt the final explanation is overdetermined, and it is probably impossible to formulate a precise equation governing the various contributing factors. Nevertheless, it is clear that both personality and circumstances conspired to create in Richard Wright a fundamental resistance to the racist attempt to fit him into the hegemonic mold reserved for "niggers."

Among the socio-political circumstances that contributed to Wright's formation the most significant is the Jim Crow extension of the fundamental structures of slave society. According to Orlando Patterson all forms of slavery are characterized by three constituent elements: the slave's "social death," his utter powerlessness, and his overwhelming sense of dishonor.[3] Defeated in battle, the slave is permitted to live in captivity rather than being killed on the battlefield. Thus the slave's status is a substitute for his death, and his powerlessness and dishonor are direct products of that status. His "social death" has two important dimensions: 1) the slave is not absolved from the prospect of death; rather death is conditionally commuted and can be revoked at the master's whim; and 2) he is incorporated into the new society as an internal enemy, as a non-being. He can possess none of the legal, moral, or cultural rights that his masters enjoy. In fact, slave cultures are structured in such a way that the slave has no socially organized existence except that which is allowed him by his master, who becomes the sole mediator between his own living community and the living death his slave experiences. The slave's condition is perpetual and inheritable, a condition that Patterson calls "natal alienation." Ultimately, honor depends on an individual's ability to impose himself on or assert himself against another within culturally accepted terms. In this sense, honor rests on personal autonomy and power, attributes which the slave lacks.

[3]Orlando Patterson, *Slavery and Social Death* (Cambridge, Ma.: Harvard University Press, 1982).

II

The most elemental and persistent manifestation of social death in Wright's life was hunger. By constantly holding the black/slave on the verge of death through virtual starvation, Jim Crow society could exploit and syphon off the entire production of his "life," including his labor, as surplus value. Starvation thus became the most efficacious means of confining the black within the realm of social death. Wright's father's ill-paid work as a sharecropper and later as an itinerant laborer, followed by his desertion of the family, the series of crippling strokes suffered by his mother, the poverty of his maternal grandparents, the inability of a black boy to earn decent wages in the South, and other circumstantial factors forced Wright to exist on the verge of starvation. The most telling evidence of the effect of this hunger on Wright's formation is the psychosomatic link that the child forges between his deep hatred for his father and physical deprivation:

> As the days slid past the image of my father became associated with my pangs of hunger, and whenever I felt hunger I thought of him with a *deep biological bitterness*. (BB, 22; emphasis added)

The absence of the father and food, of protection and nurture, together form a physical and psychic lack that comes to symbolize for Wright an essential feature of the condition of social death.[4] Hunger eventually becomes a metaphor for the intellectual deprivation, the isolation, and the "eternal difference" that are experienced as both personal and racial phenomena by Wright and other black boys in the South: "To starve in order to learn about my environment was irrational, but so were my hungers" (BB, 140). The intellectual and physical starvation imposed by the Jim Crow society becomes such a fundamental feature for Wright that he had originally intended to entitle his autobiographical work *American Hunger*. However, when he agreed to publish it in two parts, the title of the first part, *Black Boy*, designating the generic reductive manner in which all black men are perceived by a racist society, in effect became a kind of synonym, an external mark for the title of the second book, *American Hunger*, designating the inner affliction suffered by all blacks. Through the generic markers that constitute his titles, Wright implies that the external categorization of black men as "boys" is accompanied by an intellectual deprivation, by a systematic attempt to prevent them from coming to consciousness about the relations of domination in a racist society.

Eventually, the "biological bitterness" toward his father comes to include a subdued horror of the barely conscious condition under which his father existed.

---

[4]Not until the publication of *The Long Dream* in 1958, when Wright himself had become a father, was he able to return to this theme with greater equanimity and insight and to show the devastating effects of the inability of the black father to play the symbolic role of the lawgiver and protector in a white racist culture. As I hope to show in my forthcoming study of Wright, his brilliant insights make this novel at least as significant as *Native Son*.

When Wright meets him some twenty-five years after the father had deserted the family, Wright marvels at this man "with no regrets and no hope":

> how completely his soul was imprisoned by the slow flow of the seasons, by the wind and the rain and the sun, how fastened were his memories to a crude and raw past, how chained were his actions and emotions to the direct, animalistic impulses of his withering body. (*BB*, 43)[5]

This stark contrast between Wright, who had not only managed to break out of the confinement of Southern society but who had made his reputation precisely by bringing to consciousness the destructive effects of its culture, and his father, who seems to have capitulated entirely to that culture and whose consciousness had been all but extinguished, marks the kind of social and paternal negation that Wright had to overcome. The culture of social death also forced Wright to develop a deep and abiding familiarity with suffering, which he experienced at a very young age through his mother. After surviving one of her more severe strokes, his mother called him to her one night and confessed her unbearable torment and her desire to die, which elicited from him a painful response: "That night I ceased to react to my mother; my feelings were frozen. I merely waited upon her, knowing that she was suffering." As he had combined his hunger and his hatred for his father into a metaphor, so at this point he was able to cope only by turning his love and her suffering into a symbol:

> My mother's suffering grew into a symbol in my mind, gathering to itself all the poverty, the ignorance, the helplessness; the painful, baffling, hunger-ridden days and hours; the restless moving, the futile seeking, the uncertainty, the fear, the dread; the meaningless pain and the endless suffering. Her life set the emotional tone of my life, colored the men and the women I was to meet in the future, conditioned my relation to events that had not yet happened, determined my attitude to situations and circumstances I had yet to face. (*BB*, 111)

His symbolic appropriation of her suffering, however, had a dual effect on his personality. On the one hand, he transformed the tension between affection and suffering from a static symbol into the central purpose of his life; he became an unrelenting and unflinching explorer of human suffering in general: her illness invoked in him "a conviction that the meaning of living came only when one was struggling to wring a meaning out of meaningless suffering," and it made him "want to drive coldly to the heart of every question and lay it open to the core of suffering that I knew I would find there" (*BB*, 112). On the other hand, it strengthened his predisposition to withdraw from a harsh world into a brooding, meditative isolation. Because, as a poor, black child he found himself powerless to change the external racist world, he turned to an inner, imaginative world of "unlimited possibilities," to fantasies that "were a moral bulwark that enabled me to feel I was keeping my

---

[5]Wright's portrayal of his father is dangerously close to a racist stereotype of the primitive, barely conscious black. Yet as *Native Son* demonstrates, Wright's strategy requires that such stereotypes not be denied through simple negation but rather that they be exploded through a demonstration of how racist society forces blacks to conform to these stereotypes.

emotional integrity whole, a support that enabled my personality to limp through days lived under the threat of violence" (*BB*, 83-34). This inner world of feelings and fantasies grew more rapidly than the external world of facts and opportunities until Wright felt that at the age of thirteen he had a far better understanding of his feelings than he had a command of external facts (*BB*, 136). The two facets of his personality—the retreat into an inner world of fantasies that became "a culture, a creed, a religion" and the dedication to expose the causes of suffering—combined to form the driving impulse of his career as a writer.

The chronological development of negation in Wright's life begins with these two experiences that are captured in the figuration of hunger and suffering. While society forms Wright "indirectly" through these experiences, it attempts to control him more directly through the pervasive violence of Jim Crow culture. The underlying violence, which is in fact the horizon of hegemonic formation within that culture, is accurately captured by the aesthetic structure of "The Ethics of Living Jim Crow," the autobiographical preface to *Uncle Tom's Children*. The understated, casual acknowledgments of violence at the beginning and end of the sketch emphasize how physical brutality profoundly brackets black social formation in the Southern context. The first paragraph describes the house and yard behind the railroad tracks where Wright lived as a young boy. It is not the absence of the greenery of white suburban lawns that Wright laments; instead, the child delights in the cinders that cover the yard because they make "fine weapons" for the war with the white boys, an activity that the child considers "great fun."[6] In contrast to this opening, where the world is unproblematically perceived as an arsenal, the end of the preface represents the world in a latent state of siege. In his speculations on how blacks feel about racial oppression, Wright offers the answer of one of his acquaintances: "Lawd, Man! Ef it wasn't fer them polices 'n' them ol' lynch mobs, there wouldn't be nothin' but uproar down here!" (*UTC*, 15). Thus racist hegemony and the marginalization of blacks, along with the distortion of their psyches, are based on the daily use of the threat of overwhelming violence, based indeed on the ever-provisional deferral of their death sentences, which the blacks, in order to survive, eventually have to accept as a pedestrian fact of life. That is, they have to learn to live "normally" in what Wright calls the culture of "terror."

Even as a young child, his political precocity enabled him to understand, in a vague, emotional way, the fundamental structure of this culture. His early attitudes to death and fate were no doubt aided by his sympathy for the prolonged suffering of his mother, by her confessed desire to die, and by his grandmother's religious preoccupation with death—which made him "so compassionately sensitive toward all life as to view all men as slowly dying"—and her otherworldly notion of fate, which "blended with the sense of fate that I had already caught from life" (*BB*, 123-24). Wright's insight into the fundamental structures of his

---

[6]"The Ethics of Living Jim Crow," preface to *Uncle Tom's Children* (New York: Harper and Row, 1940), 3. All further references to this preface will be incorporated in the text.

political situation and his incipient decision to negate the hegemony in an uncompromising manner manifest themselves in his resolution not to accept the master/slave contract. While pondering the mysteries of his youthful, rather mythic comprehension of racial segregation and oppression—as well as the apparent anomaly of his grandmother, who looked "white" but, unlike other whites, lived with the rest of his "black" family—Wright reacts to his vague fear and knowledge of racial conflict by deciding to adhere to a basic rule: "It would be simple. If anybody tried to kill me, then I would kill them first" (*BB*, 58). The following apocryphal tale, which demonstrates his increasing commitment to the above rule and which later informs his short stories, also illustrates the dialectical relationship between the formation of Wright, as represented in his autobiographical works, and his investigation of the culture of social death in his fiction. The tale concerns a black woman who avenges the death of her husband at the hands of a white mob. Under the pretext of retrieving the body, she makes her way into the white throng; as the members of the mob stand around gloating over her and her husband's body, she pulls a gun and shoots four of them. Wright does not know whether the story is factually accurate or not, but he senses that "it was emotionally true because I had already grown to feel that there existed, *men against whom I was powerless, men who could violate my life at will.*" This tale, which gives "form and meaning to confused defensive feelings that had long been sleeping" in Wright's mind, reinforces his resolve, and he decides that in a similar situation he would emulate the woman so that he could "kill as many of them as possible before they killed me" (*BB*, 83-84, emphasis added). Wright thus demonstrates his clear understanding of the terms under which Jim Crow society obliges blacks to live: powerlessness, the conditional, instantly revocable commutation of a death sentence, and, of course, the dishonor that accompanies these conditions. This tale provides the plot of his story "Bright and Morning Star," while the decision to "kill as many of them as possible before they killed me" becomes Big Boy's fantasy in "Big Boy Leaves Home" and the actual principle on which Silas acts in "The Long Black Song." Thus the meaning of the tale is worked out in the symbolic realm of the stories and is then utilized for a better understanding of Wright's own life in his autobiographical works.

However, between the young child's vague understanding of the culture of social death and the mature writer who begins to investigate that world in *Uncle Tom's Children* lay the vast and pernicious world of social death, the most brutal and dispiriting aspects of which he had yet to experience and which were to become the subject matter of his fiction. In his entrance into that world, he was handicapped not only by being trapped within the harsh environment of his family but also by the chronic transitoriness, which was partly responsible for his poor education: before he reached the age of thirteen he had had only one year of continuous education. Wright's "real education," however, had little to do with standard academic learning. *Black Boy* is virtually silent about the details of his pedagogical life; judging from his autobiographical writings and the various biographies about him, his keen intelligence and attention were focused elsewhere. Throughout his life in the South his mind was forced to concentrate primarily on physical and intellectual survival. At first Wright's energies were occupied with enduring his maternal family, which sought to break his independent spirit and make him conform to a Southern way of life and to the code of the Adventist religion. However, as Wright later realized, his family, without being conscious of it, had been "conforming to the dictates of the whites above them," in its attempt to mold him: his formation by the hegemony had been unwittingly mediated by his family (BB, 284).

III

Wright represents and examines the most concrete and pivotal aspects of the culture of social death and the mechanisms of hegemonic formation in those portions of *Black Boy* that depict his life from the end of his formal education to his departure from the South, that is, the years between May 1925 and November 1927. These vignettes depict the ways in which the desires and aspirations of a young black person are restricted by racist dominance and hegemony; under such constraints the boundaries of the self are so limited that rarely, if ever, can he succeed in becoming a full member of civil society. Wright's anecdotes demonstrate how the individual is so effectively coerced into internalizing the external, social boundaries that he learns to restrict himself "voluntarily." Wright shows that hegemony seeks to inform the very self-conception of the young man (and his view of reality, knowledge, possibility of progress, and so forth) in order to create a subject who will become identical to the limited view of him that the ideological apparatus itself has constructed. From the hegemonic viewpoint, the external construction of the subject should, ideally, coincide with self-construction. No luxury of choice is available in this process of self-construction; rather, hegemony forces the developing black individual to accommodate himself to the very absence of choice. The black boy must be taught to reify himself and the world; that is, he must perceive his liminality and the social and political restrictions that surround him not as the historical products of social relations but as natural and even metaphysical facts. The poignancy of Wright's anecdotes lies in the narrative juxtaposition of the graphic descriptions of the hegemonic process with acute representations and analyses of his subjective reactions. The contrast between the violence, persecutions, daily limitations, and narrow horizons and Wright's rage, frustration, humiliation, and bitterness reveals the wrenching tensions that a sensitive individual undergoes when he is being subjugated by a racist society.

When Wright enters the black work force serving the Southern whites, he finds himself constantly subjected to violence designed to teach him to assume "voluntarily" the subservient place reserved for "niggers" or slaves: he witnesses black people's acceptance of white violence and its effects on them, he soon becomes a

victim of casual violence intended to teach him his "place," and, most dishearten-
ingly for him, he finds his ambitions crushed by the threat of violence. While his
black friends have learned to accommodate themselves or at least give a convincing appearance of accommodation, Wright is unable to master his reactions. His
inability to prevent his resentment from registering on his face or in his demeanor
results in his dismissal from various jobs because his employers do not like his
"looks." When he forgets to address white boys as "sir," he is hit on the head with
a bottle and thrown off a moving car. His assailants consider themselves benign
teachers: had he made that mistake with other white men, they insist, he might
have quickly become "a dead nigger" (*BB*, 200).

Such routine brutality seems to disturb Wright less than the threat of more serious violence that forces him to curb his professional ambition. Having been lucky
enough to be hired by an enlightened "Yankee from Illinois" who wants to give
him the chance to learn a skilled job in his optical company, Wright soon finds
himself forced out—the white employees resent this attempt at professional
desegregation and, fabricating a charge against him, threaten to kill him.[7] In compelling him to resign, his white colleagues win a dual victory. First, within the symbolic economy of racial segregation they correctly interpret his aspiration to learn
a "trade" as equivalent to a desire to become "white," that is, as an attempt to overcome racial difference and to work his way out of the world of social death, and in
successfully blocking his ambition they maintain the boundaries of that world.
Second, in insisting to him that suicide is the most logical solution for the dilemma
of being black ("If I was a nigger," one of the white workers tells him, "I'd kill
myself" [*BB*, 207]), they provide him with a choice between actual death, embodied in their threat to kill him, and social death, implicit in his resignation. Thus
Wright can either "voluntarily" throttle his ambition and humanity or face a violent
physical death. This process of "education" is designed to ensure that ultimately
the black man should deeply internalize the hegemonic system, that he should
accept the distinctions between himself and whites as "natural," "ontological"
species differences. As we will see, the hegemony insists that such differences
have to be accepted not just at the conscious level but even at the preconscious
one.

This episode also illustrates the manner in which Wright is forced to "collab-
orate" in his own negative formation. The white workers force him to resign by
putting him in a double bind: one of the workers, Reynolds, accuses Wright of
not using the appellation "Mr." when referring to the other white man, Pease.
Before Wright can even respond to this charge, Reynolds warns him that if he
denies the allegation he will be calling Reynolds a liar. Thus by either accepting
or refuting the charge Wright violates a cardinal rule of the Southern timocracy:
a black man can never challenge the honor of a white. This ritual, accompanied

---

[7]Michel Fabre (*The Unfinished Quest of Richard Wright* [New York: William Morrow & Co.,
1973]) does not discuss this episode at all in his biography of Wright. However, whether or not the
occurrence is factually verifiable, it does seem to possess what Wright would call an "emotional truth."

by a beating and the threat of death, succeeds in enforcing all aspects of the syndrome of social death. First, Wright is forced to acknowledge the white man as a "master" ("Mister") and, by implication, himself as a slave; second, he has to relinquish all personal dignity to his white assailants; and finally, in agreeing to resign, he has to accept both the death of his professional ambition and by implication, his own social death—he must, in a sense, commit suicide. The mortification (both shame and death) and the utter dejection produced by such an encounter would not usually be available for conscious scrutiny. However, in this case the enlightened owner's good intentions painfully foreground the effects. In his attempt to investigate the causes of Wright's resignation, he exhorts Wright, in front of Pease and Reynold, to identify the assailant. Wright attempts to speak:

> An impulse to speak rose in me and died with the realization that I was facing a wall that I would never breach. I tried to speak several times and could make no sounds. I grew tense and tears burnt my cheeks. (*BB*, 221)

Wright weeps not only because of the professional disappointment but also because of his "complicity" in his defeat: this encounter, he says, left "[me] drenched in shame, naked to my soul. The whole of my being felt violated, *and I knew that my own fear had helped to violate it*" (*BB*, 212, emphasis added). His fear thus becomes a part of his formation in a dual sense: as the title of the first part of *Native Son*, "Fear," testifies, the subjugated man carries his anxiety with him in every encounter with his masters; and to the extent that he allows his fear to "violate" his own being, he becomes an agent of the hegemony that is dedicated to negating him.

Although he *intellectually* understands the rules of Jim Crow society and the contradictions that engulf him and although the racist regulations and his predicament have a profound effect on him, Wright is still unable to transform these into an *emotional* acceptance of the hegemony. This state of mind is revealed to him at his next job, where a minor accident that would have led to a mundane reprimand turns into another dismissal and a discovery of how profoundly Wright must negate himself in order to live in the South. When Wright is scolded for having broken a bottle, each response he gives seems to infuriate the manager; when he is finally told that he has been employed for a trial period, his reply, "Yes, sir. I understand," leads to his dismissal (*BB*, 214-215). It seems that Wright's replies reveal greater self-possession than Jim Crow society can tolerate from a black, for in this system inferior creatures, that is, slaves, are not supposed to possess dignity or honor, which might imply a form of equality with the masters. The implications of this incident are drastic: in order to survive in the South, Wright must in fact *become* inferior, he must relinquish *all* vestiges of pride and self-esteem.

However, with each discovery of what is required of him, Wright seems to get more deeply mired in the conflict between his desire for intellectual understanding and the society's demand for emotional submission. Each confrontation fuels his internal struggle: "I could not make subservience an *automatic* part of my behavior. I had to feel and think out each tiny item of racial experience in the light of the race problem, *and to each item I brought the whole of my life*" (*BB*, 215; emphasis added). Having lived on the edge of this contradiction and suffered its effects over a long period, Wright's insight into his own dilemma becomes brilliantly penetrating. In order for subservience to be *automatic* it cannot be conscious; it has to become a part of one's pre-conscious behavior pattern: precisely at the point where one's behavior is unconsciously controlled by a prevailing ideology, one has succumbed to a cultural hegemony. Wright's personal imperative is diametrically opposed to this demand: he wants to *understand* each racial incident that he experiences in light of the entire social, political, and ideological system of racism and slavery. And to each incident he devotes his entire *consciousness*. Thus, whereas ideology demands an emotional, unconscious acquiescence, Wright's project entails becoming perfectly aware of the unconscious pattern of behavior. The two, it would seem, cannot exist in the same universe. It finally becomes impossible for Wright to deny that the contradiction is irreconcilable. He often wishes that he could be like "the smiling, lazy, forgetful black boys" working with him in the hotel, who had "no torrential conflicts to resolve":

> Many times I grew weary of the secret burden I carried and longed to cast it down, either in action or in resignation. But I was not made to be a resigned man and I had only a limited choice of action, and I was afraid of all of them. (*BB*, 220)

The fundamental contradiction that tortures Wright is finally laid out with syllogistic clarity: action against Jim Crow restrictions would probably lead to physical death, and resignation would certainly lead to social death. Some sixty years after the end of the Civil War, Wright and all other blacks in the South were still facing the original contract between master and slave. Afraid that if he stayed in the South he would lose control of his emotions sooner or later and "spill out words that would be my sentence of death," Wright decides to leave the South.

Thus Wright finds himself under enormous pressure, both from the white and the black communities, to conform to the rules of Jim Crow culture. Society not only expects him to follow the rules but to internalize them until he becomes totally resigned to the prevailing distribution of power. However, since he refuses to accept those restrictions, he is faced with both an external battle with society and an internal struggle with himself that fully exposes the contradictory and explosive nature of his subject position. On the one hand, he must contend against his own nature and consciousness so as not to reveal the slightest resentment, frustration, or implied criticism to his white employers; on the other hand, he must avoid capitulating to Jim Crow society while pretending to have acquiesced. Thus he has to remain constantly poised on a thin edge between feigned acceptance and silent opposition.

Yet such a contradiction, to the extent that it can be confined to an intellectual or conscious realm, can be handled relatively easily in comparison to the one that

Wright subjects himself to in order to understand the structure of this culture. For him to understand thoroughly the system and the effects of racial oppression and to bring them to the light of full consciousness, he has to be entirely open to that system, he has to internalize it fully while maintaining a space within his mind that remains uncontaminated by the racist ideology—he has to retain a vantage point from which he can observe, critique, and oppose white ascendancy. To allow one-self to be subjected to the indignities and deprivations of Jim Crow society, to think constantly about the restriction of the culture of social death and yet not be able to express one's feelings or be able to rebel against the system, is to hold together a highly explosive subject position. It is precisely this site that Wright explores in *Uncle Tom's Children* and, more systematically, in *Native Son,* after which he is able to describe and examine his own formation in the South with greater equanimity. Thus *Black Boy* is remarkable not so much for its rebellion as for the control that Wright had to exercise and the internal struggle that he had to wage against being engulfed by the racist sovereignty. Thus the autobiography charts the growth of a double consciousness, of a "duplicity" that turns the con-sciousness of its own condition into a cunning weapon. It is a remarkable docu-ment of Wright's total absorption of the racist attempt to negate him and his own total negation of that attempt.

Rejection of the hegemony, Wright learns before he is able to leave the South, has to be as total as possible under the given circumstances. Even feigned accep-tance, he finds, is in danger of becoming real. While working in Memphis, Wright reluctantly allows himself to be persuaded to fight another young black man for the entertainment of whites. Wright and his opponent agree that they will pretend to fight. However, to his great horror the boxing match suddenly becomes quite real as each fighter begins to vent his frustrations on the other. But more signifi-cantly, hatred of the racist society is turned against another black: "The hate we felt for the [white] men whom we had tried to cheat went into the blows we threw at each other" (*BB*, 265). Almost all forms of dissemblance, Wright finds, are treacherous.

IV

Only one mode of dissemblance, literature, turns out to be productive and "constructive" for Wright. Literature eventually serves his purposes not only because it is the realm of "as if," a space in which one can investigate human potentiality in ways that are immediately unconstrained by the contingencies of actual life, but also because it provides the space within which one can attempt to resolve the actual contradiction of a constrained and frustrating life. Yet Wright could gain access to this zone of symbolic dissemblance only through a prior act of social dissemblance. Southern culture had barred all blacks from entry into high culture. Not only were blacks prohibited from discussing a whole set of sub-jects (see *BB*, 253) but more crucially they could not borrow books from the

Memphis public library. Wright managed to circumvent this restriction by borrowing a library card from a sympathetic white Northerner and by pretending that the books were requested by his white master. Yet even this resourceful and cunning "triumph" contains a profound negation of Wright. He finds that within or outside the library he cannot afford to exhibit his literacy or his interest in literature: he can borrow books only on the assumption that he cannot and will not read them. In his attempt to possess any form of knowledge, he has to lead a double existence: while trying to play the role of a genial and happy black, content with his place in society, he has to satisfy his intellectual hunger, cultivate his sensibility and the consciousness of his condition, and nurture his rage in secret. After this experience whenever he brought a book to work, he "wrapped it in newspaper—a habit that was to persist for years in other cities and under other circumstances" (*BB*, 273).

Thus his subjectivity must always be hidden; it can never be displayed in public or be recognized by most whites who surround him. Not only does racist society negate Wright, but he too must negate himself, at least in public. Orlando Patterson argues that the slave can never be the subject of property, only its object; we should add that the black in Jim Crow society, like his enslaved ancestor, can never be the subject of (white) culture, only its object.

V

Yet paradoxically, Wright was able to save himself through another form of dissembling. As we have seen, Wright attributes his ability to survive the Jim Crow restrictions to his love of literature, and, as we have also seen, he was able to understand and experience the demands of the hegemony without emotionally capitulating to its control; that is, while he fully experienced himself as a degraded being, he had managed to retain a space in his mind where his *potential* humanity remained intact. Given this mode of rebellion, given his quiet but determined nurturing of his human potentiality in the abstract spaces of his mind, it is not surprising that he found an outlet in literature, which is precisely an area where the *potentiality* of human endeavour can be rehearsed and explored. When Wright, disguised as an errand boy, discovered in the segregated Memphis public library H. L. Mencken's *Prefaces,* and through it a much larger literary world, he was already predisposed to this particular mode of simulation. But because his conception of his human potential was devoid of positive content the initial function of literature for him was as negative and empty as his "humanity."

The sustained negation that he had been nurturing is first thrown into relief by the guilt that the reading of Mencken and other modern writers provokes: "I could not conquer my sense of guilt, my feeling that the white men around me knew that I was changing, that I had begun to regard them differently" (*BB*, 273). This guilt, then, becomes an index of how deeply Wright has internalized the Southern ideology and how precariously dependent upon the racist Other his negation must have been. But literature was also negative in that it depressed him. While opening up new horizons of human potentiality to him, it showed him how much he had missed by growing up in the South, and it confirmed his own view of the culture of social death: "I no longer *felt* that the world about me was hostile, killing; I *knew* it." His entire life had been shaping him, he says, to understand the realist and naturalist novel, and his complicated experience of his mother's senseless suffering was revived by reading Dreiser's *Jennie Gerhardt* and *Sister Carrie* (BB, 274). Literature thus functions as a mirror that reflects his own negation and experience of suffering.

His reading provokes him to contemplate once again his prospects in the South. He ponders various alternatives—armed rebellion, playing the Sambo role, taking out his frustrations on other blacks, escaping through sex and alcohol, and attempting to become a professional—but rejects them all as unfeasible because they would all kill something in him. To stay in the South, he knows, means to stifle his consciousness, means accepting social death at some level. Caught between the negation of his own life and the negation and distance provided by his reading, Wright implicitly opts for the only possibility that he has ever known—to use his mind as a mirror that will bring his predicament to consciousness: "I held my life in my mind, in my consciousness each day, feeling at times that I would stumble and drop it, spilling it forever" (BB, 277). In thus affirming his predisposition, literature mirrors his own mirroring mind. Having finally decided to leave the South, Wright boards the train from Memphis to Chicago and allows himself en route to think more fully about the role of literature in his life. In a highly controlled and impoverished world, where both whites and blacks had "demanded submission" and refused to affirm Wright's belief in himself, it was only through literature that he manages to keep himself "*alive* in a *negatively* vital way" (BB, 282; emphasis added). On his way North, which symbolized a utopian space where one might be able to lead a fuller and freer life, Wright could now afford to meditate more explicitly on his negative existence and the manner in which literature had helped him to bring his negation into sharper focus.

Although the South had attempted to crush his spirit, Wright feels that he had never capitulated; he had never accepted that he was "in any way an inferior being," and nothing the Southerners had said or done to him had ever made him "doubt the worth of my own humanity." But at a more concrete level, the environment had allowed him to manifest his humanity only in a negative form. He had lied, stolen, fought, struggled to contain his seething rage, and it was only by accident that he had never killed. The South had only allowed him to be himself through "rejection, rebellion, and aggression" (BB, 283-84). It had given him only the choice of becoming either a slave or rebel; he had chosen the latter, because that was the only way he could affirm his humanity. It had been an entirely negative assertion of his humanity, but he had devoted himself entirely to it:

> In a peculiar sense, life had trapped me in a realm of emotional rejection; I had not embraced insurgency through open choice. Existing emotionally on the sheer, thin mar-

gin of southern culture, I had felt that nothing short of life hung upon each of my actions and decisions. (*BB*, 282)

Since this culture could not provide him with any landmarks by which "I could, in a positive sense, guide my daily actions," Wright converted his "emotional rejection," his negation, into the very essence of his "life." Wright thus transformed himself into a dialectical negation of the culture of social death, and in each confrontation with the racist hegemony what was at stake was not some abstract notion of human dignity or freedom but his very life-as-a-negation. By carefully nurturing himself as negation and by presenting this negation in the form of his autobiographical work, *Black Boy*, Wright makes a double impact. In the first place, the *publication* and the literary success of *Black Boy* becomes an affirmation, a vindication of his strategy of negating the racist negation. In the second place, by choosing for the title of his autobiography the generic marker of racist objectification, "black boy," Wright correctly implies that he is describing the formation of all those who have been "subjectified" by racism. As Houston A. Baker Jr. implies, ontogeny in *Black Boy* recapitulates phylogeny.[8] Only if we see that the confrontation, at the individual as well as at the collective level, is between life and death, either social or actual death, can we begin to appreciate why Wright repeatedly describes his life and that of his characters such as Bigger as charged with an enormous tension. In his existential mood, with his life as an embodiment of negation constantly on the verge of extinction, Wright reads authors "like Dreiser, Masters, Mencken, Anderson, and Lewis," and finds in them an echo of his own life and "vague glimpses of life's possibilities."

At this point literature represents for Wright a world of possibilities, and it lures him into the paradoxical realm of potentialities and actualities. Jim Crow society, he says, "kept me from being the kind of person I might have been," and in leaving the South and experiencing a different kind of life he "might learn who I was, what I might be" (*BB*, 284). The paradox, of course, is that who he might be, his future potentiality, is entirely predicated on who he is, on his actuality; he would never have been concerned with his own potentiality if he were not already an embodied negation constructed around abstract potentiality. In his own way, Wright is aware of this paradox, for he immediately follows his speculations by arguing that he is leaving the South not in order to forget it, but so that he can understand it better and determine what it has done to its black children: "I fled so that the numbness of my defensive living might thaw out and let me feel the pain—years later and far away—of what living in the South had meant" (*BB*, 284). This, of course, is exactly what he accomplishes in *Uncle Tom's Children* and *Native Son*: his fictional works, written years later and far away from the South, constitute the cries of pain. He knows that he cannot really leave the South, that it has formed him and is an indelible part of himself.

[8]See Houston A. Baker, Jr., *Blues, Ideology, and Afro-American Literature: A Vernacular Theory* (Chicago: The University of Chicago Press, 1984), 147.

However, he hopes that by transplanting his experience of it to a different soil it might bloom differently:

> And if that miracle ever happened, then I would know that there was yet hope in that southern swamp of despair and violence, that light could emerge even out of the blackest of the southern night. I would know of the blackest of the southern night. I would know that the South too could overcome its fear, its hate, its cowardice, its heritage of guilt and blood, its burden of anxiety and compulsive cruelty. (*BB*, 284-85)

Wright is thus clearly aware that his potentiality consists of bringing to consciousness in symbolic form his experiences of the racist attempt to negate his actuality. His positive potentiality will manifest itself precisely in his success in bringing to consciousness his negating actuality. Thus the passage cited above embodies the twin imperatives of his life and fiction. To the extent that he is an emblem of the negation that issues from the culture of social death, his fictional rendering of his own experiences reflects that deep, deterministic connection between the environment and the individual that is a hallmark of naturalism. And to the extent that, unlike Bigger, Wright is able to transcend the limitations of his environment, his fiction represents the slave's dialectical overcoming of his condition by bringing to consciousness the structures of his social death in the symbolic realm of literature.

VI

Wright's autobiography and fiction can be best appreciated as an archaeology of negation and freedom. That is, by excavating the repressed layers of his consciousness and by insistently expressing his discoveries in the predominantly "negative" forms of his novels he defines his own negation of the prior hegemonic negation as the most fundamental form of self-affirmation: in his work racist negation becomes the opposite of what it is initially—it becomes a site of freedom. The power and the value of Wright's sustained negation is captured aptly in Baker's metaphor of the "black (w)hole." Wright, it seems to me, had dedicated himself precisely to absorbing all negation in order to negate it, and his commitment to this task was unrelenting. A hasty affirmation, a premature sense of being accepted and affirmed as a full subject by the hegemony, he seems to have felt, is always in danger of being appropriated once again by the processes of hegemonic formation. In his article in [an] issue of "Minority Discourse," Henry Louis Gates, Jr. argues that we must not think of ourselves as being condemned to "the fate of perpetual negation . . . doomed merely to 'oppose,' to serve within the academy as black signs of opposition to a political order in which we are subjugated. We must oppose, of course, when opposition is called for. But our task is so much more complex." No doubt the task of affirming is complex and important, and Gates's diverse interventions in the discursive field of the black literary diaspora are an excellent embodiment of that complexity. But as the NEH response, cited in the introduction, to the grant application for the "Minority Discourse" conference illustrates, the guardians of hegemony still consider "vernacular" literature, even though these are "English vernaculars," to be barbaric babble. From Crummell's view of African languages to the priorities of the NEH, the dominant ideology still attempts to negate minorities and therefore must be met with a similarly sustained opposition: we cannot afford the luxury of defining negation as an occasional tactic to which one resorts reluctantly. In her article, also included in [that] issue, Sylvia Wynter rightly warns us that the category "minority" is a discursive construct and not a "brute fact." However, we must also remember that Wright's most negative protagonist, Bigger Thomas, feels so oppressed that he can hardly breathe. If hegemonic formation is so powerfully negating that it can even control one's autonomous nervous system, one's ability to breathe, then we must face the empirical "fact" that some, if not all, of us are indeed reduced, some, if not all, of the time, to experiencing ourselves, ideologically and physically if not ontologically, as brute, oppressed "facts." Thus sustained negation of the hegemony may be necessary not only for the liberation of our minds but also of our voices and bodies. We must remember that not only is there a Bigger Thomas somewhere in all of us, but also a Richard Wright, whom we must allow to come to consciousness in us.

Lawd Today!

Arnold Rampersad

Posthumously offered literature, especially from an author who published steadily in his or her lifetime, is often inferior work. However, *Lawd Today!*, which first appeared in 1963, three years after Richard Wright's untimely death at the age of fifty-two, cannot with justification be called second-rate among his works. While it is certainly flawed, the tale is also quite possibly the second most important novel written by Wright, and it is clearly inferior only to the landmark *Native Son* (1940) among his novels. Far less grand in theme than *The Outsider* (1953), it is also less bleak and didactic than that existentialist story. Certainly it is more compelling than *Savage Holiday* (1954), Wright's somewhat thin and improbable accounting, according to a Freudian scheme, of a lonely white man (there are no blacks in the novel) driven to psychopathic murder. And although conspicuously less rich in characterization and plot, at least in a conventional sense, than *The Long Dream* (1957), *Lawd Today!* is nevertheless a more exuberant and spontaneous, as well as a more decisively motivated, piece of fiction than the last novel published in Wright's lifetime.

Lawd Today! is a young writer's book, one in which might be seen, sometimes in forms not entirely digested, not only the literary influences that instructed Wright in his fledgling enterprise in fiction but also some of the basic impulses that led him to begin his distinguished career as a writer. Wright started the novel, first called *Cesspool*, sometime around 1934, or about seven years after he arrived in Chicago from his native South at the age of nineteen. Near the end of his time in the South, as he relates with harrowing power in his autobiography, *Black Boy* (1945), Wright had discovered from the charged pages of H. L. Mencken that it was possible for a powerless man to use "words as weapons," and that voluminous reading and steady writing, in the face of all opposition or other discouragement, was the most effective counter to both his own profound sense of isolation and the dismal education he had received as a boy in Mississippi and Arkansas. Not long after his arrival in Chicago, he found in the leftist community there—and especially in the local chapter of the radical John Reed Club (in which he served for some time as executive secretary)—a congenial circle of younger, committed

Reprinted from Richard Wright, *Lawd Today!* (Boston: Northeastern University Press, 1991), pp. v-xi. By permission of Arnold Rampersad.

artists who shared his sense of determination that words honed and tempered into radical art could indeed make a difference in life.

Overhauled at least once by 1936, the novel made the rounds of the major commercial publishers without success or encouragement, until at last it disappeared into Wright's files not to surface publicly until after his death. Undeterred by this rejection, however, Wright continued to publish, mainly poetry (in journals such as *New Masses, International Literature,* and *Partisan Review*) and radical journalism (in places such as the Communist *Daily Worker*); but he soon emerged most impressively on the national scene in 1938 as a short story writer with *Uncle Tom's Children: Four Novellas,* which effectively launched his mature career. Two years later, *Native Son* crowned it.

Why was *Lawd Today!* rejected by publishers in the late thirties? The most consistent complaint from them apparently concerned its lack of broad, deep characterization and its skimpiness of plot. Quite possibly, however, editors were repulsed by the extreme realism in the novel, as suggested by its initial title. Although it does not contain passages that actually depict sexual intercourse, the novel is saturated with the language and situations of lust, as it records in accumulating details Wright's sense of the rough-and-ready sexual obsession of its four main characters, Jake Jackson and his friends Bob, Al, and Slim. This obsession, unrelieved by the slightest romantic element, is recounted in language and scenes of a frankness and even crudeness seldom seen previously in American literature. In addition, Wright did not conceal the fact that white women were often the objects of fantasies and desires on the part of some black men. White editors might have believed, not without reason, that the American reading public was not ready for such renegade thoughts and undisciplined language on the part of blacks.

For all its rawness, however, *Lawd Today* reveals unmistakably that Wright was already a conscious artist in its composition, and one alert to the functioning of tradition. Perhaps his most significant single debt is to James Joyce, in that the action of the novel takes place roughly in twenty-four hours (mostly on Lincoln's Birthday), as in *Ulysses*; also, the climactic visit to Rose's saloon is reminiscent of a setting of similar importance in Joyce's most famous work. From Henry James, whose prefaces and other essays on fiction Wright had taken to heart, came probably the relentness concern in *Lawd Today!* with strictness of point-of-view; we see the action of the book mainly as the "hero" Jake Jackson envisions it, from his awakening at eight o'clock one morning to his descent into bloody unconsciousness near dawn the following day.

Important, too, is Wright's sense of kinship with the major American realists and naturalists, themselves descended in some respects from Emile Zola. Not least of all, in its unpolished vigor and vitality, *Lawd Today!* reminds one almost inevitably of Stephen Crane's *Maggie: A Girl of the Streets* and Frank Norris's tale of greed, *McTeague.* Certainly Theodore Dreiser's influence is discernible, although the link between *Native Son* and *An American Tragedy* would be a more indelible token of Wright's lasting debt to Dreiser. From James Farrell, author of the *Studs Lonigan* trilogy, with whom Wright discussed at length the art of fiction, he frankly borrowed a number of devices and techniques for *Lawd Today!*, including the precise charting of the game of bridge played in the novel (like the football game described in Farrell's *Judgment Day*) and the highlighting of dreams as a guide to the largely unconscious interests and motives of Jake Jackson. From John Dos Passos, whose *U.S.A.* trilogy Wright esteemed highly, came the graphic use of newspaper headlines and radio announcements on which *Lawd Today!* depends fairly heavily for a sense both of history and of immediacy.

Lastly, epigraphs taken from the work of Van Wyck Brooks (*America's Coming of Age*), Waldo Frank (*Our America*), and T. S. Eliot (*The Waste Land*) and cited before each of the three sections of the novel indicate, along with his bows to James Joyce and Henry James, that Wright's reading and his ambitions as a writer of fiction had already taken him beyond the scope of realists and naturalists such as Dreiser, Farrell, and Dos Passos. In a real sense, these epigraphs anticipate the modernist philosophical drive that would sweep him beyond his early concerns with the matters of race and radical socialism; that drive would result most pointedly almost twenty years later in the publication of *The Outsider*.

For all these literary influences, however, *Lawd Today!* sprang first and foremost out of Wright's life and his particular experiences as a sensitive, highly intelligent black migrant hungry for a sense of achievement and trying to make his way, in the midst of the Depression, in the black South Side of Chicago. What Jake Jackson encounters in his wanderings through the city in *Lawd Today!* is essentially what Richard Wright knew on a daily basis either from personal involvement or from distanced but keen observation in Chicago. For example, like Jake Jackson and his three main friends, Wright had worked for some time in the postal service, and thus was able to describe the facilities and the regimen at the Central Post Office with deadly accuracy. "Doc" Higgins, the scheming proprietor of a barbershop and a part-time Republican Party ward boss in the novel, is not unlike the shrewd barbershop proprietor and Republican precinct captain for whom Wright himself had worked. The graphic descriptions of the hold of religion on Jake's wife, Lil, and on broad sections of the black community came no doubt from the generally oppressive place of fundamentalist religion in Wright's own family, as he saw it. Gambling, so prominent a feature of *Lawd Today!*, was virtually the chief pastime of the South Side that Wright knew. The black nationalist personalities and their ventures, the confidence men who prey on the gullible, the pimps and prostitutes who fall naturally into place as a part of the landscape of *Lawd Today!*—all were at hand, about the author, when *Cesspool* was conceived and revised into *Lawd Today!*

Because so much of the book is rooted in Wright's restless observation of the life about him, *Lawd Today!* goes beyond mere literary influence to reveal the first distinct outlines of what would be recognized as his authentic fictional vision. That vision was formed and articulated in the face of ideological and other distractions that often ran counter to it. Although Wright was a member of the Communist Party when the novel was written, it is hard to imagine that the party censors who found *Native Son* hard to swallow would have sanctioned the earlier work. *Lawd Today!* reveals Wright in his classic position as an artist and an intellectual: he was uncompromising and fiercely courageous in his moral and social criticism. Faced with social conditions that he found fundamentally intolerable, he did not hesitate to draw unflattering portraits wherever he found them appropriate. As a result, this novel is dramatically pessimistic.

Certainly it is pessimistic where the black masses are concerned. Apart from fleeting pictures of a black communist sympathizer, a bourgeois post office official who scorns Jake, and the lonely figure of a boy reading in a window at one point in the book (to Jake's bewilderment at such a waste of time), virtually all the black characters are seen as leading desperate, even demeaning lives. Wright's sense of discomfort with his community, which is to say his race, ran deep. The palms of Jake Jackson's hands are not dark but "dingy," an unfortunate term to which Wright would revert again in *Black Boy* to describe blacks. Here, as elsewhere in his work, black women seem to bear the brunt of his criticism. The masses, male or female, suggest no potential for redemption, much less revolution; instead, they are seen as creatures dominated variously by lust, avarice, sloth, superstition, and a fatal weakness for violence. If any grand visitation is at hand, it is very possibly an apocalypse—with Jake Jackson and his three friends (one is passionate about the army, another is a consumptive, and the third suffers from a venereal disease) as the four horsemen of war, disease, famine, and death. Because of such unequivocal criticism, *Lawd Today!*, like *Native Son*, is a perfect companion piece to Wright's famous catalogue in *Black Boy* of the inadequacies of the culture into which he was born. "Lawd, I wish I was dead," Jake's battered wife, Lil, moans in the last words spoken in the novel. The last lines of *Lawd Today!* are as bleak: "Outside an icy wind swept around the corner of the building, whining and moaning like an idiot in a deep black pit."

The main factor that prevents *Lawd Today!* from being thoroughly nihilistic raises provocative questions in itself. That factor is the superior quality of life among whites, who are seen only dimly and obliquely in *Lawd Today!*, but are made to look fairly attractive in that light. When a group of about fifteen black women troops through the post office, they are portrayed as "round-shouldered and dumpy-looking." In the trail of a group of white women, however, Jake hears "murmurs of laughter, light, silvery." Where the four friends perform their post office duties indifferently at best, then rush to play cards or waste their money on food, drink, and sex, the white workers are seen as generally industrious and purposeful; often they are concerned with getting an education. Behind this distinction is Wright's sense, articulated in *Black Boy* and elsewhere, of the difference between a culture and civilization, with blacks having historically been denied the means to convert the former, which admits of few virtues, into the glorious latter. It might be said with great accuracy that the main purpose of all of Wright's restless, encyclopedic reading and constant writing was to raise himself, and those who would heed him, out the shallows of what he called a culture and toward the humanist heights of civilization.

To some extent, however, *Lawd Today!* is premature on this question, in that Wright does not directly connect the lives of American blacks to the lives of American whites—as he would do with historic impact in *Native Son*. And yet there is clear evidence that Wright was moving toward this connection. The principal interplay between the two races comes with the impact of the radio program about the nobility of the life of Abraham Lincoln, which is heard intermittently but loudly throughout most of the novel. In one sense, the interplay emphasizes the failure of Lincoln's act of emancipation and seems to hold the descendants of the slaves accountable. But the bombastic language of the program, contrasting with the illiteracies of the main characters and the terseness of the narrative line, also tells us that Wright is aware of the hollowness of the national myth of freedom and the master race's manipulation of the retelling of history to suit its own ends.

On the other hand, because the white world is barely mentioned, relatively speaking, in *Lawd Today!*, the pessimism with which Wright views the black community takes on something of a cosmic significance, as underscored in the closing words of the novel. Against this pessimism is arrayed the ignorant struggle of Jake and his friends to find pleasure, if not meaning, in life. Their often frantic struggle leads to perhaps the chief appeal of *Lawd Today!*—its mixture of a sense of purposelessness and hopelessness in life, on one hand, and an almost animal vitality on the other. Not the least attractive feature of this vitality is its comedy; Wright possessed a genuine gift for farce which he seldom indulged in his later works but made a prominent part of *Lawd Today!* His pessimism predominates but is also almost matched by his wonder at the prodigious capacity of his subjects to eat, laugh, and "love." Wonder does not, however, turn to admiration or envy. Wright remains the epitome of the thinking, judging man, firm in his disapproval of what he so graphically describes.

The result is a novel almost always compelling, almost always challenging, and a worthy example of the art by which Richard Wright revolutionized not only the fictional depiction of blacks in the United States but also the American sense of identity where race is concerned.

Richard Wright's "Big Boy Leaves Home" and a Tale from Ovid: A Metamorphosis Transformed

Michael Atkinson

There is an ache in reading Richard Wright's fiction, and we feel it from first to last. It is the ache of difference, of distance between what might and should be possible for the human, and what fate and circumstance impose when that human is an outsider, is black. It is paradigmatically present in one of Wright's earliest stories, one of his most enduring and frequently anthologized, "Big Boy Leaves Home." This story continues to move us and be the object of our study, not only because of its starkly accurate social detail, a closely woven fabric of dialect and milieu, and its skill in capturing the black experience of the American South in the first third of this century, but also because it has as well a particular, and until now silent, relationship with myth, no less effective for being mute. The story is grounded in a link to myth far more specific than the broad notion of The American Myth (in which it certainly participates) or even the timeless, generalized archetypal motifs which punctuate and shape all literature (although there is no shortage of thresholds and wombs, serpents and guardians here). The pleasures and terrors of "Big Boy Leaves Home" are modeled on a classical myth, one of the most affecting and familiar—the myth of Actaeon and Diana. Rereading Wright's story in this connection can add a depth and resonance to our experience, framing the sense of social realism in a larger ontology. The parallels—and the divergences—between the myth and the story play off one another, creating a denser texture of emotional response and a suppler philosophical grasp as we read and reflect.

The similarities, and some of the differences, between the two can be foregrounded by setting the outlines of the myth and the story side by side. In Ovid's *Metamorphoses*, the most complete and accessible telling, the tale of Actaeon runs thus. Actaeon and his companions are out hunting at midday when Actaeon calls an end to the chase since "Our nets and spears / Drip with the blood of our successful hunting."[1] Nearby, in a grotto pool nestled in a valley, the goddess

Reprinted from *Studies in Short Fiction* 24.3 (Summer 1987): 251-261. Copyright 1987 by Newberry College.

[1]Ovid, *Metamorphoses*, trans. Rolfe Humphries (Bloomington: Indiana University Press, 1964) 61. Subsequent citations will be given parenthetically in the text. Although the sheer number of correspondences between Wright and Ovid argue that he was familiar with the Roman poet's telling, there

Diana, herself tired from hunting, disrobed and disarmed, bathes with her maidens. Quite by accident, Actaeon, now alone, comes upon the idyllic scene. Finding no weapon nearby, Diana flings a handful of the pond's water on the hapless hunter, taunting, "Tell people you have seen me, / Diana, naked! tell them if you can!" (p. 62). He flees from the scene, by stages transformed into a stag, a metamorphosis he does not comprehend (though he marvels at his own speed) until he pauses to drink. Then he "finally sees, reflected, / his features in a quiet pool. 'Alas!' / He tries to say, but has no words." Stunned he hears his hounds approach. "The whole pack, with the lust of blood upon them / Come baying . . . Actaeon, once pursuer / Over this very ground, is now pursued . . . He would cry / 'I am Actaeon . . .' / But the words fail" (p. 63). The hounds set upon him "And all together nip and slash and fasten / Till there is no more room for wounds." Meanwhile, his companions arrive, call for him, and rue that he is missing the good show. "And so he died, and so Diana's anger / Was satisfied at last" (p. 64).

When we look at the story of Big Boy, the similarities are striking—and the divergences are revealing as well. Big Boy and his three companions, playing hooky, wander through the woods, laughing and singing a risqué song about seeing one's mother without her underwear. One suggests they go to the swimming hole on old man Harvey's property. Initially reluctant, Big Boy consents after a tussle with the other three and they cross the fence, shed their clothes and enjoy a swim. Naked on the bank, basking in sunshine, they hear a cry—"Oh!"—and see a white woman coming over the rise, looking at them in shock. Startled and afraid, the boys start to flee, but Big Boy wants to retrieve their clothes, piled under a tree near which the white woman now stands. As he and Bobo approach the tree, she shrieks, summoning her man, who arrives on the scene with a rifle. He shoots two of the boys and is about to shoot Bobo when Big Boy wrests the gun from him and hits him with it. Though warned, the man tries to take the rifle back. Big Boy shoots him. He and Bobo flee the scene, don clothes, and return to their homes. Big Boy's family, extracting from him only confused and fragmentary details, summons elders of the black community, but they are powerless to protect him. One suggests he might catch a ride north in his son's truck, bound for Chicago the next morning. Big Boy says he will hide overnight in one of a hillside full of kilns the boys themselves dug earlier that summer. He asks them to tell Bobo to join him and runs for the kilns. There, he fantasizes the struggle to come. When the white men do arrive, they have brought their hounds and their women. The hounds find out Bobo and the men mutilate him to the singing cheers of the women. They tar and feather him, then set him afire with gasoline as Big Boy, remembering that "you could not see into the dark if you were standing in the light," witnesses the whole scene.[2] Satisfied, the mob

---

is no way of knowing which version of Ovid he might have been acquainted with. Because it is now the accepted standard, I have chosen to quote from Humphries' translation, even though it was published after Wright wrote the story.

[2]Richard Wright, *Uncle Tom's Children* (New York: Harper, 1940, 1965), 48. Subsequent citations will be given parenthetically in the text.

leaves, and Big Boy sleeps the dank night in the kiln, wakes the next morning and hears the sound of Will's truck. Unable to find his voice at first, he finally calls Will's name, hides in the truck, heading north, leaving forever his home and his people.

The points of congruence here are striking: the easy companionship, the idyllic setting, the pond, nakedness, discovery, the power of the woman, the wrenching transformation of a life, the hero's muteness, the hounds, mutilation. The divergences, too, are striking, even after we have taken into account the dilution necessary when a myth that includes the gods is shifted to a strictly human theatre. Most notably, in the story it is the woman who sees the men naked, rather than the reverse. The presence, and murder, of the male protector is an element the story adds—and then curiously effaces. And of course Wright splits the agony between the protagonist and his companion or double. But in both congruence and divergence, the myth Ovid tells provides for Wright's story a strong commentary in counterpoint. It extends and validates what we feel as we read, deepens and clarifies what we understand. If we compare their crucial structural stages, we can best see what the one tale has made of the other.

Both heroes begin in innocence. If the joy of a general kill rings a little violent to the modern sensibility, we need only remember Diana's delight in the abundant hunt, not to mention similar sentiments in the Gawain poet and Faulkner. And too, Actaeon has called a halt to the sport, unwilling to let the zest of the hunt become bloodlust. He and his companions are, in the context of their story, innocent, at rest and carefree. Likewise, Wright's story opens as an idyll still within the borders of adolescent innocence. The boys are playing hooky, hardly a crime, and the warm day is made to walk in the woods and giggle at scatological jokes that seem the timeless staple of adolescence. Mixed with this is the singing of the old hymn about the train bound for glory. Yet the story does open with a playful hint of sexual impropriety; the boys sing a dirty song:

> Yo mama don wear no drawers,
> 　A seena when she pulled em off,
> N she washed em in alcohol,
> 　N she hung em in the hall.

Stuck for the next line, they ponder rhymes. It is Big Boy that comes up with the solution:

> N then she put em back on her QUALL! (p. 18)

This innocent ribaldry, however, is given edge when we recall Ovid, for clearly it is as taboo in the realistic world to see the naked mother as it is to see the naked goddess in the world of myth. This is the forbidden woman, the forbidden vision, and it is Big Boy who names the forbidden part: "quall," a folk word with clear links to the "queynte" and "quoniam" of Middle English. They have—he has—crossed a boundary, later literally marked by their crossing the fence onto the forbidden property of old man Harvey.[3] So there is, it seems, a little less innocence in the trespass of the young black men than in Actaeon's. He at least, is unwitting, though the landscape into which he wanders is profoundly feminine: a pool in a grotto in a valley with an archway above the bathing goddess and her urn-bearing nymphs.

The essence of the idyllic moment is the principle non-differentiation, a lack of otherness. And a key element of both these idylls is the easy union Actaeon and Big Boy experience with their friends. From this immediate comradeship, Actaeon simply wanders away, taking his own path home. His separation is as swift and initially nonchalant as Big Boy's is protracted and agonizing. But both lead to tragic isolation. Big Boy's proceeds by degrees. His three companions jump him when he is reluctant to cross the fence to the swimming hole. Big Boy wins the fight by grasping Bobo's neck in a chokehold, forcing him to call off the others. Though this might for a moment seem like an antagonism between the two, it is rather like part of a brother battle after which these two are more closely united, and differentiated from the others, a fact underscored by the common alliteration of their names. At the pond, Bobo tries to throw Big Boy in. They lock in a struggle that is also a bonding, and Lester and Buck push the two of them in together.

The vestige of communality among the four is for the last time invoked after they swim. Though in the forbidden territory, and conscious of the other and the differentiation he brings (they wonder, "Whut would yuh do ef ol man Harveyd come er long right now?" "Run like hell!"), they sun and the talk is easy—suggestive of a larger and more profound political communality.

> Far away a train whistled.
> "There goes number seven!"
> "Heading fer up Noth!"
> "Blazin it down the line!"
> "Lawd, Ahm goin Noth some day."
> "Me too, man."
> "They say colored folks up Noth is got ekual rights." (pp. 26-7)

This political promise—the faintly present vision of equality and justice against which the terrifying degradation to come can alone be measured—is underscored by the most lyric passage in the story, which follows immediately. It is utterly unlike anything else in the piece.

> They grew pensive. A black winged butterfly hovered at the water's edge. A bee droned. From somewhere came the sweet scent of honeysuckles. Dimly they could hear the sparrows twittering in the woods. They rolled from side to side, letting sunshine dry their skins and warm their blood. They plucked blades of grass and chewed them. (p. 27)

[3]Crossing the threshold into the forbidden world is of course one of those omnipresent archetypal motifs which, although it is appropriate to acknowledge them when they figure significantly in the story, do not lie at the core of this more specific analysis of mythological debt. A related association would be the suggestion that the elder Harvey corresponds to the old, now infertile king whose chief function is to proscribe and to hold fast to what he has. Psychologically, he is the tyrannical father who delimits, owns, and protects the territory in which the "mother" dwells.

This experience of oneness among themselves, and of unreflective unity with nature, culminates the idyll. It is riven and terminated by the intrusion of the ultimate otherness in the very next line. "Oh!" It could be an exclamation of pure surprise. But it is not. It could be a cry of delight at the beauty of these four young men. But it is not. For this single word is uttered by the one who is the ultimate principle of difference and differentiation in the story. Not black, not male.

> A white woman, poised on the edge of the opposite embankment, stood directly in front of them, her hat in her hand and her hair lit by the sun. (p. 27)

In a muted but familiar motif symbolizing a threatened loss of virginal purity, her hat is off, her hair revealed. And like Diana the virgin moon goddess, this woman (whose name, Bertha, means "bright") is a creature of reflected light, her hair lit by the sun. As in Actaeon's case, this clear and radiant glimpse could be the culmination of the idyll rather than the shattering of it, were it not for the absolute difference between the seer and the seen. The difference between gods and humans is so great a gulf that unmediated vision of pure and naked divinity threatens life itself, from Ovid and Exodus to *Space Odyssey 2001*. The ontological difference in the myth is reflected in the sociological difference in the story: the same principle operates, a radical difference on the scale of being.

Is it axiomatic that before the mother the conscious child is always guilty? Big Boy and Actaeon share a guilt that is not born of intent but of condition, a condition marked in each by his name. "Actaeon" means "shore dweller," one who must not violate the waters even with vision, and "Big Boy" clearly marks one who is a perpetual manchild in a land without promise. In *Violence and the Sacred* René Girard proposes that it is not inequality that causes primary violence, as today we would like to believe, but the very breakdown of inequality that leads to strife and bloodshed.[4] And certainly that is true in both the myth and the story. Actaeon sees the goddess naked, as he might be privileged to see an ordinary woman. And Bertha sees the naked boys as she might see her own younger relatives—cause for embarrassment perhaps, but not for terror or revenge. However, in each case, the seeing is not ordinary; it casts itself across the barrier of difference and momentarily threatens to obscure it in the act of mutual seeing. Violence must ensue.

It is important to remember that in both cases, though the act is hedged around with sexuality, the crime is one of vision rather than sex, though clearly the two are often related in practice. And of course the differing directions of the vision, and the nakedness before it, constitute one of the chief distinctions between the story and the myth. Strikingly, in the society of this fiction, the black man must not have the power to *see*; for to see, to hold another in one's gaze as existential phenomenology describes it,[5] is to give him meaning, to object-ify him.

---

[4]René Girard, *Violence and the Sacred*, trans. Patrick Gregory (Baltimore: Johns Hopkins University Press, 1977), 49-52.

[5]See Jean-Paul Sartre, *Being and Nothingness*, trans. Hazel E. Barnes (Secaucus: Citadel, 1956), pp. 228 ff., 339, 375-9.

To fix another in one's gaze is, at root, a powerful gesture, for in doing so, one defines and dehumanizes one's object, demotes him in the scale of being, makes him a thing. But since the other is not in fact merely an object and can by free action escape denomination, final objectification must be culminated in literally making a thing of the one caught in the gaze, sadism and killing being obvious alternatives, as both myth and story demonstrate. Again, what is an ontological difference in levels of being in the myth is recast as a sociological difference in the story. But while Actaeon's crime is seeing, objectifying, what he should not see, Big Boy's crime, and the crime of his companions, is not seeing, but being seen; ironically *their crime is synonymous with their powerlessness*, their impotence as humans.

Seen, the young men's "hands instinctively cover[ed] their groins" (p. 27). Big Boy attempts the obvious human act—to recover his clothes, not to be seen totally, to cover himself, as the woman he confronts is covered. He is in effect resisting metamorphosis into an "animal": clothing and disrobing have long been used as symbols of transformation, from the hooding of Ph.D.'s and the complex formulas for assembling a bride's gear, to the investing (and defrocking) of priests.[6] In his rush for the clothes Big Boy is joined by Bobo. Ironically, their clothing lies at the foot of the tree next to which the woman now stands, as if symbolic of her power to see them only as naked and threatening, to enforce their metamorphosis into animals. Big Boy assures her that they only "wanna git [their] clothes" (p. 28). But as Bobo retrieves the bundle, her transforming gaze, her fear, is extended in the lethal power of Jim, her fiancé (in myth, one would say her votary and protector). Thoroughly dressed in an Army uniform and shouldering a rifle, he shoots Buck, who falls into the pool (the mythic locus of the goddess's power), and Lester, whose forehead falls on the toe of the woman's shoe in a perverse mockery of worship. Big Boy and Bobo refuse this obeisance. As Jim tries to shoot Bobo, Big Boy wrests the gun from him. Undaunted, the white man attempts to regain the weapon, is shot in the process, and the two young men flee, isolated forever from their dead comrades, united in their fear and their crime.

Recollecting the terms of the original myth will enhance our understanding of the shape of Big Boy's flight. Although the course of Actaeon's story runs swiftly, it is important to remember that there are two woundings: the transformative sprinkling with pondwater, which removes his humanity, and the obliterative tearing by the dogs' teeth, which destroys the last form and vestige of life. Actaeon's first wound is itself twofold. He flees the goddess with a speed that amazes him, only realizing that he has been transformed into a stag when he pauses

and finally sees, reflected,
His features in a quiet pool. "Alas!"

[6]The awesomeness in seeing the goddess naked can be appreciated by marking its rarity. The most spectacular case in point is the ritual disrobing of Inanna as she descends into the underworld. For her, eventual sacrificial nudity is death.

> He tries to say, but has no words. He groans,
> The only speech he has, and the tears run down
> Cheeks that are not his own. (p. 63)

It is significant that Diana taunts him not with his change of shape but specifically with the loss of speech she knows he will suffer: "Tell them you have seen me, / Diana, naked! Tell them if you can!" (p. 61). This second aspect of Actaeon's first wounding, his muteness, serves a dual function. It ensures that the vision of the naked goddess will never reach the consciousness of the human community and it removes the last outer sign of his humanity; only his thoughts are now human.

Though more stadial and protracted, the wounding of Big Boy also occurs in two major movements. First, he too has been sprinkled, with the blood of his fallen comrades—and their deaths constitute for him a vicarious wounding. Big Boy's demotion to animal has perhaps been more quickly sensed at the swimming hole than Actaeon's at the pond, but the wound of his muteness is revealed only gradually. In Wright's story, the structural counterpart of the reflecting pool is Big Boy's visit to his parents' shack. He too pauses in flight from the goddess, and as his mother questions him, we sense the echo of Actaeon's look into the pool.

> Whut's the matter, Big Boy?"
> Mutely, he looked at her. Then he burst into tears.
> She came and felt the scratches on his face. (p. 32)

Inarticulate and confused, he cannot give an account of what has happened, and his mother must extract the experience in fragments. She is unable to understand its seriousness until Big Boy, who already mentioned three deaths, mumbles, "We wuz swimmin, Ma. N the white woman . . ." "*White* woman?" she cries, and suddenly the impact of the crime is full upon her. Explaining to his father, she arrests his attention and brings the matter into focus thus: "Saul, its a *white* woman!" And he in turn conveys the same emphasis to the hastily called council of elders (pp. 32, 34, 38). That the white woman's very presence on the scene so immediately dwarfs the significance of the killing is a striking indicator of the power of the goddess. Big Boy's muteness has social significance, for there is no moral grammar in which his case could be made, his sentence lifted. In the white woman's extended gaze, there is no hope of innocence. Like the pool at which Actaeon pauses, the family can only reflect his desperate situation. They cannot harbor him or speak in his defense, for to do so would be to bring destruction on themselves. But one of the elders does suggest that his own son, a truck driver, could smuggle Big Boy north, if only he could be concealed until morning. Big Boy will pass the night hiding in one of the kilns he dug in the hillside out past town; and he asks that Bobo be told of his plan, so he may join him in flight.

As the next section of Big Boy's story opens, a dramatic shift in narrative is immediately apparent. The previous parts of the story have been dominated by dialogue. Though there are very good reasons to shift to an emphasis on narrative voice (quiet is necessary if Big Boy is to remain hidden; there is no one for him to talk to), this silencing of the protagonist, and of all black voices in general, also carries the symbolic weight of the wound of muteness. And as is the case with Actaeon, in this silence, we hear for the very first time the thoughts of the protagonist.[7] In Actaeon's instance, these thoughts ricochet between fear, shame, and pleading. Big Boy's blossom as alternating fantasies of an idyllic past, of ignoble defeat, and (primarily) of heroic defiance: he remembers the fun of play while digging these kilns with his three companions, imagines being torn apart by the vicious pack of bloodhounds he is certain are on his trail, and envisions standing off his white pursuers, a defiance to be memorialized in newspaper headlines: "NIGGER KILLS DOZEN OF MOB BEFO LYNCHED! . . . TRAPPED NIGGER SLAYS TWENTY BEFO KILLED!" (p. 44). These may be the adolescent and exaggerated fantasies of one at bay, but they are also a poignant reminder of the interiority of the hero, the memories and aspirations that make up his soul, the very inner freedom which the objectifying gaze seeks to eradicate.

Hiding in the kiln, the womb-like cavity in the earth which he has killed an inhabiting snake to gain, the silent Big Boy listens to a rising crescendo of white voices. Unwittingly they bring him news: some of the lynch mob have put the torch to his parents' shack, the last communal reflector of his humanity. And too the voices bear the sanction of their mission: "Ef they git erway notta woman in this town would be safe" (p. 46). As with Diana, perpetuation of symbolic, not physical, virginity is at stake. Bertha herself and the other women of the town are there to witness the sacrificial purification. The mission is clear: no mention of the murder of Jim Harvey is made, effectively eliminating him again from the symbolic economy of the story, retaining the myth's focus on the crime against the feminine.

The hounds approach. They have found the snake Big Boy killed, and his discovery seems imminent. The reigning irony of the Actaeon myth—the hero torn by his own hounds—is missing here, in two ways. First, though a black might well own hounds, in the myth they figure as symbols of the hero's power, and here the black man is powerless. Big Boy even thinks of the whites and the bloodhounds synonymously—terrifying, atavistic and without human values—"Gawddam them white folks! Thas all they wuz good fer, t run a nigger down lika rabbit!" (p. 44). Further diluting the irony, it is not Big Boy who is discovered, but Bobo, silently in hiding nearby. Though Big Boy has imagined being torn by hounds, it will not be his to endure directly.

---

[7]The phenomenology of speech and silence are as suggestive here as the phenomenology of vision. (See Walter J. Ong, "A Dialectic of Aural and Objective Correlatives," *Critical Theory Since Plato,* ed. Hazard Adams [New York: Harcourt, 1971], 1159-1166.) The power of speech is the principal sign by which we intuit the interiority of the other, though that can only be pointed to, never truly revealed to us. The other, by his speech, may demonstrate a subjective freedom—a humanity—which is similar to ours. In life, we can never experience the thoughts of the other, but in fictions of course we can, through indirect and direct quotation of a character's mental processes. In this section of his story, Wright modulates his prose seamlessly between the literate, reportorial voice of the narrator and the colloquial dialect in which Big Boy's thoughts express themselves directly.

As the mob presses to see the prize the dogs have found, the women raise their voices in song. Big Boy, inwardly compelled to witness though aching at the sight, shrinks from the mob's firelight. But then he remembers an important fact which might well serve as the story's epigraph: *"you could not see into the dark, if you were standing in the light"* (p. 48; my italics). In the white mob's consciousness, nothing "inside" the black man could be seen. His interiority, his soul, is invisible. In the light of their fire, Bobo appears, even to Big Boy, as just a "long dark spot" (p. 48). To Big Boy, and perhaps Wright, the souls of the whites are similarly obscured—but he does not have the capacity to *see* them in that primal, defining, life altering sense.

The mob crowds around to the call, "LES GIT SOURVINEERS!" (p. 49). They will remember him by dismembering him, taking a finger, an ear—what else?—to recall the night on which they quite literally turned a human being into an object. This ritual tearing asunder—which the Greeks called *sparagmos*—is one of the most consistent features of tragic and ironic myth: Actaeon, Pentheus and Orpheus rent, Osiris scattered, Christ's body pierced and sacramentally distributed, Oedipus and Gloucester blind, Shylock calling for his pound of flesh. But, as Northrop Frye points out, sparagmos signifies not only the dismemberment of a hero, but also the fragmentation or disappearance of the heroic—"the sense that heroism and effective action are absent" or for the time impossible.[8] That double sense counts in Wright's story: Bobo is mutilated and Big Boy cannot act heroically to save him. The thought never crosses his mind, even in the sort of fantasy he was able to sustain earlier. The scene is the story's most humiliating: it is a ritual or metaphorical as well as literal killing, for something in Big Boy dies too.

Actaeon also suffered a wounding, at the teeth of the dogs that were once his.

> So they run him
> To stand at bay until the whole pack gathers
> And all together nip and slash and fasten
> Till there is no more room for wounds. (p. 64)

"Till there is no more room for wounds"—surely this is one of the most heart-rending lines of the tale. And one of the most ontologically significant. For when there is no more room for wounds, there is no form, even at the physical level, no identity to support those wounds. With no ground against which the wounds can be gauged or measured, woundedness itself becomes a condition of blank, of non-entity. Disfigurement does not complete the sparagmos of Bobo; he must be transformed, metamorphosed into a non-being on whom there is "no more room for wounds." And how does one make the black man into a non-entity? By denying his difference, of which there are two methods: by covering him with a caricature of his own blackness or by robbing him of his blackness, making him a parody of the white. Both of these seemingly contradictory maneuvers occur in the subsequent tarring and feathering of Bobo, as it is witnessed by Big Boy.

[8]Northrop Frye, *Anatomy of Criticism* (Princeton: Princeton University Press, 1957), 192.

Since he is seeing things in the light of the mob's fire—that is, as they see them—he is only able to see Bobo as a "long dark spot" when the mob pours tar over him. They have given him—made him over in—their own parodic cast of darkness, blackness: again, "you could not see into the dark if you were standing in the light." And then the feathers. After the tar has horribly accentuated his blackness and his suffering, symbolically enough Bobo is covered with feathers. With this applied whiteness, he is denied his own identity, both racially and humanly; he is made to look like a ridiculous animal, in an amplified recapitulation of the metamorphosis at the pond.

But that is not the final transformation. For once blackness has been travestied, then covered with whiteness, a new and extinguishing blackness must erase all traces save the physical, "objective" souvenirs. And so Bobo is doused with gasoline and set afire, like the shack of Big Boy's parents. He has become truly a wound that leaves no place for wounds, black again as the mob would have him black—a non-entity, beyond recognition. For Big Boy, both friends and family home have been eradicated. Diana taunted Actaeon to "tell *them* if you can," thus placing a premium on preventing a social grounding for Actaeon's vision; so the mob in Wright's story is keen to eliminate anything which might permit a social validation for Big Boy's seeing.

After Big Boy has witnessed and numbly internalized Bobo's death, he himself is threatened with discovery by one of the hounds. This dog he takes by the neck and, despite its vigor, strangles it—a token vengeance on the mob, but in fact only a defense of his increasingly isolated self. Again, the sparagmos or dismemberment of Bobo is matched by the enforced sparagmos or disappearance of effective action in Big Boy. He can preserve himself, no more.

Big Boy wakes curled beside the dog he has killed. The morning also brings the sound of the truck. This night of sparagmos and muteness is broken, if not dispelled, when Big Boy attempts to speak: "He tried to call to Will, but his dry throat would make no sound" (p. 51). In a second try, he finds his voice, and with it contacts Will, whose name points to Big Boy's only remaining means and motive for survival. He has eluded the fate of Actaeon—at least on a literal level. And the familiar motifs of the rebirth archetype appear to reinforce this: after Big Boy emerges from the womb-like kiln, utters his first cry, and joins his fate to Will, a rooster crows, and rays of sunlight penetrate even into the back of the truck in which he hides.

But there is a negative element here too. In the kiln, he has been hardened. It is will alone that sustains him, not feeling or compassion or justice. Though the ultimate wounding has been vicarious, it is deep. The numbness that pervades his experience radiates out from this story and informs Wright's subsequent fiction. As we know from Wright's autobiographical account of his life previous to writing this story, he had few illusions that a move north could bring unalloyed good. The fact that Wright's later protagonists often grounded their sense of liberation and worth in a gratuitous violence quite equivalent to what the whites perpetrate here soberly mutes any tendency we might have to romanticize the story's ending. The survival in this story is a survival numbed by the violence it has internalized, and that numbness only increases in the fiction that follows. To that degree, in the story as in the myth, the goddess has her victory.

Ontology and difference, seeing and being seen, idyll and isolation, speech and silence, transformation and wounding—these are the structures of understanding that emerge to guide us when we bring Richard Wright's story into alignment with its mythic source. In their crosscut, they give us a new and deepened perspective on the human condition as it is portrayed in our century, and twenty centuries before.

The Voice in *12 Million Black Voices*

Jack B. Moore

Richard Wright's (and Edwin Rosskam's) *12 Million Black Voices* has met a curious critical reception. Contemporary response to it was unusually complimentary, particularly considering its clearly uncomplimentary portrait of the terrible conditions of life that white Americans had forced upon black Americans. Many of these reviews were not only positive but enthusiastic. Compared to the contemporary responses to his later non-fiction works such as *Black Power* (1954), *The Color Curtain* (1956), *Pagan Spain* (1957), and *White Man, Listen!* (1957) the book was a smashing critical success. But so far *12 Million Black Voices* has not elicited the kind of in-depth analyses—with a few notable exceptions—that a popularly conceived major work by a major writer deserves. And while book-length, comprehensive treatments of Wright and his creative works ordinarily deal at some point with the text's ideas, its art has not been extensively addressed. An unfortunate result of this relative scarcity of criticism scrutinizing the creative foundations of Wright's polemic in deference to his political vision, has perhaps been to underscore the long-held belief that he is primarily a writer of power (when successful) and not so much a writer of craft and skill. Ironically, this embodies in a way the racist stereotype that blacks are physically strong but lack intelligence.

John M. Reilly is one critic who has dug deeply into the technic of *12 Million Black Voices*. In two brief, perceptive articles he has focused upon the language Wright used to tell his story, "a language akin to the style of the popular blues, spirituals, and sermons," and the form which Reilly identifies as "simulated oral utterance derived from the spontaneous arts that shape the orations of the preacher, . . . a secularization of the sacred moral voice of the folk. Employing techniques of the sermon, it is rooted in localized tradition." Among the techniques Reilly discusses as part of this sermonizing tradition are personifications ("Lords of the Land"), "tag phrases such as 'gangster-politicians,' " and a "pattern of style that allows the narrative to rise to climax, to fall, and to rise again. Wright he terms a "preacher-narrator."[1]

Reprinted from *Mississippi Quarterly* 42.2 (1989): 415-424. By permission of Jack B. Moore and *Mississippi Quarterly*.

[1]"Reconstruction of Genre as Entry into Conscious History," *Black American Literature Forum* 13 (Spring 1979) 3; "Richard Wright Preaches the Nation," *Black American Literature Forum* 16 (Fall 1982), 117, 118.

Reilly is very helpful and correct in emphasizing these traditions within the black experience to explain Wright's skill in attracting and holding an audience for his political and spiritual message. It is surely no accident that smack in the physical middle of *12 Million Black Voices* Wright placed a sermon. But Wright's art sprang from and fed upon many sources, and I think there are other explanations elucidating the form and technique of his book. I believe Wright was also consciously or unknowingly using the art of the documentary film to reach his audience. Wright was quite sensitive to films. He possessed what Michel Fabre terms a "passion for film-making," and wrote a number of film scripts including one "inspired" by the Fisk Jubilee Singers, and of course the screenplay for *Native Son*. In 1942 he contacted the great documentary film-maker John Grierson concerning a film he wanted to work on about the underground railroad.[2]

He even thought about some of his fiction in cinematic terms. In discussing "How Bigger Was Born," he says, "I wanted the reader to feel that Bigger's story was happening now, like a play upon the stage or a movie unfolding on the screen. . . . Wherever possible, I told of Bigger's life in close-up, slow motion."

The documentary was a popular form of film during the 1930's and early 1940's, often used to present history or slices of history in a somewhat simplified manner entwining kinetic visual images and sound and narrated text to teach a lesson to massed audiences. It was accessible to black Americans generally and to whites along a fairly broad social and demographic scale. Aimed generally at this popular audience, it was sometimes an art and not merely an entertainment. Some documentaries were like disguised sermons with very specific lessons to deliver, and many were quite mixed internally in mood and tone and level of sophistication. At the very least, Wright's (and photo-director Rosskam's) production paralleled in many of its contextual elements the work of the era's many fine film documentarians, while concurrently taking its place in the evolution of the photojournalistic book, as so many commentators have pointed out.[3]

Much of the language and vision of the book could be that of the black minister; a great deal is not. The voice at the start of section two, for example, "Inheritors of Slavery," is not a minister's voice, but a narrator's voice speaking over the print of a picture.

> The word 'Negro,' the term by which, orally or in print, we black folk in the United States are usually designated, is not really a name at all nor a description, but a psychological island whose objective form is the most unanimous fiat in all American history: a fiat buttressed by popular and national tradition, and written down in many state and city statutes: a fiat which artificially and arbitrarily defines, regulates, and limits in scope of meaning the vital contours of our lives, and the lives of our children's children.

[2]Michel Fabre, *The Unfinished Quest of Richard Wright* (New York: William Morrow and Company, Inc., 1973), 353, 261.

[3]Richard Wright (photo-direction by Edwin Rosskam), *12 Million Black Voices, A Folk History of the Negro in the United States* (New York: Viking Press, 1941), 30. Citations of this book will hereafter be placed in parentheses in the text.

The book's language here, which reads as though something heard over the book's pictured images, is delivered neither by a minister nor an orator, but by a narrator's voice that can become when necessary either the minister's or orator's voice. Sentences such as "How did this paradoxical amalgam of love and cruelty come to be?" (p. 24), and "Eastern industry, which had begun to flood the nation with commodities, was owned by men who wielded a new type of authority" (p. 26), sound as though they were spoken by an authoritative narrator who is presenting, as the book's sub-title indicates, a history lesson, but a special variety of history lesson, highly selective and compacted, that reproduces in its structure the central problem of its subject. "Standing now at the apex of the twentieth century, we look back over the road we have traveled and compare it with the road over which the white folk have traveled, and we see that three hundred years in the history of our lives are equivalent to three thousand years in the history of the lives of whites! The many historical phases which whites have traversed voluntarily and gradually during the course of Western civilization we black folk have traversed through swift compulsion" (p. 145).

Wright's telescoping of black history in his text (with pictures) re-creates the nature of development which he feels traumatized black life and impeded its progress in the United States. Compacted and jammed in upon itself, black life as Wright portrays it in *12 Million Black Voices* has survived and achieved, despite the series of shocks it was forced to experience during slavery and the fake emancipation that followed it when black people were chained to the land by the demands of cotton growing. "Imagine," he says, "European history from the days of Christ to the present telescoped into three hundred years and you can comprehend the drama which our consciousness has experienced! Brutal, bloody, crowded with suffering and abrupt transitions, the lives of us black folk represent the most magical and meaningful picture of human experience in the Western world" (p. 146). His method as a writer was to "telescope" in a documentary the complex history of this black experience, to offer a meaningful picture (or pictures) with text that to be accurate had to be "Brutal, bloody, crowded with suffering and abrupt transitions," like black life itself. He attempted what he had called for in "Blueprint for Negro Writing," a "foreshortened picture" of black people "being transplanted from a 'savage' to a 'civilized' culture in all its social, political, economic and emotional implications."[4] As the narrator of this story, his "We" becomes even more functional, for although "We" is many people, it speaks with one voice (one capable of varying its sounds) and thereby reinforces the idea of black trauma, as though all the "crowded" sufferings and shocks were endured by a single entity in a single though extended lifetime. Wright's technique is both timely—it was not unusual for film documentaries such as Willard Van Dyke's and Ralph Steiner's *The City* (1939) to employ the "we-you" narrative formula[5]—and ancient. The African *griot* also functioned as a story teller, communicating history and mythic awareness while serving as a timeless representative of his tribe.

---

[4]*New Challenge* 2 (Fall 1937), 61.

[5]William Stott, *Documentary Expression and Thirties America* (New York: Oxford Press, 1973), 28.

The prose of *12 Million Black Voices* is more cadenced, rhythmic, and filled with parallelisms and lists—is more oral and aural—than any of Wright's other book-length works. In some paragraphs, hardly a sentence seems without a triad or more of connected images. These Whitmanesque sequences (Reilly refers to a group of fifteen "short, nearly chantable paragraphs"[6]) often present successive or overlapping pictures in some linked or contrapuntal fashion. The narrator speaks of "Bloody riots" that erupt over "trifling incidents. . . an altercation between a black boy and a white boy on a beach, over the wild rumor that a white man has slapped a black boy in a store, over the whispered tale that some white man has spoken improperly to a black girl, over the fact that a black man has accidentally stepped on a white woman's foot, over the gossip that a black woman has talked back to a white woman . . . streetfighting . . . flares in Pittsburgh, Chicago, Washington, New York, Atlanta, and East St. Louis" (p. 123). These are catalogues, but they are also cuts in a montage, in films a technique for telling a story quickly, for making a point or creating an impression rapidly, by juxtaposing brief, often particularly scenic and suggestive images that in themselves are undeveloped but that accumulated in a sequence tell a story or deliver a message. The technique has come to be pervasive in films of all sorts, and writers were early sensitive to it. John Dos Passos, in his influential trilogy *U. S. A.*, for example, creates the feel of jumbled Western history at the end of World War I by tying together seemingly unrelated news snippets in "Newsreel XXIX":

TWO TROLLIES HELD UP BY GUNMEN IN QUEENS

Over the cowshed
I'll be waiting at the kakakitchen door

SPECIAL GRAND JURY ASKED TO INDICT BOLSHEVISTS

Montage is an intensely visual method of communication that was frequently used in but hardly unique to documentary films. Pare Lorentz's classic *The Plow That Broke the Plains* (released in 1936) is replete with montages accompanied by inspirational or informative narration. In one famous sequence a bomb explodes followed by headlines of World War I and signs of surging wheat profits. Fields are suddenly worked night and day by men on large machines and the narrator almost shouts "wheat will win the war!" as wheat grains spill thickly into piles and more machines churn in synchronized maneuvers over the plains, and then military tanks plow over battlefields. Finally images of a victory celebration are juxtaposed with cuts of more farm machines massed as though on parade over the land. Many segments of arguably the decade's most popular and certainly its most frequently seen documentary "The March of Time" employed montage to visualize and simplify history. The August 16, 1935, episode on the Army's preparedness for war— a ludicrous claim in history's light—shows for example a map of the United States indicating various points of entry some unnamed enemy might take, then focuses

[6]"Richard Wright Preaches," 118.

on a route through the St. Lawrence seaway. In shots that would be missed by the blink of an eye, bugles blow, General Douglas MacArthur ponders his desk, the "War Council" is alerted, messages are sent by phone and telegraph, more bugles blow, and trains, army vehicles, and even wagons are mobilized and carry troops and supplies to the front, accompanied by appropriately rousing music.

The technique is another way of telescoping history, and so once again, Wright employs a method enabling him to compact the black experience and thereby communicate its uniqueness, its forced compression. His montages span and link time and space, helping to picture the new diaspora for example. "Night and day, in rain and in sun, in winter and in summer, we leave the land. Already, as we sit and look broodingly out over the turning fields, we notice with attention and hope that the dense southern swamps give way to broad, cultivated wheat farms. The spick-and-span farmhouses done in red and green and white crowd out the casual, unpainted gingerbread shacks. Silos take the place of straggling piles of hay" (p. 98). The passage is cadenced, filled with pictures and movement, and it is highly oral. It is simplified history—just like a documentary.

12 Million Black Voices is divided into four sections, and these are further subdivided into scenes with minor movements of their own within the greater rhythms of the larger units. One such subsection (pp. 59ff.) begins "Lord, we know that this is a hard system!" Some of the concepts in this sequence are abstract, yet still are presented in relatively clear verbal pictures describing the oppression of cotton workers: "For longer than we can remember, cotton has been our companion; we travel down the plantation road with debt holding our left hand, with credit holding our right, and ahead of us looms the grave, the final and simple end." But the sequence concludes with a modulated affirmation of black life achieved through time by the growth of children that embodies the growth and survival of the race, which nature seems to affirm. "Yet we live and our families grow large . . . like black buttercups, our children spring up on the red soil of the plantations. . . . A child is a glad thing in the bleak stretches of the cotton country. . . ."[7] The sequence ends with the narrator declaring exultingly that "our gold is in the hearts of the people we love." The following paragraph begins another sub-sequence simply and quietly as the narrator states that "Our way of life is simple" and eventually concludes with a return to images of black children (also depicted in accompanying photographs), "born to us in our one-room shacks," who grow up "fetching pails of water from the springs" and "minding the younger children" (p. 62). Wright's verbal montages, the text's photographs, and the narrator's voice again telescope black history, now despairing, now hoping, always returning to the vision of attainable progress. Moods are communicated through the narrator's voice, and the images he delivers, and cry out for filmed presentation, which the print montages strongly suggest.

The narrator presents contrasting images, often within the same sentence, that offer strange pictures of life in the South and portray what seems to be a distortion

---

[7]Ellipses added.

of the natural order as though the South were an expressionistic jungle of bizarre violence. "Most of the flogging and lynchings occur at harvest time, when fruit hangs heavy and ripe, when the leaves are red and gold, when nuts fall from the trees, when the earth offers its best" (p. 41). Sometimes the juxtapositions are threaded along tightly bound sequences mixing horror with jokes. Less than a page following the brutal photograph of a lynched black male slumped back against a tree, his knees buckled, his eyes shut, his slack body held up from the neck by a rope, the narrator sets down a pair of comic verses, chants of the sort sung by black children as joking outcries against white bigotry

> I don't like liver
> I don't like hash
> I'd rather be a nigger
> than poor white trash

and

> White folks is evil
> And niggers is too
> So glad I'm a Chinaman
> I don't know what to do.

The juxtaposition stuns. William Stott has pointed out that Wright's text was written before Edwin Rosskam selected the photographs for it, and claims that Rosskam chose the Farm Security Administration photos partly because they were easily available and free.[8] But the book's readers would not have been aware of this background information. They would read lines about black bodies swung from ropes, see the photograph of the lynched black man and then "hear" the comic verses. They would experience the fusion of sight and sound.

A black minister might have included children's songs and comic jibes in a sermon attacking white racism, might have mixed materials from various levels of the black experience to deliver his message, but so might have a documentary. "The March of Time," so popular during the thirties that it was parodied in Orson Welles's *Citizen Kane*, with which Wright was familiar, often mixed sequences that were now somber, now jaunty. Its very first issue in 1935 dealt with the conflict within Japan between advocates of democracy and militarism, attempts of New York's "21 Club" to trick prohibition agents, England's comic battle against angry car drivers to install traffic lights, and the quixotic struggle of an American tourist to make the French repay its war debts to America—all in twenty-two minutes of "pictorial journalism."

"The March of Time" was rather like a sponge among documentaries, soaking up the techniques of other documentaries and releasing its tricks and style to future documentarians and moviemakers who were magnetized by its art and its (it must be admitted) schlock-filled mannerisms. The series often employed sharp changes in music to underscore turns in its mood, cuing the audience that they

[8]Stott, 232.

were expected to make a momentary adjustment in their emotional response to what was being shown. *12 Million Black Voices* contains no sound track, but who cannot hear in the mind's ear the sounds of spirituals in the sequence at the center of the book where Wright incorporates a sermon (in the finished book interspersed with photographs of women singing in a choir, and an ecstatic, solitary, white-robed gospel singer) and describes black churchgoers "lifted far beyond the boundaries of our daily lives" (p. 73)? Just two paragraphs later, Wright's narrator projects the sights and sounds of a Saturday night crossroad's dancehall:

> Shake it to the east
> Shake it to the west
> Shake it to the one
> You love the best

and

> I love you once
> I love you twice
> I love you next to
> Jesus Christ.

The narrator's mixing of sacred and profane in black life, his show of how they merge, might be termed a metaphysical montage, a demonstration of how technique and subject become fused (the merger of spiritual and jazz) to demonstrate a fact of black life.

As simple, visual histories, documentaries were also of course frequently interwoven with facts stated directly. Wright often employs this technique. At the conclusion of "Inheritors of Slavery," and the start of "Death on the City Pavements" Wright embeds facts and statistics suggesting the plight of disfranchised and dispossessed black men and women at the nadir of the reconstruction period and the beginning of the black rise. "From 1890 to 1920, more than 2,000,000 of us left the land" his narrator says (p. 89). "Harlem's black population doubled between 1900 and 1920" (p. 93).

My point is not that Wright imitated "The March of Time" in *12 Million Black Voices,* or any other specific documentary, though it is not difficult to find parallels between some well-known documentary films and Wright's book. Lorentz's popular *The Plow That Broke the Plains* and *The River* (released in 1937) share many elements with *12 Million Black Voices* including simplified history; children as symbols of devastated poor people's hope (in *The River* a baby grasps a plow in a dusty-dry field as the narrator says "many were disappointed but the great day was coming, the day of new causes, new profits, new hopes"); an authoritative narrator speaking highly cadenced prose images uses "we" to dramatize that he embodies the Americans whose history he is telling (in *The River* he speaks of "black spruce and Norway pine; Douglas fir and red cedar; scarlet oak and shagbark hickory; we built a hundred cities and a thousand towns, but at what a cost?" and in *The Plow* the narrator offers pictures of "what we did with" the land); the ways cotton tied people to cycles of poverty (the narrow of *The River* intones that "poor land makes poor people, poor people make poor land"). Rather, I suggest that he was influenced by the styles, by many of the techniques of this quintessentially 1930's popular and commercial art form in his own formulations for his book. Who reads *12 Million Black Voices* and examines its photographic images without *hearing* the text delivered in a very personal fashion? This is the particular power of the book's appeal. The voice Wright established to represent *12 Million Black Voices* is unique, as it would have to be to represent the sounds of such a varied, rich culture. It is sometimes portentous in the same way as the famous "Voice of Fate" Westbrook Van Voorhis memorably employed throughout "The March of Time" but far more flexible, and often simpler, more conversational, like Thomas Chalmers in *The Plow That Broke the Plains*, far less distanced from his subject matter and his audience. The narration is often poetic, but far grittier than the lyrical sound of Pare Lorentz's text for his award-winning *The River.* And befitting the voice of a people, the narrator's voice is finally an exceptionally forceful voice—but even in exhorting it is personal; the "we" always seems to speak directly to "you" before it.

12 Million Black Voices is essentially simplified history, similar to a film documentary, featuring a series of connected photographs and a text filled with visual imagery, delivered by what seems a speaking voice. Whether or not the text was written first and the photographs slotted into it, the finished product is at its best a seamless fusion of pictures—verbal and photographic—and sounds, words as though spoken and the unplayed music so strongly suggested by Wright's prose. There is smooth visual continuity between the prose that says "some of the neighborhoods in which we live look as though they have been subjected to an intensive and prolonged aerial bombardment" (p. 114) and the photograph immediately following that shows an exact pictorial replica of Wright's words. The book's art is the art of blending sights and sounds, facts, statistics, songs, images, folk stories, and stark history, to deliver the message that *"we are you"* (p. 146), that the teller of this tale, the folk mass, is also its audience, the mass of Americans black or white or whatever, to whom the book's message has been presented.

This blending is demonstrated in the narrative-documentary's conclusion, which itself blends juxtaposed images of sight and sound: "We are with the new tide. We stand at the crossroads. We watch each new procession. The hot wires carry urgent appeals. Print compels us. Voices are speaking." The listener-reader-viewer is told "Men are moving! And we shall be with them" (p. 147). The written (to be listened to) verbal text merges with a final photograph of a young black boy outside a shack, looking up into the sun. "And we shall be with them" means that we shall be with him, the boy, and that "we" are now blended, merged with the old "we" who has voiced our documentary of the mind, ear, and eye. Hokey? "Sentimental"?[9] Perhaps, but also very effective, like the end of Clifford Odets' "Waiting for Lefty" where "we" who are no longer just an audience agree to "strike! STRIKE!" Effective, like the end of a good documentary that has taught us simple history, and moved us.

<hr />

[9]Stott's evaluation, p. 234.

The Paradoxical Structure of Richard Wright's "The Man Who Lived Underground"

Patricia D. Watkins

Most critics of Richard Wright's novella "The Man Who Lived Underground" focus on its existential content.[1] However, because these critics generally ground their usually brief analyses on the story's plot rather than close textual analysis, their comments about man's "essence" and "existence" seem inadequate, justifying Robin McNallie's complaint that critics "have settled too easily for broad overviews of 'Man' instead of focusing on the story's particulars" (77). Along the same lines, only a few critics mention—let alone discuss—the story's naturalistic content. When they do mention it, these critics assure their audiences that Wright "surpassed" and "moved beyond" the naturalistic perspective to the more "universal," "sophisticated," and "philosophical" existential perspective.[2] Despite its current low repute, however, naturalism, like existentialism, makes a statement about man's essence and existence. Thus, to focus on the story's existential content while ignoring or minimizing its naturalistic content is necessarily to risk distorting what Wright says in it about man and man's life. More importantly, such a focus disregards a major basis of the story's paradoxical structure—paradoxical because at every level, from the dictional to the philosophical, Wright pairs contradictory and seemingly irreconcilable parts.

At the heart of the paradox is the story's simultaneous existence as a naturalistic (thus deterministic) fable and an existential (thus anti-deterministic) fable. The result of this yoking of fables is a protagonist who is simultaneously portrayed as an animal, whose fate is controlled by forces independent of his will, and a god, whose will becomes, in effect, the First Cause of his fate. The paradoxical structure of the story demands first that the protagonist be considered in terms of his

Reprinted from *Black American Literature Forum* 23 (Winter 1989): 767-783. Copyright © 1989 Indiana State University.

[1]See, for example, Fabre, "Richard Wright"; Bone, 25-31; Gounard; Ridenour; Bakish; Brignano, 148-55; Margolies.

Portions of "The Man Who Lived Underground" were originally published in 1942. An expanded version of the story was published in *Cross Section*. All references to the story in this text are to the version appearing in Wright's *Eight Men* (1961).

[2]Ridenour, 54; McNallie, 83. See also Goede and Widmer.

role in both the naturalistic and existential fables, and finally that the apparent contradictions related to the fables and the protagonist's role in them be reconciled. This structural approach will disclose a more accurate picture of the protagonist's (and, by extension, Wright's conception of man's) essence and existence than has been developed by evaluating the protagonist in terms of one fable alone.

"The Man Who Lived Underground" has all of the features of the classic naturalistic fable. Its working-class protagonist Fred Daniels has been falsely accused of murder. He escapes from the police and takes refuge underground in the sewers. After a few days of tunneling through the sewers and secretly observing the people who live above ground, he leaves the underground and confronts the policemen who earlier forced him to sign a confession of guilt. When Daniels tries to lead them into the sewers so that they can see people as he has seen them, one of the officers shoots and kills him. Thus, Daniels suffers the classic fate of the naturalistic protagonist: He is "wiped out."

Wright's presentation of Daniels' story epitomizes the naturalistic method described by Émile Zola in such works as *The Experimental Novel, The Fortune of the Rougons,* and *Thérèse Raquin.* Wright literally renders Zola's dictum that man be considered an animal. Throughout the story Wright compares Daniels to animals, sometimes explicitly and sometimes implicitly. For example, Wright uses a series of similes that explicitly compare Daniels' actions to those of an insect, a dog, an eel, and a cat (35, 41, 53, 73). Wright implicitly compares Daniels to an animal by writing that Daniels "slithered through" the entrance to the cave that serves as his underground home (41). Wright's placing Daniels underground to "live" is another implicit comparison of Daniels to an animal, most particularly a rat. Mildred W. Everette points out that Daniels lives like a pack rat, burrowing from place to place underground and dragging stolen items to his "underground den" (321). Eventually Daniels dies like a rat that he encountered when he first entered the sewer. As Everette notes, the wording that describes the death of the rat as it spins in the sewer current after Daniels has killed it is the same wording that describes the death of Daniels as he spins after the police officer Lawson has shot him (320).

As Zola also dictated, Wright observes the effect that heredity has on the fortunes and character of his protagonist. A significant role played by heredity is Daniels' inheritance of compulsive animal drives—especially the need to satisfy his hunger and thirst. The need to find food and clean water drives Daniels from one location to another while he is underground. The need to find food influences Daniels' character as well, turning him into a thief who steals a lunch pail from a furnace tender and fruit from a grocer.

Racial identity does not directly determine what happens to Fred Daniels. Rather, environment—specifically, economic and social forces—seems to be a more important determinant of Daniels' fortunes. Before his arrest Daniels worked at the home of a Mrs. Wooten, presumably as a servant. Hence, Daniels is at the lower end of the economic and social scale, like the white night watchman who shares his fate. This fate is to be the victim of policemen who "solve" cases by using brute force. Having falsely accused and then tortured the night watchman, the policemen let him shoot and kill himself; having falsely accused and then tortured Daniels, one of the same policemen shoots and kills him.

On all counts, therefore, "The Man Who Lived Underground" exemplifies the naturalistic fable: It shows man living like an animal and dying like an animal, which is to say that, like an animal, man is the subject of internal and external forces over which he lacks control.

Paradoxically, as Wright compares Daniels to animals, he simultaneously compares him to Christ. This animal/Christ linking is a subparadox within a broader animal/God paradox. The first suggestion that Daniels is Christlike occurs early in the story when he dreams that he can walk on water (42). Less obviously but just as tellingly, references to daylight and darkness, which indicate that Daniels stays underground for three days, reveal his story to be virtually the mirror image of Christ's: Christ was executed, lay dead in a cave for three days, and then rose on the third day; Daniels lives in a cave for three days, rises on the third day, and then is executed.[3]

Daniels' identification with Christ is further suggested in the confrontation of Daniels with the Black worshippers in a church when Daniels returns above ground on the third day. Their paradoxical encounter, during which the worshippers reject the savior that they pray for, is a sustained example of dramatic irony, based on the reader's awareness and the worshippers' lack of awareness that Daniels is a Christ. The congregants sing a hymn that invokes "the Lamb" to "*Tell me again your story*" (75, emphasis added). Daniels comes to them shouting, ". . . I want to *tell* 'em" (75, emphasis added). Some of the congregation, not recognizing that the invoked spirit has arrived, say of Daniels, " 'He's filthy. . . He stinks' " (75). Others begin another hymn, which speaks of a "*wondrous sight . . . Vision sweet and divine*" (76). The sewer-filthy Daniels is, indeed, a "wondrous sight," and if the congregation recognized him for the Christ that he is, they would see that he is a "vision sweet," even though he does stink. Finally, the congregants sing:

Oh, wondrous sight, wondrous sight
Lift my heavy heart above
Oh, wondrous sight, wondrous sight
Fill my weary soul with love (76)

Love is exactly what Daniels wants to fill these souls with. Though he does not know what to say to the congregation when he confronts them, by the time that he gets to the police station he knows both his message of love and his method for spreading it. Speaking to Lawson he exclaims, " 'Mister, when I looked through all

---

[3]Daniels' first day underground begins in the daytime and ends when, after encountering the Black worshippers in a church, he sees the light of street lamps shining through the perforations of a manhole cover and realizes that "it must be night" (33). His second day underground begins as Daniels notices that "daylight spilled from a window above his head" in the basement of a jewelry store (43), and it ends after he burglarizes the store's safe while "moonlight floated in from a wide window" (54). On the third day, Daniels arises from the underground for the final time, stepping "into a hot glare of sunshine" (73).

of those holes and saw how people were living, I loved 'em. . . .' " (86). Daniels believes that, if the policemen follow him to his underground home, the love that he feels will multiply; ". . . they would feel what he had felt and they in turn would show it to others and those others would feel as they had felt, and soon everybody would be governed by the same impulse of pity" (89). The Black congregants, however, do not give Daniels the opportunity to deliver the message of love that they pray for. They push him out of the church into the street. Their action provides a final parallel between the situations of Daniels and Christ. Rejected by his own people, Daniels is executed by the centurions of the ruling class. Thus his fate—to die like a rat and to be killed like Christ—is paradoxically the fate of animal and God.

Daniels' divinity is not limited to his Christlike life and death. Rather, it is the broader divinity usually associated with Jean-Paul Sartre's existential dictum "Create yourself and your world." For a humanistic existentialist like Sartre, God is dead. Since there is no God, man is free—obligated, in fact—to define himself and to act based on his own will rather than on some God-given, predetermined idea of what man is and how he should live. In other words, since God is dead, man is free to become his own god. In existential terms Daniels becomes his own god (just as in naturalistic terms he is an animal). Daniels must be considered in existential terms because he experiences the range of emotions—a sense of isolation, anxiety, guilt, and freedom—that are experienced by the typical existential protagonist when he discovers that he exists in a universe without God.

According to Michel Fabre's chronology, Wright wrote "The Man Who Lived Underground" before he received formal instruction on Nietzsche, Kierkegaard, and other existentialists, and before his first meeting with Sartre (299). Thus, in his story Wright may not be consciously working out the major themes of twentieth-century existentialism. Nevertheless, Wright's rendering of existential themes is understandable in terms of standard explanations of twentieth-century existentialism, which, like the centuries-old existential attitude, seeks to understand how man should live in a chaotic universe on which no God imposes an order that man can comprehend.

No God imposes a comprehensible order on the universe of "The Man Who Lived Underground." In this universe God is dead—or at least absent. Thus, dreaming of a drowning mother and her baby, Daniels loses sight of the baby and begins calling, "*Where is it* and the empty sky and sea threw back his voice" (42). The "empty sky" metaphor has been used by other twentieth-century American authors to suggest God's absence from the affairs of men—absence either because He does not exist or because He does not choose to involve Himself. For example, to signify God's non-existence, Nathanael West uses the "empty sky" metaphor in *Miss Lonelyhearts*, wherein the protagonist "searched the sky. . . . the gray sky looked as if it had been rubbed with a soiled eraser. It held no angels, flaming crosses, olive-bearing doves, wheels within wheels" (174-75); ". . . it was canvas-colored and ill-stretched. He examined it. . . . he found nothing" (204-05). To signify God's lack of involvement, Zora Neale Hurston uses the "empty sky" metaphor in *Their Eyes Were Watching God*, wherein the protagonist "looked hard at the sky for a long time. Somewhere up there beyond blue ether's bosom sat He. Was He noticing what was going on around here? . . . The sky stayed hard looking and quiet. . . . God would do less than He had in His heart" (264). In the dream of Fred Daniels the empty sky reveals his subconscious awareness (provoked by the corpse of a real baby that he has seen earlier floating in the sewer) that no God will appear to rescue even the most "innocent" of creatures—a baby—from death. Later, while Daniels is waiting to learn the combination of a jewelry store safe, he "looked with a baffled expression at the dark sky" (51). At this point Daniels consciously begins to realize that God is absent.

When the typical existential protagonist realizes that there is no God watching him or watching over him, he feels isolated, alone in the universe. During his three-day ordeal underground, Fred Daniels is constantly aware that he is "alone" (31, 40, 43, 92). In addition, the typical existential protagonist feels angst—a combination of fear and dread—when he realizes that he is solely responsible for his actions because, since there is no God, man lacks a God-given, pre-defined nature that he can use to excuse his actions as well as an absolute standard of good and evil to help him choose among alternative actions. During his three-day ordeal Daniels experiences angst—most clearly as he prepares to emerge from the underground for the last time: "He did not know how much fear he felt, for fear claimed him completely; yet it was not a fear of the police or of people, but a cold dread at the thought of the *actions* he knew he would perform if he went out into that cruel sunshine" (73, emphasis added). Daniels' fear and dread in this case are existential, or ontological. They are not the same as his "ordinary," or situational, fear and dread, which arise when he faces harm (from the rushing sewer waters, for example, or from the police). Instead, they are the angst that arises when he must act.

In addition to feeling alone and anxious, the typical existential protagonist feels guilty. Fred Daniels experiences both "ordinary" and existential guilt. Early in the story, Daniels experiences "ordinary," or situational, guilt when he transgresses religious and social codes, for example, when he wants to laugh at the church congregants the first time that he sees them (32). The guilt that he suffers arises from his wanting to do something that his religious training makes him feel that he should not do. That Daniels has such training, that he is a religious man is clear: Who but a religious man would worry that God might "strike him dead" (32), and of whom but a religious man would it be claimed that "he knew most of the churches in this area [where he was hiding] above ground . . ." (32)? Not surprisingly, therefore, Daniels feels guilt when he wants to laugh at the people worshiping God. He feels the same ordinary guilt when he steals the furnace tender's food and while he burglarizes the jewelry shop safe (40, 54).

Unlike his ordinary guilt, the existential, or ontological, guilt of Daniels does not derive from any violation of religious or social codes. It cannot, for existentialists recognize no legal or ethical absolutes against which man can judge his actions and find himself guilty. Rather, as Donald V. Marano explains, existential guilt derives from man's possession of consciousness, which allows him to discern his inherent weakness and inadequacy: his powerlessness to bring himself into existence and his powerlessness to guarantee that he will cease to exist even if he commits suicide; his powerlessness to keep that which is outside himself (for example, the heat from a fire) from impinging on his consciousness unwilled; his physical, intellectual, and moral inability to be or do all that he wants to be or do (42-45). The term *guilt*, therefore, embraces "not only human deficiencies, since they all bespeak the discrepancies between what a man is and what he aspires to be" (46). As Marano concludes, man, because of his finitude, is innately guilty (45).

Fred Daniels first becomes aware of existential guilt as he listens to the church congregation singing:

> He felt that their search for a happiness they could never find made them feel that they had committed some dreadful offense which they could not remember or understand. . . . Why was this sense of guilt so seemingly innate, so easy to come by, to think, to feel, so verily physical? It seemed that when one felt this guilt one was retracing in one's feelings a faint pattern designed long before; it seemed that one was always trying to remember a gigantic shock that had left a haunting impression upon one's body which one could not forget or shake off, but which had been forgotten by the conscious mind, creating in one's life a state of eternal anxiety. (68)

In other words, Daniels credits the congregation's guilt not to their actual ability to judge themselves guilty of a specific religious or legal violation (in which case their guilt would be "ordinary," everyday guilt) but rather to their consciousness of an innate sense of failure and inadequacy. The guilt that Daniels attributes to them, therefore, is existential guilt.

Daniels recognizes this same existential guilt in the boy who is beaten for stealing a radio stolen by Daniels himself. Watching the beating, Daniels says to himself, "Perhaps it was a good thing that they were beating the boy; perhaps the beating would bring to the boy's attention, for the first time in his life, the secret of his existence, the guilt that he could never get rid of" (69). Likewise, Daniels recognizes existential guilt in the night watchman, who is accused of stealing the jewelry stolen by Daniels: "The watchman was guilty; although he was not guilty of the crime of which he had been accused, he was guilty, had always been guilty" (70). Convinced at last that all men are guilty in a way that is unrelated to any legal or religious infraction, Daniels leaves the underground, enters the police station, and—even though he knows that he has not murdered anyone—confesses, " 'I'm guilty' " (85).

Daniels' emotions of isolation, fear, and guilt are predictable consequences of an awareness of the absence of God in the universe. As the existential protagonist accepts the absence of God, he recognizes his freedom to create himself and his world—in short, his freedom to be his own god. Near the end of his second day underground, Daniels takes the first step toward creating himself and his world and hence becoming his own god: He begins rejecting his aboveground values and identity.

One aboveground value that Daniels rejects is money. Given a dime by a woman who mistakes him for a clerk at a grocery store, Daniels "fl[i]ng[s] the dime to the pavement with a gesture of contempt" (49). He shows the same contempt for even larger sums of money when he pastes hundred dollar bills on the walls of his cave. His rejection of the valuation of money above ground is a liberating act. After pasting the money on the walls, Daniels "slapped his thighs and guffawed. He had triumphed over the world aboveground! He was free!" (62).

A second aboveground value that Daniels rejects is time. On his second day underground, Daniels' enslavement to time ends when he prepares to nail valuable watches onto the same dirt wall on which he has just pasted the hundred dollar bills. Taking the watches from a box, he "began to wind them up; he did not attempt to set them at any given hour, for there was no time for him now" (62). Once again, rejecting a value of the world above ground is a liberating act for Daniels, for as he contemplates the watches, he recognizes the restrictions that time places on people who, unlike him, have not escaped time's tyranny: "The gold watches ticked and trembled, crowning time the king of consciousness, defining the limits of living" (66). When he first went underground Daniels realized that he had "to kill time or go aboveground" (35). Because Daniels succeeds in killing time by refusing to acknowledge its existence, he is able to return above ground no sooner than he *wills* to do so. Thus, his ability to reject time, which the people above ground value, helps him to become free.

As Daniels rejects the values of the world above ground, he begins to create his own values, the second step toward "creating his own world." Steeped in his new sense of freedom, Daniels initially concludes that "anything . . . was right, any act a man took to satisfy himself, murder, theft, torture" (64). Such an attitude allows him to justify his having taken someone else's money. In his mind, "He had not stolen the money; he had simply picked it up, just as a man would pick up firewood in a forest" (62). The attitude that anything is right also contributes to Daniels' desire to laugh at the boy and the watchman who are accused of having stolen items stolen by Daniels himself (69, 70). Even as he smiles, however, Daniels begins to feel the pity that ultimately characterizes life above ground. He discards the amorality of the Nietzschean superman and assumes the attitude of the existentialist who chooses his actions mindful of the effect that his choices have on humanity: ". . . every man ought to say to himself, 'Am I really the kind of man who has the right to act in such a way that humanity might guide itself by my actions?'" (20). So writes Sartre to explain how man should evaluate his actions since the death of God eliminates any fixed reference for judging whether an act is "good" or "evil." Such thinking seems to guide Daniels, for he abandons his anything-is-right attitude and replaces it with an attitude of love and pity for mankind, the attitude that he hopes will guide humanity's actions when it sees the new world that he has created underground. This new world is symbolized by his dirt cave, wherein watches, rings, diamonds, and money have lost their value and function merely as decoration.

In addition to creating his own world, Daniels creates himself. He does so after he sheds his aboveground identity—literally, his name. When he first goes underground Daniels knows his name and types it on the typewriter that he sees in an office. When he drags the typewriter to his cave, however, his name is "on the tip of his lips," but he cannot remember it. His response is a "vague terror" (61). By the time that Daniels enters the police station, however, not only has he forgotten his name but he no longer cares that he has forgotten it. When asked his name by a policeman, "He had opened his lips to answer and no words came. He had forgotten. But what did it matter if he had? It was not important" (78).

As he sheds his aboveground identity, Fred Daniels acquires a godlike identity. Part of his divinity is the sense of freedom that he attains. Daniels feels *freedom from* the rules and the enslavements (to time, to money) of the world above ground; and he feels *freedom to* make his own rules—initially, to steal and even murder if he chooses to. Thus, playing God as he stands over the sleeping night watchman, Fred "smiled indulgently; he could send a bullet into that man's brain and time would be over for him . . ." (58). Seeing the night watchman being beaten a short time later, Daniels feels "a great sense of power" as he again realizes his godlike ability to control the watchman's fate (70).

Another part of his divinity is the sense of distance from mankind that Daniels feels. This sense becomes evident when Daniels listens to war news on a radio while staring at the stolen diamonds that he has strewn over the floor of his cave. On this occasion Daniels has the illusion of looking down from the sky, godlike, on the actions of men at war with each other (64-65). The violence that the radio announcer reports and the violence that Daniels himself has witnessed and experienced above ground lead to his final avatar—a Christ on a mission of mercy to mankind that ends in his death.

In sum, Daniels experiences or possesses a variety of emotions and attitudes—a sense of isolation, angst, guilt, freedom, creation, and divinity—that are often related to existential protagonists. In one other way, too, is Daniels' experience typical of the existential protagonist's. The pattern of his experience is consistent with the archetypal pattern of the existential fable. As described by William V. Spanos, this fable portrays the protagonist in "flight from a dark, threatening agent who pursues the fugitive protagonist into an isolated corner (often, the underground), where he must confront his relentless pursuer, whereupon, in a blinding moment of illumination he discovers the paradoxically benevolent aspect of his persecutor" (10). Briefly, in "The Man Who Lived Underground" the existential pattern works like this. The police chase Fred Daniels into the underground, ignoring his declaration of innocence and proclaiming him guilty. His underground experience causes Daniels to realize the truth—that he is, in fact, guilty. Because it is the policemen who are responsible for Daniels' going underground and thereby learning the truth, they are malevolent and benevolent. That Daniels' story may be so interpreted is possible because of three paradoxes—oxymora, stated or implied—that define Daniels' perception of the people, artifacts, and atmosphere of the world above ground.

Daniels perceives that the people of the world above ground are dead. Some are physically dead, like the woman whom Daniels is accused of having murdered, the baby that he encounters in the sewer, the corpse that he sees in the undertaking establishment, and the night watchman, who commits suicide. Others in the world above ground are spiritually dead. They are the paradoxical living dead. The oxymoron *living dead* is implied in the description of the crowd that Daniels sees in a movie theater: "These people were laughing at their lives. . . . They were shouting and yelling at the animated shadows of themselves. . . . sleeping in their living, awake in their dying" (38). The churchgoers, similarly involved with shadows rather than reality, are also among the living dead. Their pursuit of shadows is apparent in their prayers to an absent God for "a happiness they could never find" (68). The pursuit of shadows by the congregation stands in ironic contrast to their rejection of Daniels, the only real divinity that they will ever see. Their preference for shadows rather than reality links them to the other dead people whom Daniels encounters.

Daniels also perceives a link between death and the artifacts of the world above ground. He drags a number of these artifacts to his underground home: a gun, a typewriter, a radio, a bloody meat cleaver, money, diamonds, rings, and watches. The oxymoron *serious toys* defines his perception of these items (55). Daniels himself treats the artifacts like toys, using them in "games" of make-believe. With the gun, he pretends to be a gunfighter in a movie; with the typewriter, he pretends to be a secretary in an office; and with the diamonds he pretends to be a rich man taking a morning stroll (58, 61, 63). His games trivialize—that is, reduce to the level of toys—the artifacts as they are used above ground by the people whose roles he plays. The "serious" nature of these "toys" becomes clear, however, when Daniels connects them to all of the dead persons—the physically dead and the spiritually dead—above ground:

> He stood in the dark, wet with sweat, brooding about the diamonds, the rings, the watches, the money; he remembered the singing in the church, the people yelling in the movie, the dead baby, the nude man stretched out upon the white table : . . He saw these items hovering before his eyes and felt that some dim meaning linked them together, that some magical relationship made them kin. He stared with vacant eyes, convinced that all of these images, with their tongueless reality, were striving to tell him something. . . . (59)

What these images are probably striving to tell Daniels is that the world above ground is "a wild forest filled with death" (62). The artifacts of this world are connected to death if for no reason other than that their disappearance results in beatings and even loss of life for those who are accused of stealing them.

Daniels' perception of the atmosphere of the world above ground is synopsized by the phrase *dark sunshine* (65). This oxymoron stands in the atmosphere of Daniels' underground world. At the beginning of the story, the light of the world above ground is stressed (32, 36, 43, 46, 54), just as the darkness of the underground is stressed (28, 29, 31, 32, 33, 35, 59). At the turning point of the story, however, the world above ground acquires the quality of darkness, and the world underground acquires the quality of light. This turning point is the sequence of events that begins when Daniels drags to his cave the artifacts that he has found above ground. In this sequence, Daniels attaches a light bulb and a string of electric wire to some wiring that runs into his cave. The result is, as Spanos puts it in explaining the existential myth, "a blinding moment of illumination," or as Wright puts it in the story, "the sudden illumination blinded him" (60). The illumination signals the new awareness that Daniels is about to gain, for awakening from a nap that he takes after lighting his cave and decorating it with the stolen artifacts, Daniels realizes that the worshippers in the church, the boy being beaten, and the night watchman being tortured are all guilty. This realization of everyman's guilt is the turning point in Daniels' life, for it makes him ready to stop proclaiming his own innocence, to acknowledge his guilt, and to return above ground. From this point, too, Daniels begins to see the world above ground as not only a place of death and cruelty—suggested by the phrases "dead world of sunshine," "obscene sunshine," "dead sunshine," and "cruel sunshine" (55, 63, 66, 73)—but also a place of darkness, of "dark sunshine." This world is dark in the sense that it does not illuminate but instead cloaks, veils, or obscures the truth—namely, that all men are guilty. In contrast, the "dark light" of the underground allows Daniels to see his— and others'—guilt.

When Officer Lawson burns the confession that Daniels signed three days earlier, Lawson, in effect, nullifies Daniels' new-found knowledge that he, like all men, is guilty. Daniels' response is predictable: "He stared, thunderstruck; the sun of the underground was fleeing and the terrible darkness of the day stood before him" (83). In other words Lawson's act extinguishes the "dark light" of the world underground, which has enabled Daniels to see the truth of everyman's guilt, and restores the "dark sunshine" of the world above ground, which does not allow man to see that truth. The atmosphere of the world above ground reeks of death because of its people and their artifacts. But perhaps the most crucial quality of that world—crucial because there is no remedy for death, although there is a remedy for ignorance—is that it provides only a dark light that does not allow man to see "the *secret of his existence*, the *guilt* that he could never get rid of" (69, emphasis added).

To return to the pattern of the existential fable as Spanos describes it, "The Man Who Lived Underground" portrays a protagonist, Fred Daniels, in flight from the accusation that he is guilty. To escape the policemen who are making this accusation, Daniels goes underground. Before being chased underground, Daniels was like the other dead people above ground: He attended movies (58, 63), believed in a God who watches and watches over mankind, and considered himself innocent as long as he had not violated any law. The dark light of the underground, however, allows Daniels to see the nature of human existence—its tropism (to use Nathanael West's metaphor) toward shadows, or fiction, rather than reality, or truth, and its core of suffering, death, and guilt. The result for Daniels is a blinding moment of illumination, a spiritual birth. Because the policemen forced him underground, they are midwives to that birth. Thus, the agents who initially seem to be wholly malevolent emerge as paradoxically benevolent.

In its structure as well as in its themes of isolation, anxiety, guilt, and freedom, "The Man Who Lived Underground" thus epitomizes the existential fable. A tale of existential triumph and a tale of naturalistic defeat, the story is in the paradoxical position of presenting both a philosophy of determinism and a philosophy that rejects determinism. As a deterministic philosophy, naturalism sees man as merely an animal whose fate is controlled by forces unrelated to his will. In contrast, existentialism presents man as a free agent whose duty is to exercise his will, the possession of which raises him above the level of other animals. "The Man Who Lived Underground" embodies both postures.

One reason that "The Man Who Lived Underground" can embody both naturalistic and existential postures is that Wright has so skillfully crafted his story that the actions that can be attributed to Daniels' will can also be attributed to forces independent of Daniels' will. For example, the existential interpreter can argue that Daniels *wills* to go underground and that Daniels *wills* to return above ground and confront the policemen who have previously tortured him. His decision to return above ground represents a victory of will over animal instinct: "He had to act, yet he was afraid" (72). Once resolved to leave the underground, Daniels moves purposefully and rationally, "his actions . . . informed with precision, his muscular system reinforced from a reservoir of energy," and his mind set on self-preservation—as, avoiding being sucked under by the sewer current, he sighs, "thankful that he had missed death" (72-73). Because Daniels has successfully eluded the police for three days and because they are no longer even looking for him, his decision to return above ground effectively makes Daniels the First Cause of the events that culminate in his death.

On the other hand, the naturalistic interpreter can argue that Daniels' return above ground is caused by insanity, which occurs because Daniels was forced underground. A major sign of Daniels' insanity is his laughter when he sees the boy and watchman being beaten for his thefts and his numerous outbursts of laughter in the presence of the police when he turns himself in to them (77, 81, 90). The existential interpreter can counter that Daniels' laughter is not the inappropriate laughter of an insane man but the wise laughter of the man who gets the cosmic joke—namely, that man's position in the universe is absurd, because no matter how good a life he lives he is guilty and no matter how much he may want to live he is going to die. The naturalistic interpreter and the existential interpreter can continue their rebuttals *ad infinitum*, so tightly has Wright woven the threads of his paradox.

A second reason that "The Man Who Lived Underground" can embody both naturalistic and existential postures is that existentialism recognizes that man *is* a part of nature and is consequently subject to nature's laws. In "Notes from Underground," Dostoevsky's proto-existential underground man (the putative ancestor of Fred Daniels) acknowledges his inability to conquer the laws of nature, which he visualizes as a stone wall: "Of course I cannot break through the wall by battering my head against it if I really have not the strength . . ." (853). (However, with the same mettle that Daniels demonstrates when he conquers time, Dostoevsky's underground man immediately makes clear that while his body is subject to nature's laws, his spirit will not be.) The laws of nature to which Daniels is subject are the need to eat, drink, eliminate (a typically naturalistic detail), rest, and sleep. Some of his actions, therefore, are definitely determined by his animal nature. That these actions spring from this source is consistent with naturalism's determinism and compatible with existentialism's antideterminism.

A final reason that "The Man Who Lived Underground" can embody both naturalistic and existential postures is that existential triumph does not preclude naturalistic defeat. Indeed, the existential hero is *likely* to suffer, for existentialism posits a universe of chaos and death. To triumph in such a setting—that is, to act as he should—existential man must recognize that he is free to act, and he must accept the responsibility for his actions, not attempting to attribute them to some force (for example, God, the laws of society, definitions of "human nature") outside his will. The existential hero triumphs when he breaks free of those forces that would enslave him and acts in order to be himself, whatever self he chooses to be. Thus, when Daniels exercises his will by papering his cave with money, he feels that he has "triumphed over the world above ground" and senses that he "[i]s free" because he is living the life that he has chosen for himself rather than conforming to the life prescribed for and by the people above ground (62). Again, Daniels triumphs when he exercises his will by choosing to go to the police station and attempting to lead Officers Lawson, Murphy, and Johnson to his underground world. That Lawson kills Daniels does not negate Daniels' triumph. Rather, Daniels' feat illustrates the fact that one cannot count on others' actions, over which one has no control, to bring about an event. As Sartre puts it, ". . . no God, no scheme, can adapt the world and its possibilities to my will" (29). Further, Daniels' death underlines the existential truth that the only certainty in man's life is that he will die. Hence, the existential triumph of Daniels is compatible with his naturalistic defeat—the death that he suffers as a result of someone else's will.

Even though key naturalistic revelations about man's essence and existence are assumed in existential theory, it is a mistake to focus exclusively on the existential vision of "The Man Who Lived Underground" and to ignore or minimize the story's naturalistic vision. To do so is to risk misapprehending Wright's portrait of man as it is revealed through Fred Daniels: It is to risk not seeing man as *equally* god and animal, and man's existence as *equally* free and tied to necessity. It is a question of focus and emphasis, the answer residing in the structure of the story, which suggests paradox at every turn. When the paradoxical structure of "The Man Who Lived Underground" is considered, it is clear that man is not simply a god in the existential sense or an animal in the naturalistic sense; nor is man's existence the existence of a god or an animal. Rather—and purely existential interpretations of the story have not revealed this point—the structure of "The Man Who Lived Underground" suggests that man is a paradox whose existence is a paradox. A paradoxical existence is an absurd existence; it makes no sense. In Wright's story man's existence is paradoxical, absurd: In this world innocent men are guilty, men's toys cause death, men reject the savior that they pray for, light leaves men blind while darkness gives sight, dead men live above ground, and a dead man who goes underground comes to life. In this world, too, man is paradoxically, absurdly, both beast and god.

Naturalism is presently out of fashion. It is considered simplistic in its reduction of man to the level of an animal or victim, formulaic in its social protest, and false in its conception of the work of fiction as a kind of scientific experiment in which the writer "objectively" records the details of his protagonist's life and environment. Because of its recognized weaknesses, naturalism is routinely ignored or belittled by Wright's critics. Such dismissal is an error, however, for naturalism, like existentialism, served as an emotional, philosophical, and creative wellspring of Wright's literary career. In "The Man Who Lived Underground" naturalism and existentialism have a synergistic relationship that emphasizes the paradox that Wright, a born naturalistic and existential philosopher, must have seen as inherent in man's essence and existence. Conceivably, one using existentialism as an approach to "The Man Who Lived Underground" could arrive at the same conclusions about man's paradoxical essence and existence that I have reached by using a structural approach. That the former has not been done reveals the danger of not taking into account the structure of a work, which, because it reveals a work to be more than the sum of its parts, necessarily reveals a work to be more than any one of its parts. Naturalism is clearly as much a part of "The Man Who Lived Underground" as is existentialism, and both are merely subordinate parts that contribute to the total meaning of Wright's story.

Approaching "The Man Who Lived Underground" from a structural perspective also permits an appreciation of Wright's consummate craftsmanship in constructing a story whose every component—most notably character, story, plot, setting, imagery, diction, and tone—is generated by and integrated within a paradoxical structure. Seen from a structural perspective, "The Man Who Lived Underground" is a warning to any critic of Richard Wright who would peremptorily disregard his naturalism or categorically dismiss his art.

Works Cited

Bakish, David. "Underground in an Ambiguous Dreamworld." *Studies in Black Literature* 2.3 (1971): 18-23.

Bone, Robert. *Richard Wright.* U of Minnesota Pamphlets on American Writers 74. Minneapolis: U of Minnesota P, 1969.

Brignano, Russell Carl. *Richard Wright: An Introduction to the Man and His Works.* Pittsburgh: U of Pittsburgh P, 1970.

Dostoevsky, Fyodor. "Notes from Underground." 1864. Trans. Constance Garnett. *The Norton Anthology of World Masterpieces.* Gen. ed. Maynard Mack. 4th ed. 2 vols. New York: Norton, 1980. 2: 846-934.

Everette, Mildred W. "The Death of Richard Wright's American Dream: 'The Man Who Lived Underground.' " *CLA Journal* 17 (1974): 318-26.

Fabre, Michel. "Richard Wright: The Man Who Lived Underground." *Richard Wright: A Collection of Critical Essays.* Ed. Richard Macksey and Frank E. Moorer. Englewood Cliffs: Prentice, 1984. 207-20.

——. *The Unfinished Quest of Richard Wright*. Trans. Isabel Barzun. New York: Morrow, 1973.

Goede, William. "On Lower Frequencies: The Buried Man in Wright and Ellison." *Modern Fiction Studies* 15 (1969-70): 483-501.

Gounard, J. G. "Richard Wright's 'The Man Who Lived Underground': A Literary Analysis." *Journal of Black Studies* 8 (1978): 381-86.

Hurston, Zora Neale. *Their Eyes Were Watching God*. 1937. Urbana: U of Illinois P, 1978.

Margolies, Edward. "The Short Stories: *Uncle Tom's Children*; *Eight Men*." *The Art of Richard Wright*. Carbondale: Southern Illinois UP, 1969. 57-89.

Marano, Donald V. *Existential Guilt: A Phenomenological Study*. Atlantic Highlands: Humanities, 1973.

McNallie, Robin. "Richard Wright's Allegory of the Cave: 'The Man Who Lived Underground.'" *South Atlantic Bulletin* 42.2 (1977): 76-84.

Ridenour, Ronald. " 'The Man Who Lived Underground': A Critique." *Phylon* 31 (1970): 54-57.

Sartre, Jean-Paul. "Existentialism." Trans. Bernard Frechtman. *Existentialism and Human Emotions*. New York: Philosophical Library, 1957. 9-51.

Spanos, William V. *A Casebook on Existentialism*. New York: Crowell, 1966.

West, Nathanael. *Miss Lonelyhearts & The Day of the Locust*. 1946, 1950. New York: New Directions, 1962.

Widmer, Kingsley. "Black Existentialism: Richard Wright." *Richard Wright: A Collection of Critical Essays*. Ed. Richard Macksey and Frank E. Moorer. Englewood Cliffs: Prentice, 1984. 173-81.

Wright, Richard. "The Man Who Lived Underground." *Cross Section: A Collection of New American Writing* Ed. Edwin Seaver. New York: Fischer, 1944. 58-102.

——. "The Man Who Lived Underground." *Eight Men*. Cleveland: World, 1961. 27-92.

Richard Wright's *The Outsider* and Albert Camus's *The Stranger*

Yoshinobu Hakutani

Although the likeness in theme, character, and event between *The Outsider* and *The Stranger* has been pointed out, it has not been studied in any detail. In general, critics have regarded Wright's philosophy in *The Outsider* as nihilistic. Charles I. Glicksberg, in "Existentialism in *The Outsider*" and "The God of Fiction," saw parallels between Wright and Camus in the treatment of the metaphysical rebel, calling Cross Damon's philosophy most consistently nihilistic.[1] More recently, critics have demonstrated Camus's influences on Wright in his conception of Cross Damon.[2] Edward Margolies in his comparison of Damon and Meursault pointed out that "both men kill without passion, both men appear unmoved by the death of their mothers; both men apparently are intended to represent the moral and emotional failure of the age."[3]

It would be quite tempting to compare the two works if they were the products of the same age and the particular philosophy they dealt with was in vogue. It is a well-established fact that Wright lived and wrote *The Outsider* in France, where he maintained a close contact with such influential writers as Camus, Sartre, and de Beauvoir. Moreover, Camus's indifferent philosopher can conveniently be placed side by side with Wright's protagonist, who contemplates human existence through his exhaustive reading of Nietzsche, Hegel, Kierkegaard, and Dostoevski. One sus-

---

Reprinted from *Mississippi Quarterly* 42.4 (1989): 365-378. By permission of Yoshinobu Hakutani and *Mississippi Quarterly*.

[1]Charles I. Glicksberg, "Existentialism in *The Outsider*," *Four Quarters* 7 (January 1958) 17-26; "The God of Fiction," *Colorado Quarterly* 7 (Autumn 1958), 207-220.

[2]Michel Fabre specifically indicates that Wright's composition of *The Outsider* "was influenced in subtle ways by his reading of *The Stranger* in August 1947. He read the book in the American edition at a very slow pace, 'weighing each sentence,' admiring 'its damn good narrative prose,' " and commented:

> It is a neat job but devoid of passion. He makes his point with dispatch and his prose is solid and good. In America a book like this would not attract much attention for it would be said that he lacks feeling. He does however draw his character very well. What is of course really interesting in this book is the use of fiction to express a philosophical point of view. That he does with ease. I now want to read his other stuff.

See Michel Fabre, "Richard Wright, French Existentialism, and *The Outsider*," in Yoshinobu Hakutani, ed., *Critical Essays on Richard Wright* (Boston: G. K. Hall, 1982), 191.

[3]Edward Margolies, *The Art of Richard Wright* (Carbondale: Southern Illinois University Press, 1969), 135.

pects, however, that the comparison of the two novels would never have been made unless the two novelists were both caught up in the philosophical context of existentialism. This meant that the literary likeness was taken for granted. Meursault kills a man; he is charged with a murder, tried, and convicted in a world of court, jury, and judge. Damon, on the other hand, kills more than one man, not only an enemy but a friend, a mentor, and an ally, and is responsible for the suicide of a woman he loves. But he is never charged with a crime, brought to a trial, or convicted. Unlike Meursault, who encounters his death in the world of daylight in Algiers, Damon is himself murdered by two men, the agents of the Communist party, on a dimly lit street in New York. *The Outsider,* therefore, is fiction of a different order, brought together with *The Stranger* in an assumed definition of human existence in the modern world. Although the two novels are regarded largely as existentialist, giving attention to the crucial details that differentiate the narratives makes Meursault and Damon radically different in their ideology and action.

It is time to reexamine *The Outsider* and the black tradition and experience that underlies it. Comparing this novel with an avowedly existentialist novel like Camus's *The Stranger* will reveal that Wright's novel is not what critics have characterized. Contrary to disclaimers, Cross Damon is not a black man in name only. Not only is his plight real, but all the incidents and characters he is involved with, which at times appear to be clumsily constructed symbols, nonetheless convey well-digested ideas. He is not "pathetically insane" as a reviewer described him.[4] The book bewildered black reviewers as well, not because of Wright's novel philosophy, but because Wright seemed to have lost contact with his native soil.[5] But a detailed comparison of this novel with *The Stranger,* a novel of another culture and another tradition, will show not only that Wright's hero is not simply an embodiment of a half-baked philosophy, but that he is a genuine product of the African-American experience. Such a reevaluation of the book will also clarify misconceptions about Wright's other books as well.

The disparity between the two books becomes even more apparent if it is seen in the light of the less fashionable literary philosophy, naturalism. To some American writers, such as Stephen Crane and Theodore Dreiser, naturalism is a doctrine that asserts the indifference of the universe to the will of man.[6] Camus,

---

[4]James N. Rhea, *Providence Sunday Journal*, March 22, 1953.

[5]See Saunders Redding, *Baltimore Afro-American*, May 19, 1953; Arna Bontemps, *Saturday Review* 36 (March 28, 1953), 15-16; Lloyd L. Brown, "Outside and Low," *Masses and Mainstream* 6 (May 1953), 62-64.

[6]The indifference of the universe is most poignantly described by Stephen Crane in "The Open Boat":

When it occurs to a man that nature does not regard him as important, and that she feels she would not maim the universe by disposing of him, he at first wishes to throw bricks at the temple, and he hates deeply the fact that there are no bricks and no temples. Any visible expression of nature would surely be pelleted with his jeers.

See *Great Short Works of Stephen Crane* (New York: Harper & Row, 1958), 294. Dreiser describes the forces of nature in *Sister Carrie*:

Among the forces which sweep and play throughout the universe, untutored man is but a wisp in the wind. Our civilisation is still in a middle stage, scarcely beast, in that it is no longer wholly

though his naturalistic vision is not conveyed with Dreiser's massive detail or ana-lyzed by Zola's experimental method, nevertheless constructs his novel to drama-tize a climactic assertion of universal indifference. Wright's novel, on the other hand, is filled with the events and actions that exhibit the world's concerns with the affairs of man. The outside world is indeed hostile to Damon, a man of great will and passion. Refusing to be dominated by it, he challenges its forces. But Meursault, remaining much of a pawn, is not willing to exert himself against the forces which to him have no relation to existence.

Heredity and environment, the twin elements in naturalistic fiction, are more influential on human action in *The Stranger* than they are in *The Outsider*. Though heredity has little effect on Meursault's behavior, environment does play a crucial role. Meursault is consistently shown as indifferent to any of society's inter-ests and desires: love of God, marriage, friendship, social status. He is averse to financial success or political power; he receives only what is given or acts when acted upon. He is, like Dreiser's Sister Carrie, "a wisp in the wind"; he is more drawn than he draws.[7] This explains his passivity. Camus painstakingly accounts for human action just as Zola or Dreiser demonstrates the circumstances under which it occurs.

Camus shows that Meursault, who had no desire to kill the Arab, merely responded to pressures applied by natural forces. The blinding sun and the glitter-ing knife held by the Arab caused Meursault to fear and forced him to pull the trigger. If the man with the knife had been a Frenchman, Meursault would not have acted with such rashness. Given the history of Arab-French colonial rela-tions, Meursault's antagonism toward the Arabs might have subconsciously trig-gered his action. Camus's emphasis in this narrative, however, is placed on the ele-ments of chance, that is, the blinding sun and the glittering knife, rather than on the social elements such as the disharmony between the French and the Arabs.

This idea of chance and determinism is absent in Wright's concept of human action exhibited in *The Outsider*. Each of the four murders committed by Damon is premeditated, the suicide of a woman is directly related to his actions, and his own murder is a reprisal for the actions he could have avoided. In each case it is made clear that Damon had control over his action; in each murder he was capa-ble of exerting his will or satisfying his desire. In marked contrast to Meursault, Damon exerts himself to attain the essences of his own existence. They are the very embodiments of the abstract words of society—friendship, love, marriage, success, equality, and freedom—to which he cannot remain indifferent. Wright takes pains to show that they are not empty dreams. The fact that Damon has been deprived of them at one time or another proves that they constitute his existence.

---

guided by instinct: scarcely human, in that it is not yet wholly guided by reason . . . As a beast, the forces of life aligned him with them; as a man, he has not yet wholly learned to align himself with the forces. In this intermediate stage he wavers—neither drawn in harmony with nature by his instincts nor yet wisely putting himself into harmony by his own free-will.

See *Sister Carrie* (New York: Doubleday, Page & Co., 1900), 83.
[7]Cf. *Sister Carrie*, 83-84.

The Outsider represents a version of existentialism in which human action is viewed as the result of an individual's choice and will. To Wright, the individual's action must be assertive and, if need be, aggressive. This is perhaps why he was more attracted to Sartre and de Beauvoir than to Camus. In an unpublished journal Wright wrote:

> Sartre is quite of my opinion regarding the possibility of human action today, that it is up to the individual to do what he can to uphold the concept of what it means to be human. The great danger, I told him, in the world today is the very feeling and conception of what is a human might well be lost. He agreed. I feel very close to Sartre and Simone de Beauvoir.[8]

If Wright's protagonist is considered an existentialist actively in search of an essence in the meaningless existence, Meursault seems a passive existentialist compelled to do nothing in the face of the void and meaningless universe. Focused on the definition of existence, their views are alike: Damon at one time says, perhaps uncharacteristically, "Maybe man is nothing in particular."[9] The point of disparity in their world view, however, is the philosophy of the absurd. While Meursault is convinced of the essential absurdity of existence, Damon is not. If one judges life inherently meaningful as does Damon, then it follows that his action to seek love, power, and freedom on earth is also meaningful. Conversely, however, if one judges life absurd as does Meursault, then it follows that his action is also absurd.

What is absurd is this dilemma of Meursault between his recognition of chaos and his search for order. It is the conflict between his awareness of death and his dream of eternity. It is the disparity between the essential mystery of all existence and one's demand for explanation. The fundamental difference in attitude between Meursault and Damon is that Meursault seeks neither order, nor a dream of eternity, nor explanation, while Damon is passionately in search of such an essence. Meursault's passivity, moreover, stems from Camus's attitude toward his art. Camus tries to solve the existentialist dilemma by arguing that an artist is not concerned to find order, to have a dream of eternity, or to demand explanation, but to experience all things given. The artist describes; he does not solve the mystery of the universe that is both infinite and inexplicable.

Whereas Camus's hero resists action, Wright's is compelled to act. Wright endows his hero with the freedom to create an essence. Damon's revolt is not so much against the nothingness and meaninglessness of existence as it is against the futility of man's attempt to make illogical phenomena logical. In the eyes of the public, Damon is as guilty of his murder of the fascist as Raskolnikov is guilty of his murder of the pawnbroker in *Crime and Punishment*.[10] Both crimes result from premeditated actions; Meursault's killing of the Arab is accidental.

---

[8]See Fabre, p. 186.

[9]Richard Wright, *The Outsider* (New York: Harper & Row, 1953), 135. Later page references to this edition are indicated in parentheses.

[10]As Damon's murder of the fascist Herndon is analogous to Raskolnikov's murder of the pawnbroker, Damon's killing of his friend Joe is similar to Raskolnikov's killing of the pawnbroker's sister, Lizaveta. In the case of Joe or Lizaveta, the murderer has no malice toward the victim but intentionally kills the victim to protect himself from prosecution.

Some critics find a contradiction in Damon's view of the world. Earlier in the story, Damon considers man "nothing in particular" (p. 135), but at the end of his life he asserts, "We must find some way of being good to ourselves. . . . Man is all we've got. . . . I wish I could ask men to meet themselves" (p. 439). Likewise his inaction initially makes him see nothingness and meaninglessness in human existence but in the end his action results in his realization of loneliness and "horror" on earth (p. 440). In short, what appears to be a contradiction in Damon's view of existence is rather a reflection of activeness and aggressiveness in his character.

The chief difference in philosophy between the two books derives from the differing philosophies of the two novelists, Wright and Camus. Though both men are regarded as rebels against society, their motives for rebellion differ. Damon rebels against society because it oppresses him by depriving him of the values he and society share, such as freedom in association and opportunity for success. Meursault is aloof from society because he does not believe in such values. Moreover, he does not believe in marriage or family loyalty. His obdurate attitude toward society is clearly stated in Camus's preface to the American edition of *The Stranger*:

> I summarized *The Stranger*—a long time ago, with a remark that I admit was highly paradoxical: "In our society any man who does not weep at his mother's funeral runs the risk of being sentenced to death." I only meant that the hero of my book is condemned because he does not play the game. In this respect, he is foreign to the society in which he lives; he wanders, on the fringe, in the suburbs of private, solitary, sensual life. And this is why some readers have been tempted to look upon him as a piece of social wreckage. A much more accurate idea of the character, at least one much closer to the author's intentions, will emerge if one asks just how Meursault doesn't play the game. The reply is a simple one: he refuses to lie. To lie is not only to say *more* than is true, and, as far as the human heart is concerned, to express more than one feels. This is what we all do, every day, to simplify life. He says what he is, he refuses to hide his feelings, and immediately society feels threatened.[11]

If Meursault is characterized by his refusal to play society's game, Damon is a type of person who cannot resist playing such a game. If society is threatened by Meursault's indifference to it, it is Damon rather than society that feels threatened.

This estranged personality of Meursault is reflected in his relationship with his mother. Some critics have used his calm acceptance of the bereavement as evidence for his callousness.[12] But the fact that he does not cry at his mother's funeral would not necessarily suggest that he is devoid of emotions. Had Meursault thought her death would have spared her the misery of her life or that death would be a happier state for man, he should not have been aggrieved by the passing away of his mother. What makes him a peculiar character, however, is the fact that an experience which would be a traumatic one for others is for him devoid of any

---

[11]Albert Camus, *Lyrical and Critical Essays*, ed. with notes Philip Thody, trans. Ellen C. Kennedy (New York: Knopf, 1968), 335-337.

[12]See, for instance, Robert de Luppe, *Albert Camus* (Paris: Temps present, 1951), 46-47.

meaning. *The Stranger* thus opens with the protagonist's unconcerned reaction to his mother's death: "Mother died today. Or, maybe, yesterday; I can't be sure."[13] But as the story progresses he becomes a more sensitive individual. He is indeed disturbed during the vigil by the weeping of his mother's friend. And every detail, whether it is the driving home of the screws in the coffin lid or the starting of the prayers by the priest, is minutely described. Throughout the story there is no mention of Meursault's disliking his mother. He fondly reflects on her habits and personality; he affectionately calls her *Maman*.

By contrast Damon's relationship with his mother betrays not only the estrangement between them but also his hostility to the racist society that had reared her. His mother, the product of the traditional Christianity in the South that taught black children subservient ethics, tries to mold her son's character accordingly. It is only natural that Damon should rebel against such a mother, who moans, "To think I named you Cross after the Cross of Jesus" (p. 23). He rejects his mother not only because she reminds him of Southern Negro piety but because she is an epitome of racial and sexual repression:

> He was conscious of himself as a frail object which had to protect itself against a pending threat of annihilation. This frigid world was suggestively like the one which his mother, without knowing it, had created for him to live in when he had been a child. . . . This God's NO-face had evoked in his pliable boy's body an aching sense of pleasure by admonishing him to shun pleasure as the tempting doorway opening blackly onto hell; had too early awakened in him a sharp sense of sex by thunderingly denouncing sex as the sin leading to eternal damnation. . . . Mother love had cleaved him: a wayward sensibility that distrusted itself, a consciousness that was conscious of itself. Despite this, his sensibilities had not been repressed by God's fearful negations as represented by his mother; indeed, his sense of life had been so heightened that desire boiled in him to a degree that made him afraid. (pp. 17-18)

The young Damon's desire to free himself from such a bondage is closely related to his inability to love any black woman, as shown by his relationship with Gladys, his estranged wife, or Dot, his pregnant mistress. The only woman he loves is the white woman Eva, the wife of his Communist friend Gil Blount. Damon falls in love with Eva despite, and partly because of, the fact that a black man's desire for a white woman is taboo. He feels an affinity to her, for he discovers that she, too, is a fearful individual and that she had been deceived into marrying her husband because of a political intrigue. Damon is tormented by the envenomed abstraction of racial and political myths. Unlike the white phonograph salesman, who seduces the wife of a black man in "Long Black Song," he is permanently frustrated. Since *The Outsider* portrays a rich variety of racial and political animosities, his love life is defined in terms of the forces beyond his control. To him the consummation of his love for Eva means the ultimate purpose of his new existence. It is understandable that when that goal appears within reach

---

[13]Albert Camus, *The Stranger*, trans. Stuart Gilbert (New York: Vintage Books, 1942), 1. Later page references to this edition are indicated in parentheses.

and yet is taken away from him, he finds only "the horror" that he has dreaded all his life (p. 440).

Meursault's relationship with women, on the contrary, is totally uninhibited socially and psychologically. His relationship with Marie is free from the kinds of racial and political entanglements which smother Damon's relationship with Eva. Meursault, the perfectly adjusted man, does not suffer from any kind of repression. His action for love is motivated from within according to logic rather than convention or sentiment. In his life, love of woman is as natural an instinct as is eating or resting; love is more akin to friendship than marriage. He helps Raymond, for he says, "I wanted to satisfy Raymond, as I'd no reasons not to satisfy him" (p. 41). Meursault is kind and benevolent as Damon is not; he is relaxed and content as Damon is tense and frustrated.

Meursault's indifference to existence is epitomized by his love life. His attitude toward Marie bears a sort of impersonal, superhuman mode of thought. To the public such an attitude is inhuman, unconventional, and unethical. His view of love is no different from that of death; interestingly enough, his sexual relations with Marie begin immediately after his mother's death. If death occurs beyond man's control, so does love. His meeting with her takes place by mere coincidence and the relationship that develops is casual and appears quite innocent.

> When I was helping her to climb on a raft, I let my hand stray over her breasts. Then she lay flat on the raft, while I trod water. After a moment she turned and looked at me. Her hair was over her eyes and she was laughing. I clambered up on to the raft, beside her. The air was pleasantly warm, and, half jokingly, I let my head sink back upon her lap. She didn't seem to mind, so I let it stay there. I had the sky full in my eyes, all blue and gold, and could feel Marie's stomach rising and falling gently under my head. We must have stayed a good half-hour on the raft, both of us half asleep. When the sun got too hot she dived off and I followed. I caught up with her, put my arm round her waist, and we swam side by side. She was still laughing. (pp. 23-24)

Even when a marriage proposal is made by Marie, his indifference remains intact: "Marie came that evening and asked me if I'd marry her. I said I didn't mind; if she was keen on it, we'd get married" (p. 52).

Meursault's indifference is also reflected in his reaction to the crime of which he is accused. Partly as a corollary to the nature of the crime, he is passive rather than active. Unlike Damon, he commits a crime without malice or intention. He kills the Arab not because he hates the victim but partly because he sympathizes with his friend Raymond, whose life has been threatened. Given this situation, it would be more natural for him to defend his friend than the hostile stranger. Meursault's crime is a crime of logic; it is not a murder. Camus's purpose for using crime in *The Stranger* is to prove that society, rather than the criminal, is in the wrong. Camus's intention is to prove that his hero is innocent, as well as to show that Meursault's logic is far superior to society's. When crime appears innocent, it is innocence that is called upon to justify itself. In *The Stranger*, then, it is society, not the criminal, that is on trial.

Because Meursault is convinced of his innocence, he attains at the end of his life his peace of mind, a kind of nirvana:

> With death so near, Mother must have felt like someone on the brink of freedom, ready to start life all over again. No one, no one in the world had any right to weep for her. And I, too, felt ready to start life all over again. It was as if that great rush of anger had washed me clean, emptied me of hope, and, gazing up at the dark sky spangled with its signs and stars, for the first time, the first, I laid my heart open to the benign indifference of the universe. (p. 154)

Damon is also convinced of his innocence at the end of his life. What the two novels share is not only that the hero is prosecuted by society, but that society—the prosecutor, jurors, and judge—seems to him to be always in the wrong. Camus's hero refuses to play society's game; as a result he is sentenced to death by society. Society expects him to grieve over his mother's death and refrain from having a casual affair with a woman during the mourning. But Wright's hero, induced to play society's game, loses in the end. He is tempted to participate in the normal activities of society such as a love affair and a political association. Tasting his agonizing defeat and dying, he utters:

> I wish I had some way to give the meaning of my life to others. . . . To make a bridge from man to man . . . Starting from scratch every time is . . . is no good. Tell them not to come down this road . . . We must find some way of being good to ourselves . . . We're different from what we seem. . . . Maybe worse, maybe better . . . But certainly different . . . We're strangers to ourselves. (p. 439)

The confession at the end of his life suggests that he, unlike Meursault, has always felt obliged to justify his actions. He has finally realized that they always collided with society's interests and values. As an outsider, he trusted no one, not even himself, nor did society trust him. While maintaining in his last breath that "in my heart . . . I'm . . . innocent" (p. 440), he is judging society guilty. While Meursault is a victim of his own crime, Damon is a victim not only of his own crime but of society's. Meursault, who refuses to justify his actions, always feels innocent: "I wasn't conscious of any 'sin'; all I knew was that I'd been guilty of a criminal offense" (p. 148).

Although both novels employ crime as a thematic device, the focus of the author's idea differs. Camus's center of interest is not crime but its consequences—its psychological effect on his hero. Before committing his crime Meursault is presented as a stranger who finds no meaning in life. After he is sentenced to death he realizes for the first time that his life has been enveloped in the elusive beauty of the world. "To feel it so like myself, indeed, so brotherly," he says, "made me realize that I'd been happy, and that I was happy still" (p. 154). In *The Outsider* crime is used, like accidental death or suicide, to create a new life for the hero. He murders the fascist Herndon as a reprisal; he intentionally kills the Communist Blount out of his desire for a white woman. In stark contrast to Camus's hero, to whom death has brought life and happiness,

Wright's hero in the end is once more reminded of his own estrangement and horror.[14]

The two novelists' divergent attitudes toward the problems of crime and guilt are also reflected in the style and structure of their works. *The Stranger* is swift in pace and dramatic in tone, and displays considerable subjectivity, involving the reader in the consciousness of the hero. The reader's involvement in the hero's dialectics is intensified because the book consists of two parts dealing with the same issue. The first part involves the reader in a few days of Meursault's life, ending with his crime; the second re-involves the reader in the same experiences through the trial in court. Since the hero's experiences are viewed from different angles, they never strike one as monotonous or repetitious. The chief reason for the juxtaposition is for the hero, and for Camus, to convince the reader that what appears to society to be a crime is not at all a crime in the eyes of an existentialist.

This juxtaposition also elucidates the discontinuity and unrelatedness of Meursault's experiences in the first half of the story despite the reordering and construing of those experiences in the second half. As the incidents and actions in the first half are discontinuous, so is time. No days are referred to in Meursault's life except for Saturday and Sunday, his days off. Of the months only August is mentioned since Meursault, Mason, and Raymond plan to have their vacation together; of the seasons only summer. By the same token, there is no mention of the day of the month. And Meursault's age is unknown; he is merely "young."[15] As there is nothing unique about his concept of time, there is nothing unique about his experience. As points in time are discontinuous, so are the experiences. At his trial the prosecutor accuses him of moral turpitude, for Meursault shed no tears at his mother's funeral and casually started an affair with Marie immediately after. To Meursault, his mother's death, his behavior at the funeral, and his love affair are not only devoid of meaning in themselves, but discontinuous, unrelated incidents.

Similarly, the threatening gesture of the Arab, the sweating in Meursault's eyebrows, the flashing of the sun against his eyes, and the firing of his revolver occur independently of one another. If his eyes were blinded by the sun and the sweating of his eyebrows, his pulling the trigger on the revolver would not have been a logical reaction. When he is later asked by the prosecutor why he took a revolver with him and went back to the place where the Arab reappeared, he replies that "it was a matter of pure chance" (p. 110). If he does not believe that he is "morally guilty of his mother's death" (p. 128), as charged by the prosecutor, it would be

[14]The kind of fear Damon suffers at the end of his struggle is clearly absent in Meursault's life. A critic, in comparing Meursault to Clyde Griffiths, the hero of Theodore Dreiser's *An American Tragedy*, comments: "Passivity in *L'Etranger* is strength, and only the strong can be indifferent. When Meursault receives this almost Buddhist illumination, he loses the two great distractions from life: hope and fear. He becomes happy, rather than terrified, in the face of his expected execution; he no longer hopes for some wild chance to deliver him from it. This prisoner is alone and freed from within." See Stropher B. Purdy, "*An American Tragedy* and *L'Etranger*," *Comparative Literature* 19 (Summer 1967), 261.

[15]The most precise analysis of Camus's concept of time is presented in Ignace Feurlicht, "Camus's *L'Etranger* Reconsidered," *PMLA* 78 (December 1963), 606-621.

impossible for him to admit that he is morally guilty of the Arab's death. This is precisely the reason why he tells the priest, "I wasn't conscious of any 'sin'; all I knew was that I'd been guilty of a criminal offense" (p. 148).

Swift and intensive though Camus's probing of Meursault's character is, the reader is deliberately kept from coming to an easy conclusion about Meursault's guilt. By contrast, the reader is instantly made aware of Damon's guilt in unambiguous terms. In *The Outsider* truly heinous crimes are constructed in advance with all the plausible justifications. Before the reader is made aware of Damon's guilt, the author has defined in unequivocal terms the particular traits in Damon's character and the particular forces in society that had led to his crimes. In so doing Wright creates a clear pattern by which Damon's motives for crime are shown. Whereas there is no such relatedness in Meursault's motives for action, there emerges in *The Outsider* a chain of events that can scarcely be misinterpreted. The murder of the fascist is committed side by side with that of the Communist.[16] Damon kills both men with malice: he murders Herndon because of his hatred for the racist as he does Blount because of his passion for the white woman. Unlike Meursault, Damon is conscious of his guilt in the instant of committing crime.

Since Damon's actions are predetermined and interrelated, Damon is constantly made conscious of the passage of time. The problems in his manhood and marriage, for example, are related to those of his childhood. His desertion of his wife is analogous to his rejection of his mother just as the Communists' rule over workers in modern times is akin to slavery in the past. *The Outsider* opens with a scene at dawn in which Damon and his friends "moved slowly forward shoulder to shoulder and the sound of their feet tramping and sloshing in the melting snow echoed loudly" (p. 1). Like Jake Jackson in *Lawd Today,* Damon, bored with his routine work, finds the passage of time unendurable. In *The Stranger,* Meursault is least concerned with time; he never complains about the monotony of his work. In fact, he dislikes Sundays because he is not doing his routine job. Damon, on the contrary, wishes every day were Sunday, or reminisces about Christmastime in a certain year.[17] More importantly, Meursault says whether he dies at thirty or at seventy it doesn't matter. For him life has no more significance than death.

For Damon life is all that matters. If his earlier life is not worth living, a new one must be created. Therefore, a freak subway accident, in which he is assumed dead, offers him another life and another identity. All his life he plans his action

---

[16]Another example of this relatedness in Damon's actions is, as Margolies observes, the pattern in which Damon rejects the black women as he destroys the Communists and fascist: "When Cross murders two Communists and a fascist, his motives seem to derive more from what he regards as his victims' desire to enslave him psychologically, rather than from any detached, intellectualized, conscienceless 'compulsion' on his part. What the Communists and fascist would do to Cross if they had him in their power is precisely what his mother, wife, and mistress had already done to him. In a sense, Cross murders his women when he crushes his enemies" (Margolies, p. 133).

[17]Damon's friend Joe Thomas reminds Damon of their happy days in the past. Joe speaks, "Remember that wild gag he pulled at Christmastime in 19 . . . .?. . . When the hell was that now? Oh, yes! It was in 1945. I'll never forget it. Cross bought a batch of magazines, *Harper's, Atlantic Monthly, Collier's, Ladies' Home Journal,* and clipped out those ads that say you can send your friends a year's subscription as a Christmas gift" (p. 5).

with hope for the future and with denial of the past. Such attitude is emblematic of the African-American tradition, the deep-seated black experience, as expressed in the spirituals. While Edgar Allan Poe's writings sometimes smack of morbid romanticism, that erotic longing for death, the spirituals reverberate with energy and vitality and convey the sense of rejuvenation. However violent and destructive Damon may appear, he inherently emerges from this tradition. Meursault, on the other hand, is the very product of the nihilistic spirit that hovered over Europe, particularly France, after World War II.

Despite Wright's effort to relate Damon's actions to his social and psychological backgrounds, *The Outsider* remains an imperfect work. Some of its faults are structural rather than philosophical. Given the kind of life Damon has lived, it is not difficult to understand his nihilistic view of the world stated earlier in the book that "man is nothing in particular" (p. 135), or his conciliatory vision that man "is all we've got. . . . I wish I could ask men to meet themselves" (p. 439). But, as some critics have pointed out, it is difficult to believe that a young man with such mundane problems, renewing his life through a subway accident, suddenly emerges as a philosopher discussing Nietzsche, Heidegger, and Kierkegaard.[18] While in *The Stranger* the two parts of the story are so structured that each enlightens the other, those in *The Outsider*, the hero's life before and after the accident, are constructed as though they were two tales.

This weakness notwithstanding, *The Outsider* is unquestionably a powerful statement made by an outsider who refuses to surrender his will to live. One can scarcely find among black heroes in American fiction such a courageous and tenacious, albeit violent, man. As compared to Bigger Thomas, Wright's celebrated hero, Damon stands taller and poles apart simply because Damon is endowed with an intellectual capacity seldom seen in Afro-American fiction. Small wonder that when the novel came out, critics in general, both white and black, who were unfamiliar with such a character, failed to appreciate Wright's intention and execution in the book.[19]

The strengths of *The Outsider* become even clearer as this novel is compared with *The Stranger*. Although Damon professes to be a nihilist, as does Meursault,

---

[18]J. Saunders Redding, a distinguished black critic, considers *The Outsider* "often labored, frequently naive, and generally incredible." See his review in *Baltimore Afro-American* (May 19, 1953), in John M. Reilly, ed. *Richard Wright: The Critical Reception* (New York: Burt Franklin, 1978), 225-227. Another reviewer finds it impossible to relate Wright's "passionless slayer" to the Cross Damon of Book I, and says, "We can identify with the first Cross Damon, but not the later one. Wright goes out of his way to make this identification impossible." See Melvin Altshuler, "An Important, but Exasperating Book," *Washington Post* (May 22, 1953) in Reilly, pp. 203-204.

[19]Orville Prescott's *New York Times* review was a typical white critic's reaction to *The Outsider*. With due respect for Wright's previous successes, Prescott politely insisted that Wright must have deplored Damon's moral weakness and irrational behavior at the end of the book, and further remarked, "That men as brilliant as Richard Wright feel this way is one of the symptoms of the intellectual and moral crises of our times" (*New York Times*, March 10, 1953). Saunders Redding, quoted earlier, noted that Wright's brand of existentialism, instead of being a device for the representation of truth, "leads away from rather than toward reality" (*Baltimore Afro-American*, May 19, 1953). Arna Bontemps was even sarcastic: "The black boy from Mississippi is still exploring. He has had a roll in the hay with the existentialism of Sartre, and apparently he liked it" (*Saturday Review*, 36 [March 28, 1953]: 15-16).

he is never indifferent to human existence as is Meursault. Camus's hero is called a stranger to society as well as to himself; he is indifferent to friendship, marriage, love, success, freedom. Ironically, Damon, who seeks them in life, fails to obtain them. It is ironic, too, that Meursault, to whom they are at his disposal, is indifferent to them. Wright's hero, an outsider racially as well as intellectually, struggles to get inside. Damon wants to be treated as an individual, not as a second-class citizen or a person whose intellectual ability is not recognized. On the other hand, Camus's hero, an insider but a stranger, strives to get outside.

It is hardly coincidental, then, that both novels are eloquent social criticisms in our times. *The Outsider* is an indictment against American society, for not only does Wright maintain Damon's innocence but he shows most convincingly that men in America "hate themselves and it makes them hate others" (p. 439). *The Stranger*, on the other hand, is an indictment against French society, for Camus proves that while the criminal is innocent, his judges are guilty. More significantly, however, comparison of the two novels of differing characters and traditions reveals that both Wright and Camus are writing ultimately about a universal human condition.

Richard Wright and the Art
of Non-Fiction: Stepping Out
on the Stage of the World

John M. Reilly

Writers have several lives—at least to critics they do. First is the life construed as biography and serving to explain how the subject took a place in the institution of literature. Marking influences, establishing stages of development, and explaining connections among, say, family origin and social definition and the literary texts, the standard biography proffers a theory of mediations in the guise of a life record. The second life, ostensibly the declared object of the biographer, actually exists beyond the horizon of literary genre, already lived, already past, before the biographer begins the act of recovery. Since this "real life" took place in a series of moments amidst complex social interconnections in the immediacy of what was once present but is now past perfect, it is no longer available for examination, except under the aspect of basic chronology. This literal life is obliquely glimpsed through the biographer's anecdote or contemporary testimony and requires a shaping interpretation or imaginative decoding before it assumes meaning.

The writer's third life is the self-created product of memory as it is given expression in an autobiographical text. This is the "real life" recalled and shaped by the reflective power of the subject-author who transforms the completed past into the forever present. In autobiography, lived experience becomes, on the one hand, a controlled reenactment that replaces the events that were lived in a diffused way with a vision of destiny. On the other hand, and as the result of the imagined reenactment, autobiography becomes the life itself, complete and knowable in a way that the elusive reality of the past can never be (Olney 244–45).

By this reasoning on the multiple lives of an author, two more types, more or less partial, remain to be identified. Surely someone listening to this scheme has already thought to suggest that critical writing, even though it falls short of complete biography, nevertheless becomes a variety of life writing insofar as it presents interpretation linking texts and, thus, posits a process of development that stands for some part of the authorial life. This is correct. The critic explicating the products of imagination inevitably implies a thought experiment when the critic's sub-

Reprinted from *Callaloo* 9.3 (Summer 1986): 507-520. By permission of John M. Reilly and The Johns Hopkins University Press.

ject is literary theme, a generic or stylistic investigation if the intent is formal analysis, or a projection of self and philosophy if the critical focus is upon language or structure; and in any case, whether it is an experiment, investigation, or projection that is implied by the critic's analysis, the critical writing proposes a biography.

Recognition of criticism as biography leads us to the final version of the writer's life, the partial life writing that emerges as the subject-author uses personal experience for rhetorical tactic or as the structural framework of a text. Not so much implied as it is deliberate, this version of a life is what we find in the non-fiction of Richard Wright when he is not intent upon creating a story of self sufficiency enlarged to fill the generic requirements of autobiography, but still feels impelled to draw upon deeply personal sources for his conception of contemporary history.

To reveal this latter version of Wright's life while admitting that, after all, it results from the engagement of a critic with Wright's text, we must propose a plot in which *The Color Curtain* and *White Man, Listen!*, for example, are the significant events. We might as well call the plot a fiction because, while we can have confidence that the pattern of life and history Wright invested in his texts existed in reality, such reality is inaccessible to us except by interpretation of texts. So, then, with a bow of acknowledgment to Michel Fabre (*Unfinished Quest*) and Edward Margolies (*Art of Wright*) whose writings have set the framework of discourse on the exile writings of Richard Wright, let us start by saying that the significance of *The Color Curtain* and *White Man, Listen!* is that they mark the resolution of a crisis that had beset Wright's life ever since he took up permanent residence in Europe.

Despite the fresh perspective that exile offered Wright, he seems very quickly to have become pessimistic. The first published evidence is contained in two letters on the condition of European politics that he addressed to Dorothy Norman for publication in her journal *Twice-A-Year* (65-73). The letter dated 28 February 1948 speaks of deep divisions in European life. The intellectuals are talking about European unity, while the masses speak of hunger. The hunger is real, and since governments seem unable to cope with the threat it represents, the ideas of political unity are futile. Superimposed on the economic crisis Wright observed, was a feeling among the French that they were helpless objects in the struggle between the US and USSR. The second letter dated 9 March 1948 develops the idea of Left and Right mirror images represented in the Soviet Union and the United States. The conception of revolution has changed since Lenin, Wright says; now the masses wait while Left and Right armies prepare a struggle without regard for human consequences.

The bleak results Wright saw forthcoming from the international power struggle would not be, he said, the consequences of the ideas held by either side. Instead, they would result from the

> social system which is common to both of them, that is, unbridled industrialism which is the yardstick of all values. As things stand now, the only difference is that Russia has taken over industrial methods and applied them with a ruthlessness which we cannot use because of our traditions of individual freedom. . . . (72)

Wright's equation of the United States and the Soviet Union is perhaps to be expected from someone equally distanced from bourgeois capitalism and Stalinist Communism, but heed the tone of his discussion of the drift toward totalitarianism in the advanced countries of the West:

> What is happening here in Europe is not only a contest between Left and Right, but a total extinction of the very conception of what it has meant to be a human being for 2000 years. Those of us who work on the Left helped in making things confused; and those who work on the Right, bit by bit, did the very thing which they accused the Left of doing. . . .
>
> The Right and Left, in different ways, have decided that man is a kind of animal whose needs can be met by making more and more articles for him to consume. . . . If man is to be contained in that definition, and if it is not to be challenged, then that is what will prevail; and a world will be built in which everybody will get enough to eat and full stomachs will be equated with contentment and freedom, and those who will say that they are not happy under such a regime will be guilty of treason. How sad that is. We all were accomplices in this crime. . . . Is it too late to say something to halt it, modify it? (73)

Just a few years earlier, in the manuscript that would become *American Hunger,* Wright had written with confidence and a degree of satisfaction in the role of the detached and objective intellectual whose imaginative insight even permitted empathy with the "spectacle of glory" to be seen in the ritual trial of a Communist renegade. In the letters to Norman, however, Wright cannot go beyond a categorical opposition of Left and Right while expressing the note of self-reproach ("Those of us who work on the Left helped in making things confused") that obscures the privileged viewpoint of an intellectual working by means of a higher, more authentic reason than that employed by the ruthless agents of totalitarianism.

At the heart of these analyses Wright produced for *Twice-A-Year* lies disillusionment with politics, a sense that the practice to which he had devoted so many years of his adult life, including the critical period of his literary apprenticeship, had been misdirected. The will of the young devoted party member and the later vision of the persona Wright had developed in his autobiography as the intellectual refusing organizational discipline yet faithful to a goal of revolutionary social change seemed to him now in the later 1940s, to have served utterly cynical ends.

This same distrust informs Wright's first exile novel, *The Outsider.* In language that is striking because of its apparent acceptance of a decidedly conservative notion of a fixed human nature activated by something like original sin, Wright allows his protagonist Cross Damon to strip the covering of Marxism from his Communist nemeses and characterize their motives as

> something more recondite than mere political strategy; it was a *life* strategy using political methods as its tools. . . . Its essence was a voluptuous, a deep-going sensuality that took cognizance of fundamental human needs and the answers to those needs. It related man to man in a fearfully organic way. To hold absolute power over others, to define what they should love or fear, to decide if they were to live or die and thereby to ravage

the whole of their beings—that was a sensuality that made sexual passion look pale by comparison. It was a noneconomic conception of existence. . . . (198)

With the help of critics we have learned to read *The Outsider* as a rehearsal of existentialism carried to a logical extreme (Singh). The famous quotation in which Wright stated that *The Outsider* was his first literary effort "projected out of a heart preoccupied with no ideological burden save that of rendering an account of reality as it strikes my sensibilities and imagination" (Ford 91) seems to be evidence that the work was meant as a declaration of the end of an illusion and that Richard Wright associated the viewpoint of Cross Damon with his own.

The matter is more complicated than that, however, for it is just as easy to read the novel as a critique of existentialism which in the end is just as much despairing. The evidence for a distinction between Wright and Cross Damon rather than an identification is found in the representation of Damon's own sensual love of power and his absolute refusal to accept, let alone create, any limits on his right to behave as a vengeful god. Damon's story relates not merely an extreme existentialism but also the career of an exaggerated individualist acting out the ultimate fantasy of the hard-boiled private investigator who permits no contingencies to stand in the way of his pursuit of a solution to his case, acknowledges no sanctions from society or other persons that would control or frustrate his will, and renders the final preemptive solutions to his inquiries without a shiver or justification. Moreover, Cross Damon the detective is also an intellectual, and serving the way he does as the protagonist of the English-speaking countries' most popular genre of literary entertainment—the thriller—he typifies the Western intellectual hero.

The place assumed by *The Outsider* in a critic's fiction of the crisis in Wright's exile years should be clear. The disillusion with politics consequent to his observation of the opening events of the Cold War in Europe led Richard Wright to compose a narrative in which he would draw upon his own knowledge of organized political movements and their functionaries to lay bare their base motives. To demystify the ideology of Left and Right for his readers, he created a protagonist formed out of his own experience. Once under way, however, the novel revealed more than Wright originally planned; for even though he did not present Cross Damon as an autobiographical surrogate, Wright provided Damon with the insights of the author. The critique of Damon that issues from *The Outsider* could not help but also be a critique of the Westernized intellectual, Richard Wright himself.

Wright had effectively boxed himself in. Physically exiled, full of second thoughts about the consequences of political action, he had reached an intellectual nadir; yet he could not abandon the convictions about the world that the experiences of racism and alienation had taught him without ceasing to be a writer, and he could not abandon the stance of the intellectual either, for like his knowledge of Afro-America, the identity of intellectual was the foundation of his artistic integrity. To resolve his crisis and break through despair, Wright needed a compelling subject to restore optimism of will, the means to project confidently his self-created identity of intellectual, and a literary form that would empower him to speak, as he had done in *12 Million Black Voices* and the fiction of his earlier years, with the force of an agent of contemporary history.

This compelling subject Wright found in the emerging nations of Africa and Asia. Like Lenin and Sartre who turned to the so-called underdeveloped world when their hopes seemed "increasingly inapplicable to European conditions" (Hughes 47), Wright discovered with a thrill of recognition that the Third World could re-establish for him the arc of intellect and feeling. Elsewhere I have discussed at some length the first published evidence of that thrill of recognition, the study of the emerging nation of Ghana in *Black Power* ("Discovery" and "Self-Creation" 222-26), so rather than repeat myself here, let me proceed to other significant texts.

In "Princes and Powers," an essay on the 1956 Congress of Black Artists and Intellectuals sponsored by *Presence Africaine* with Wright's help, James Baldwin describes Leopold Senghor's declaration in a keynote speech that the heritage of all Blacks is undivided. The proof of his point, according to Baldwin, was a poem by Richard Wright filled with African tensions and the classic work *Black Boy,* which Senghor assured his audience would upon analysis reveal its true source to be African (Baldwin 31-32). The declaration of the application of *Négritude* is hardly unexpected, and possibly the characterizations of Wright's work by Senghor might be demonstrated by such an analysis as he calls for. The point of the report in "Princes and Powers," however, is that Wright at the same conference in 1956, two years after the appearance of *Black Power,* implicitly discounted what he seems to have understood to be a mystique of race. Instead, Wright opened his own speech by describing himself, much as he does in the introductory pages of *Black Power,* as at once a Westerner and a Black, one who is thereby privileged to see "both worlds from another, and third, point of view" (44). As Baldwin proceeds to report Wright's speech in further detail, and as we read it in the version published in *White Man, Listen!* under the title "Tradition and Industrialization" (44-68), it is an historical accounting, like Cross Damon's, of the decline of religious authority in the West and, with it, the religious justification of colonialism. Moreover, Wright insists, the effect of colonialism was eventually liberating, because it freed Africans from the "rot" of their prerational past. Hardly designed to announce total solidarity with Third World leaders, the speech by Wright displays a rationalist, Western self-image and employs a more or less Marxist framework of historical analysis. In other words, the speech is characteristic of the familiar persona Wright had created for himself in *Black Boy* and *American Hunger,* except that as he took a vantage point on his new subject—the colonial experience—the despair he had expressed toward conditions in America and Europe—the West itself—seemed now to be replaced by an enthusiasm for historical discourse.

It should be noted that Wright delivered his speech in reply to Senghor during the year following his trip to Bandung to collect material for *The Color Curtain,* an experience like the earlier trip to Africa responsible for the enthusiasm. The subject of *The Color Curtain,* besides the Third World itself, is the politics of transition from colonialism to independence. What strikes Wright first about the emergence of former colonies into independence is the apparent irrelevance of conventional political designations to a description of the new states; therefore, he calls the first section of the report on Bandung "Beyond Left and Right," and announces in the second section that race and religion, not standard politics, are the dominant concerns of the delegates. In the period of despair about left and right politics evidenced in the letters to Dorothy Norman's *Twice-A-Year,* one might expect from Wright ready confirmation of the wisdom of dispensing with outmoded and manipulative categories. In *The Color Curtain,* however, cynicism comes less easily than it had. The Third World's rejection of Western political configurations must be carefully examined for motive and consequence.

In fact, as readers of *The Color Curtain* will recall, the book is constructed as though it were a work of empirical social investigation. In an effort to get to know the Asian personality about which he confesses to knowing very little, Wright consulted Otto Klineberg for help in devising a questionnaire consisting of no less than 80 questions meant to uncover the respondents' background, experience with colonialism, and general opinions (Fabre 422). To establish a base line of comparison, Wright first administered the questionnaire to an Indonesian-born Dutch journalist; then he presented his questions to an Eurasian woman, a Westernized Asian educator of middle age, a full-blooded Indonesian student of political science, and a journalist from Pakistan. With the same evident empirical bent, Wright also records later conversations about relations between the West and Asia with an Indonesian student of sociology whom he encountered on an airplane and a Japanese newspaperman met on another flight; and, once in Jakarta, he continues interrogatory conversations with the editor of an independent Socialist daily newspaper about the basic statistics and political environment of Indonesia, with his hosts in the home where he was quartered, who tell him about the political history of the Republic, with a Westernized politician, and a Moslem political leader. Documentary detail continues to pick up in the second chapter of *The Color Curtain.* Opening this section with words suggesting he had built a data base, "I was now ready to go to Bandung to the Conference," Wright proceeds to paraphrase and quote twelve leaders of delegations. The same manner of citation continues in the third section of the book where, in a consideration of the issue of Communism at the conference, he focuses attention upon speeches by Chou En-Lai and Nehru.

In none of his reported conversations, including those in "Racial Shame at Bandung," the fourth section of the book, does Wright make an attempt to preserve a sense of natural verbal exchange or to create verisimilitude. Instead he emphasizes the content of informal talk as though it were delivered without inflection, tone, or the dynamics of dialogue that provide "color" and reveal animation. Throughout *The Color Curtain,* the people Wright meets are treated solely as informants, vessels without character. He may attribute personal traits to his informants in the sense that he considers them exemplary of what Edward Margolies calls "fractured personalities" (part one), but Wright renders them flat. They are spokespeople without unique voice.

Despite the fact that Richard Wright's *The Color Curtain* is presented in subtitle as *A Report on the Bandung Conference*, we have no trouble in seeing that the text hardly conforms to the conventions of the non-fiction genre of reportage. Except for the anecdotal flavor of incidents in which Wright relates how he was given preferential treatment by bureaucrats because of his skin color (113-14) or explained to a white woman why her Black roommate was behaving surreptitiously (because she was concealing her hair-straightening) (182-87), and the description of the topography and people seen on the drive up the mountain slopes to Bandung (scenes which Wright says remind him of Africa) (129-30), Wright does little to render the outward drama of a global meeting without precedent in past history.

Constructed as though on the model of an empirical investigation, *The Color Curtain* gains overt structure as Wright proposes the topics of inquiry: how the respondents to his questionnaire feel about nationalism or industrialism; their attitudes toward the use of nuclear weapons; their views of trade unions; generational differences and the sentiments they may have toward the Russian Revolution. The context for such empirical investigation is suggested by Wright's citation of Western newspaper accounts that show an incapacity to comprehend the meaning of Bandung, the data about education and development he derives from the conversations with Indonesians, and the testimonials he notes from Afro-Americans who do see the meaning of Bandung. Yet, this overt structure does not provide the plot for *The Color Curtain*.

A brief example or two may serve to suggest what the real plot of the text is. Eschewing the potential for external drama in recounting the various interviews as they occurred, Wright instead presents the results of those interviews as he thought them over on his journey to Indonesia. Rather than the gathering of data, he gives his readers the tentative sorting of the data, noting how accidents of birth determine responses to his questions, judging whether or not the respondent would be likely to gain influence in the Asian future, and commenting on the relative sense of reality that seems apparent in the answers that his questions elicited. The control manifest in this "processing of data" appears as well in the records of conversations that took place once Wright reached Indonesia. Tersely presented, without reference to need for translation, interpretation or editing, the statements by native Indonesians are always subordinate to Wright's questions. The true subject of *The Color Curtain*, therefore, becomes the intellect of Richard Wright. His report on Bandung brackets perception outside his text and carries narration at once to conceptions. The welter of new impressions that confront a foreign visitor, such as Wright was, is absent from the text; the attempts by the foreign visitor to gain understanding by tentative hypothesis have no place in the record, even though Wright explains his need for questionnaire by lack of knowledge; and what is perhaps most striking in the peculiar drama of Richard Wright's confrontation of the Third World in Indonesia is the tone and manner of surety. This tone can lead to no other conclusion but that Wright already knows what he will find, or at least already possesses the framework to contain any new data, ideas or positions he will encounter at Bandung.

Implored by the contours of Wright's mind, *The Color Curtain* also can be seen as providing the necessities for lifting the despair surrounding his thought at the time he wrote *The Outsider*. He had found his compelling new subject in the Third World, and the measure of the effect it had in reviving his optimism can be seen in the unrelieved control he exercises in the text over this new subject. Insofar as that control is expressed in the manner of an intellectual, firm in his conviction of the power of his reason and the value of the self-sufficient stance that intellectuals believe mark their role in the world, *The Color Curtain* also shows Wright reaffirming his self-created identity. The third thing I have suggested was necessary to resolve Wright's crisis, namely, a form that would once again empower him as an historical agent, requires more discussion, however.

As he had inverted the form of the private eye's investigative story in *The Outsider* and thereby challenged the suppositions of individualistic narrative that underlie the bourgeois novel itself, so too in his non-fiction beginning with *Black Power* and continuing through *The Color Curtain* and *White Man, Listen!* Richard Wright undertook an adaptation of conventions that eventually converted journalism into a vehicle for a theory of contemporary reality inspired by a vision of a new people entering history. There can be little doubt that in passages such as the following interpretations of answers he secured from Asians to his questionnaire, Wright is characterizing a collective rather than individuals. Of the middle-aged Indonesian educator, Wright says: "His approach implied a denial of collective thought-processes, of mass organic experiences embedded in the very lives and social conditions about him" (55). Because of the man's distrust of mass participation in politics, his preference for some sort of benevolent aristocracy that would foster a re-examination of ethical issues, Wright concludes that his influence upon Asian reality would be negligible. The Indonesian political science student who described for Wright the scars that humiliation by the West had left upon him, is said by Wright to know "both East and West, without really believing in either of them. There was another and other world that he and his kind had to create" (62). And the Pakistani journalist who also tells Wright that the West has made the Asian feel a sense of shame leads Wright to say that it was clear to him "that the East held by the West as a fond image does not exist any more; indeed, the classical conception of the East is dead even for the Easterner . . . He lives in his world, but he does not believe in it any longer; he holds on to its values with too much self-consciousness to live by them. In fact, his pretentious clinging to those old values signifies that he is trying to save face" (70-71).

With his analysis of each of these exemplary figures in the limited group he sampled, Wright readily disposes of religion and valorization of traditional life by Asians as the result of oppositional experience. As the Western colonialists denigrated the signs of traditional Asian life, the objects of Western scorn assumed unrealistic value simply because of the oppositional experience. "The West," says

Wright paraphrasing his Pakistani informant, "has made the Easterner feel a sense of shame, and this shame is very widespread and is really an inferiority feeling" (65). Wright feels no need to give credence in his analysis to the inherent value of religion or the continued vitality of traditional patterns of life, because he is convinced that the revolutionary changes brought about by colonialization cannot be reversed. The dialectic of history has force greater than individual preference or even a national program that may be developed by the newly-freed nations of the Third World. All of his observations confirm the point. For example, arriving at the Jakarta airport and proceeding by car into the city, Wright observes a hurly-burly scene that reminds him of Accra in Africa. To Western eyes the cities present "a commercial aspect, naked and immediate, that seems to swallow up the entire population in petty trade. . . . The spectator who is acquainted with colonial practice," says Wright, "knows at once where this feverish activity comes from: one must sell to earn money to buy products shipped from Europe" (93-94). Then, in a passage that echoes Marx in *The Communist Manifesto*, declaring that "The bourgeoisie, wherever it has got the upper hand, has put an end to all feudal, patriarchal, idyllic . . . pitilessly torn asunder the motley feudal ties that bound man to his 'natural superiors' and . . . left no other nexus between man and man than naked self-interest, than callous 'cash payment' " (323). Wright tells the readers that in Jakarta "family relations have been replaced by factory and financial relations, and the resulting picture of brutal and direct commercial activity is of a nature unknown even in cities like London, New York, or Paris . . ." (94). Elsewhere in *The Color Curtain*, Wright generalizes the point to include all of the colonialized world as well as Indonesia: "The trampling by a powerful West upon the traditional and customary Asian and African cultures, cultures sacred and beyond rational dispute, left vast populations at the mercy of financial and commercial relations which compounded the confusion in Asian and African minds" (73). Thus, to Wright the material history of the domination of East by West constitutes a late chapter in the spread of the enormous power of capitalism. What capitalism once did in Europe and America, its compulsion to secure raw materials, markets and extension of trade has accomplished also in Asia and Africa. This dynamic material process at the base of Wright's conception of modern Asia and Africa explains colonialism as a rupture in the continuum of time that renders religion and traditional values vestigial. Religion might remain important to Asians and Africans, but largely because it satisfies their self-conscious needs to differentiate themselves from their Western oppressors, they elevate religion to a prominence it no longer can occupy in the West, and that is no longer justifiable, except as psychological defense, in the East. To be sure, the masses retain deep-seated religious feelings, but for the leaders of the emergent East who are intent upon revolutionary transformation of their rational life, religion, like the ideas surrounding race, is an instrumentality. Thus, as Wright sat listening to Sukarno address the Conference, he says he "began to sense a deep and organic relation here in Bandung between race and religion, *two of the most powerful and irrational forces in human nature. Sukarno was not evoking these twin demons; he was not trying* to create them; he was trying to organize them . . ." (140). In *Black Power*, Wright had already written of a national leadership that synthesized modern mass politics with tribal traditions for the purpose of creating an independent, industrializing nation state. He would dramatize that strategy again in his essay "The Miracle of Nationalism in the African Gold Coast" (*White Man, Listen!* 106–37) and here in *The Color Curtain* he attributes the same strategy to the Chinese Communists (163).

Considered rhetorically, the attention Wright pays to the political synthesis of values and forces resonant of an Asian and African past with the vanguardist practices of modern revolutionary movements enforces the point that a new people have been created by modern history. Metaphors of awakening or renaissance, however attractive or effective they would seem, never appear in Wright's analysis. Instead, Wright underlines the novelty of the historical development he observes by characterizing the subjects of his analysis as "more Western than the West, their Westernness consisting in their having been made to break with the past in a manner that but few Westerners could possibly do" (71) and explaining the conference as "the last call of westernized Asians to the moral conscience of the West!" (202).

With such language, as well as in his discussions of political strategy, Wright moves beyond consideration of the material forces of history. Seeking to describe the significance of Bandung, Wright's categories of analysis become predominantly those that relate to consciousness. The Marx of *The Communist Manifesto* may have suggested the descriptions of a society founded upon a cash nexus in Jakarta and Accra, but in weight and extent the greater part of the analysis of history in *The Color Curtain* resembles writings of the younger Marx of 1844 in its attention to alienation as a condition of life under capitalism. So we see that it is the historical production of consciousness that Wright outlines by the inferences he draws from his questioning of Asians, just as it is consciousness Wright describes when he characterizes the uniquely disaffiliated condition that marks the Third World elites who must lead their nations.

Wright's theory of contemporary history becomes indivisible from the form he devised for its certification. If the terrain of history is to be understood as consciousness, which is at one and the same time an historical product and the agency of historical change, then it is entirely appropriate, perhaps even obligatory, that the process of description should occur within a personalized intellectual drama that enables the author to deploy evidence and advance a thesis according to the tempo of the man thinking.

However, before this observation of the functional congruity of form and purpose leads me by default to a judgment that *The Color Curtain* is an entirely successful example of non-fictional art, I must hasten to acknowledge the book's weakness, for by that means we uncover its final importance in the critic's version of a life enacted through *The Color Curtain*.

The essential weakness of the book lies in features of its rhetoric that permit it to be read as a Cold War document. For example, Tillman Durdin reviewing the book in the *New York Times Book Review* wrote that Wright correctly posed the crucial question of Bandung in the concluding chapter. Wright asks, according to Durdin, "whether the sensitive and resentful people represented there are to be brought out of their present state of poverty, ignorance and economic backwardness under the aegis of a blood Communist totalitarianism or through wise and generous aid from the West that will link them with our freer, democratic system" (1). Other commentators on the book, like Addison Gayle, remark that Wright portrays Communism at Bandung as absolute evil (259)—that's why he displays such concern about Chou En-Lai's approach to the delegates—and quotes Carlos Romulo of the Philippines, explaining that the white Western world "which has fostered racism has done many another thing," including giving the new nations "basic ideas of political freedom, justice and equity," as well as a science "which in this generation has exploded the mythology of race" (153). This apparent support of Cold War clichés seems particularly egregious in the final pages of *The Color Curtain* where it threatens to cast the leaders of the Third World whom Wright has been characterizing previously as figures beyond the ideology of left and right in the role of Western dependents. The base of secular, rational thought in the West must become one with the shaky base of similar thought that exists in the East, says Wright, lest "the tenuous Asian-African secular, rational attitudes will become flooded, drowned in irrational tides of racial and religious passions" (219). Alternatively, if the West remains unavailable to the elites of the Third World, they may adopt the methods of Stalinism with its "drastic practices of endless secular sacrifices" (220).

In these passages, Wright's language has become so abstract that it ceases any longer to evoke reality. He speaks of unifying bases of thought as if they were political organizations. He asserts a faith that *only* the rational, secular, and beneficent power of the West is available to developing countries. The result of such apparently innocent conviction and hasty summarizing is that rather than proposing as a conclusion to his contemporary theory of history a resolution that reaches beyond ideology, Wright speaks words that encourage one to read his statements as jingoism.

What explains this excess? Let me suggest that we return to the reported incidents of the final chapter of *The Color Curtain* for explanation. The controlling problem of that section Wright states this way: "Can Asian and African leaders keep pace with the dynamics of a billion or more people loosed from their colonial shackles, but loosed in terms of defensive, irrational feelings?" (206). This is, of course, reiteration of Wright's historical vision of the emergence of a new people in history, though this time the thesis is expressed to evoke prediction and strategy. Historicist that he is, Wright immediately finds analogy for the Third World challenge in "the convulsive terror that must have gripped the hearts of the Bolsheviks in Russia in 1920. . .":

> Lenin, no matter what we may think of him today, was faced with a half-starving nation of 160,000,000 partly tribalized people and he and his cohorts felt that they could trust nobody; they were afraid of losing their newly gained power, their control over the des-

tinies of their country. Now, today, there were one and one-half billion people loosed from domination and they too were afraid of losing their freedom, of being dominated again by alien powers, afraid of a war for which they were in no way prepared. What Lenin had faced in Russia in 1920 was here projected on a stage of history stretching over continents and augmented in terms of population a thousandfold. (207)

The analogy of the Soviet Union implies, and the whole of Wright's exposition of his theory of contemporary history in *The Color Curtain* confirms, that the primary issue to be decided in the modern world is an answer to the revolutionary's constant question: "What is to be done?" Lenin the Westernized Russian intellectual had asked it once, and now the new intelligentsia of Africa and Asia have put the same question at the head of their agenda. The leadership of the Third World will not simply allow events to take their course any more than they will risk their new freedom. What's more, whatever program develops as the plan for action, it will constitute deliberate intervention. Just a few pages before the abstract passages about the contrast between the brutal means of Stalinism and the merging of bases of thought, those words that encourage a Cold Warrior interpretation, Wright reports a conversation with an American liberal who proposes a gradual training process of 150 Indonesian student a year. The liberal who calls himself a Jeffersonian Democrat says, according to Wright, "We will help, but we won't interfere" (211). Wright rejects such hesitancy out of hand. Interference or intervention call it what you will, is absolutely essential by Wright's reasoning if cataclysmic war waged with the two-edged sword of Western technology or a repetition of the excesses of Stalinism are to be avoided.

Certainly Wright can be said to share an innocence born of hope about the possibility of Western intervention in the Third World, but there can be no doubt that he had to raise the issue, had to insert in his report on Bandung a colloquy about the power of historical actors to direct events. The famous letter to Nkrumah with which he had concluded *Black Power* had amounted to the same thing. Telling Nkrumah to militarize the people, force march them into the future, Wright had assigned to the leader of the Gold Coast popular movement the charge to make history, consciously and deliberately. The form that the call to make history deliberately and consciously takes in *The Color Curtain* may be politically naive, but the compulsion for Wright to issue the call in all of the non-fiction that he wrote in exile arises from the deepest recesses of the author's being, his feeling that ultimately, contemporary reality must be understood through projection of autobiographical will into history. As consciousness was the terrain of history, there was no doubt in Wright that his own consciousness was exemplary not only of the Afro-American condition, but now it was also the proof of the changing contemporary world's history as well.

Here is the key passage for evidence of the autobiographical content of *The Color Curtain*, a section appearing early in the book where Wright explains to his wife how he expects to produce a report on the monumental meeting of twenty-nine newly independent nations:

> . . . I feel that my life has given me some keys to what they would say or do. I'm an American Negro; as such, I've had a burden of race consciousness. So have these people. I worked in my youth as a common laborer, and I've a class consciousness. So have these people. I grew up in the Methodist and Seventh Day Adventist churches and I saw and observed religion in my childhood; and these people are religious. I was a member of the Communist Party for twelve years and I know something of the politics and psychology of rebellion. These people have had as their daily existence such politics. (15)

This is the basis for identification that transcends for Wright any limitations he may feel because of his lack of detailed knowledge of Asia or Africa. The passage reveals as well an outlook that dissolves secondary differences among the colored peoples of the world and permits him the equations we have seen between the appearance of Jakarta with Accra, of the peasants in the hills of Indonesia with the country folk of the Gold Coast. For Wright, the life of the colored masses has become unitary.

Yet it is not just mass life, but the condition of the vanguard of the Third World with which Wright forges his alliance. The passage about the congruity of Afro-American and Third World experience quoted just above is immediately followed by two sentences that, lacking any transition, seem at first like non sequiturs:

> These emotions are my instruments. They are emotions, but I'm conscious of them as emotions. I want to use these emotions to try to find out what these people think and feel and why. (15)

But, of course, the sentences are not non sequiturs. They are declarations of Wright's deeply held conviction that as consciousness is the terrain of history, his own consciousness, developed by imagination working on the matter of experience, provided the reliable guide to contemporary reality. In this respect, then, autobiography provides the final subject and method to *The Color Curtain.* He is one with the self-aware elite of the Third World, except for the crucial difference of the fact that he has possessed the capacity to see himself self-reflexively for more than a decade, while, for all he knows, the elite intellectuals of the Third World have only recently grasped the unique situation of double-consciousness that is the birthright of all sensitive Afro-Americans. In the autobiographical manuscript that became *Black Boy* and later *American Hunger,* Wright had represented himself as both typical of American Blacks and peculiarly qualified to serve as their spokesperson by virtue of a comprehensive imagination that allowed him to step aside, in mind at least, from the crushing experience of racism and to see the troubles of daily life as issues of history. As far as life in America went, he had it whipped in mind with a conception of reality that dominated the chaos and absurdity of American experience (the allusion to the words of Ralph Ellison's nameless protagonist is deliberate here). Now in *The Color Curtain* Wright steps out onto the stage of the whole world, offering his experience as the template for contemporary history, his emotions as instruments for understanding reality more powerful than the empiricism of conventional social science or the colorful style of description customary in non-fiction reportage.

Once before, Wright had spoken of the emergence of a people into history. That was in *12 Million Black Voices* where he wrote, "The seasons of the plantation no longer dictate the lives of many of us; hundreds of thousands of us are moving into the sphere of conscious history" (241). Since 1941, however, life had put Richard Wright through changes, not the least of which was the crisis of conviction he experienced as he entered exile at the inception of the Cold War. For a time doubtful even of the intellectual's persona he had created for himself, he tested the premises and consequences of a completely individualistic philosophy and literary genre in *The Outsider* and met despair in the career of his kinsman Cross Damon. Too rationalistic to immerse himself in mass life, yet radically incapable of abandoning the desire to make sense of the history that had created him, Wright made a secular salvation for himself out of his discovery of the Third World. The elite Westernized leaders of Africa and Asia he conceived as his alter egos, his own imagination and experience the force mediating their entry into conscious history. As that formulation provided him resolution for his crisis of belief, it also became the essence of his art of non-fiction.

Works Cited

Baldwin, James. *Nobody Knows My Name: More Notes of a Native Son.* New York: Dial Press, 1961.

Durdin, Tillman. Review of *The Color Curtain. New York Times Book Review* (18 March 1956): 1.

Fabre, Michel. *The Unfinished Quest of Richard Wright.* New York: William Morrow, 1973.

Ford, Nick Aaron. "The Ordeal of Richard Wright." *College English* 15 (1953): 87-94.

Gayle, Addison. *Richard Wright: Ordeal of a Native Son.* New York: Doubleday, 1980.

Hughes, H. Stuart, "Jean-Paul Sartre: The Marxist Phase." *Ramparts* 5 (1967): 47-51.

Margolies, Edward. *The Art of Richard Wright.* Carbondale: Southern Illinois UP, 1969.

Marx, Karl. "The Communist Manifesto." *Capital, The Communist Manifesto, and Other Writings,* Ed. Max Eastman. New York: Modern Library, 1932.

Olney, James. "Some Versions of Memory/Some Versions of Bios: The Ontology of Autobiography." *Autobiography: Essays Theoretical and Critical.* Ed. James Olney. Princeton: Princeton UP, 1980: 236-67.

Reilly, John M. "Richard Wright's Discovery of the Third World." *Minority Voices* 2 (1978): 47-53.

——. "The Self-Creation of the Intellectual: *American Hunger* and *Black Power.*" *Critical Essays on Richard Wright.* Ed. Yosihinobu Hakutani. Boston: G. K. Hall, 1982: 213-27.

Singh, Amritjit. "Richard Wright's *The Outsider:* Existentialist Exemplar or Critique." *CLA Journal* 27 (1984): 357-70.

Wright, Richard. *The Color Curtain: A Report on the Bandung Conference.* Cleveland: World, 1956.

——. *12 Million Black Voices. Richard Wright Reader.* Eds. Ellen Wright and Michel Fabre. New York: Harper & Row, 1978: 144-241.

——. "Two Letters to Dorothy Norman." *Twice-A-Year* 16 (1948): 65-73.

——. *The Outsider.* New York: Harper, 1953.

——. *White Man, Listen!* New York: Doubleday, 1957. Anchor Edition, 1964.

A Long Way from Home:
Wright in the Gold Coast

Kwame Anthony Appiah

One does not react to Africa as Africa is, and this is because so few can react to life as life is. One reacts to Africa as one is, as one lives; one's reaction to Africa is one's life, one's ultimate sense of things. Africa is a vast, dingy mirror.

Africa is dangerous, evoking in one a total attitude toward life, calling into question the basic assumptions of existence. Africa is the world of man; if you are wild, Africa's wild; if you are empty, so's Africa. . . .

—*RICHARD WRIGHT, Black Power*

Africa has played its various roles in Western symbolic geography with an astonishing versatility. Its early role as homeland of the pious Ethiopians is unjustly less well-remembered than its more recent triumph as the heart of darkness; but after twenty-five centuries of continuous performances, this is, perhaps, understandable.

But the story of Africa has its less familiar episodes, and among the most intriguing, I think, is a curious byway in the history of Afro-America's African dream. From the earliest days of the African resettlement schemes that produced Liberia and Sierra Leone, New World blacks have reversed the Middle Passage. Those whose literacy and education allowed them to record their response—priests and scholars like Alexander Crummell and Edward Wilmot Blyden—produced works bearing impressive testimony to the powerful image of Africa that dominated the culture they sought to escape.

Driven by a love of Africa that was rooted in the romantic racism of the nineteenth century, these proto-nationalists were still unable to see her for what she was—even when they no longer saw her darkly through the glass of distance; even when they had stared her in the face. Alexander Crummell and Edward Blyden begin the record of Afro-Americans who have taken the dream to Africa with them, and have travelled there without awakening.

Crummell, though born and raised in New York, was Liberian by adoption. On July 26, 1860—the thirteenth anniversary, by Crummell's reckoning, of Liberian Independence—he addressed the citizens of Maryland county, Cape Palmas, on the subject of "The English Language in Liberia." He claimed that the Africans

Reprinted from *Richard Wright*, ed. Harold Bloom (New York: Chelsea House, 1987), pp. 173-190. By permission of Kwame Anthony Appiah.

"exiled" in slavery to the New World had been given by divine providence "at least this one item of compensation, namely, the possession of the Anglo-Saxon tongue." Crummell, who loved Africa enough to give the best years of his life to it, believed that English was a superior language to the "various tongues and dialects" of the indigenous African populations; superior in its euphony, its conceptual resources, and its capacity to express the "supernal truths" of Christianity.

Blyden, with Africanus Horton and Martin Robinson Delany, was one of three contemporaries of Crummell's who could also lay claim to the title of "Father of Pan-Africanism." Like Crummell, Blyden was a native of the New World, Liberian by adoption, and a priest; and, for a while, they were friends and fellow workers in the beginning of Liberia's modern system of education.

These men shared a conception of the destiny of their race, a conception that lay at the heart of their Pan-Africanist convictions: Africa was the proper home of the Negro and the Afro-American was an exile, who should, in Blyden's words, "return to the land of his fathers. . . AND BE AT PEACE." Yet they also shared a distaste for Africa's indigenous culture and traditions. Not only did they scorn Africa's languages—Blyden believed that "English is undoubtedly, the most suitable of the European languages for bridging the numerous gulfs between the tribes caused by the great diversity of languages or dialects among them"—but they each had little faith in African customs and, most especially, traditional—or, as they would have said, "pagan"—religions.

Outside the areas where Islam had brought some measure of exogenous civilization, Blyden's Africa is a place of "noisy terpsichorean performances," "Fetichism," and polygamy; it is, in short, in "a state of barbarism." Crummell's Africa

> is the victim of her heterogeneous idolatries. . . . Darkness covers the land and gross darkness the people. . . . Licentiousness abounds everywhere. Moloch rules and reigns throughout the whole continent, and by the ordeal of Sassywood, Fetiches, human sacrifices and devil-worship, is devouring men, women, and little children.

For Crummell and Blyden, Africa was not so much a *tabula rasa* as a slate to be erased.

It is surprising that even those Afro-Americans like Crummell and Blyden, who initiated the nationalist discourse on Africa in Africa, inherited a set of conceptual blinders that made them unable to see virtue in Africa, despite their need for Africa, above all else, as a source of validation. Since they conceived of the African in racial terms, their low opinion of Africa was not easily distinguishable from a low opinion of the Negro; and, through the linking of race and Pan-Africanism, they left contemporary African cultures with a burdensome legacy.

The centrality of race in the history of African nationalism, both widely assumed and often ignored, is derived from the typical experience of those who led the post-war independence movements. A great many colonial students from British Africa were gathered in London in the years after the Second World War, united in their common search for political independence from a single metropolitan state. They were brought together too by the fact that the British—those who helped as well as those who hindered—saw them first as Africans. But they were able to articulate a common vision of post-colonial Africa through a discourse inherited from pre-war Pan-Africanism, and that discourse was the product, largely, of black citizens of the New World.

Since what bound those Afro-American and Afro-Caribbean Pan-Africanists together was the partially African ancestry they shared, and since that ancestry existed in the New World through its various folk theories of race, a racial understanding of their solidarity was, perhaps, an inevitable development. This was reinforced by the fact that a few crucial figures—Kwame Nkrumah among them—had travelled in the opposite direction to Crummell, seeking education in the black colleges of the United States.

It was the Pan-Africanism gained from his American experience that made Nkrumah open to the small army of New World blacks who beat a path to his door in the early 1950s, when, as first prime minister of the Gold Coast, he began the process that led, in fewer years than most Europeans expected—and than many Africans had hoped—to the decolonization of Africa. In July 1953, he rose in the Gold Coast parliament to argue for "self-government now"; and in proposing what he called the "motion of destiny," he drew attention explicitly to the connection between the Afro-American situation and the African one:

> Honourable Members . . . The eyes and ears of the world are upon you; yea, our oppressed brothers throughout this vast continent of Africa and the New World are looking to you with desperate hope, as an inspiration to continue their grim fight against cruelties which we in this corner of Africa have never known—cruelties which are a disgrace to humanity; and to the civilisation which the white man has set himself to teach us.

Nkrumah knew that despite what decolonization meant to Africans, to Afro-Americans it was a beacon of hope. He would not have been surprised to hear James Baldwin say to Robert Penn Warren a decade later:

> For the first time in American Negro history, the American black man is not at the mercy of the American white man's image of him. This is because of Africa. For the first time in the memory of anybody now living, African states mean Africa. It's still, you know, very romantic for an American Negro to think of himself as an African, but it's a necessary step in the recreation of his morale.

I

Sitting in the gallery on the July day when Nkrumah tabled his motion was one of those Afro-Americans who found their way to Nkrumah's Gold Coast. He was there at the prime minister's invitation, and he listened with rapt attention. His name was Richard Wright, and *Black Power,* the book that records his visit, holds a special place in the literature of return that begins with Crummell and Blyden.

It also holds a special place in its author's career. As John M. Reilly, one of the book's more devoted readers, has argued, *Black Power* was written at a crucial moment in Wright's literary development, the result of "an intellectual crisis manifest in the implicitly nihilistic philosophy" espoused by Cross Damon, the protagonist of his novel *The Outsider*. What Wright needed in order to resolve this crisis was a "newly compelling subject that would permit him to reaffirm his writer's identity." In *Black Power*, Reilly claims,

> Richard Wright wished to build a bridge of words between his self and the world. He succeeded, and we acknowledge the accomplishment by discovering within the constructions of language the prerequisite endeavor to create his expressive self.

Reilly correctly describes the project of self-fashioning that haunts this book, but he misrecognizes its shape: for the *failure* of that "bridge of words between his self and the world" is precisely what the success of that "prerequisite endeavor to create his expressive self" demands.

Although self-expression is the book's latent objective, this is hardly the impression left by the book's preface, "Apropos Prepossession," which opens with these words:

> In today's intellectual climate—a climate charged with ideological currents in the service, paid or voluntary, of some nation, party, movement or interest—it behooves a writer reporting in nonfictional terms on vital material to lay before the reader his working frame of reference, his assumptions and preoccupations.

Generically, the stilted diction signals a work of "scientific" ethnography, a transparent conduit answering only to the facts. As he says a little later:

> In presenting this picture of Africa, I openly use, to a limited degree, Marxist analyses of historic events. . . If anyone should object to my employment of Marxist methods to make meaningful the ebb and flow of commodities, human and otherwise, in the modern state, to make comprehensible the alignment of social classes in modern society, I have to say that I'll willingly accept any other method of interpreting the facts; but I insist that any other method *must not exclude the facts*. (his emphasis)

In striking contrast to the preface, the opening of the first chapter marks an abrupt generic shift. Here, where he is concerned to explain the circumstances of his trip to Africa, his dissertative style is promptly abandoned as inadequate to the task.

The chapter begins with a moment after luncheon on Easter Sunday in the Wrights' home in Paris, when "we were stirring the sugar in our cups." "We" are Richard and Ellen Wright and their guests, among whom is Dorothy Padmore, "wife of George Padmore, the West Indian author and journalist." The Padmores were friends of Nkrumah's, influential actors in the culture of Pan-Africanism that spanned the three continents of the triangular trade that had created the black diaspora. Out of the silence, Mrs. Padmore turned to me and asked:

> "Now that your desk is clear, why don't you go to Africa?"
> The idea was so remote to my mind and mood that I gaped at her a moment before answering.
> "Africa?" I echoed.

"Yes. The Gold Coast," she said stoutly.

"But that's four thousand miles away!" I protested.

"There are planes and ships," she said.

My eyes glanced unseeingly about the room. I felt cornered, uneasy. I glanced at my wife.

"Why not?" she said.

A moment ago I had been collected, composed; now I was on the defensive, feeling poised on the verge of the unknown.

"Africa!" I repeated the word to myself, then paused as something strange and disturbing stirred slowly in the depths of me. I am an African! I'm of African descent.

It is a scene, one is bound to observe, that evokes nothing so much as Conradian dread; a dread intensified, no doubt, by the thought that Wright, the Afro-American, already has the horror stirring "in the depths" of him, even in the tranquillity of Paris. The melodramatic language of this opening passage—the language, dare I say, of a bad Edwardian novel—is, as I suggested, oddly in conflict with the high purpose announced in Wright's preface and the "scientific" language of the informational discourse that he has promised. The relation between the book and this vignette echoes strangely the relation between *Native Son* and the famous essay which precedes it (since the second edition), the preface which tells us "How Bigger Was Born." Just as that preface prepares one for a sociological reading of the novel, this initial scene-setting prepares one for a novelistic reading of the sociology. At the start, *Black Power* is a book that doesn't seem to know where it's going.

II

Wright chose a stanza from Countee Cullen's famous poem "What Is Africa to Me?" as the first epigraph of his book:

What is Africa to me?
Copper sun or scarlet sea
Jungle star or jungle track,
Strong bronzed men, or regal black
Women from whose loins I sprang
When the birds of Eden sang?
    One three centuries removed
    From the scenes his fathers loved
    Spicy grove, cinnamon tree
    What is Africa to me?

At one level, the whole book is an intensely personal answer to this oldest of Afro-American questions. But Wright's invocation of descent on the first page does not serve to introduce the straightforward racialism of Blyden or Crummell. For he asks immediately "But am I African?"; and goes on to wonder how he will feel in the presence of someone whose ancestors might have sold his ancestors into slavery—to wonder, we might say, if he can feel African—and then to ask how "the

Africans" will think of him. From his first response—"Africa?"—the scattered question marks of the next few pages largely indicate rephrasings of a central mystery, the puzzle that is the insistent theme of the book: what can Africa mean to an Afro-American who does not share—at least, officially—what Blyden called "the poetry of politics" that is "the feeling of race"?

> Had three hundred years imposed a psychological distance between me and the "racial stock" from which I had sprung? . . . But am I African? . . . What would my feelings be when I looked into the black face of an African, feeling that maybe his great-great-grandfather had sold my great-great-grandfather into slavery? Was there something in Africa that my feelings could latch onto to make all of this dark past clear and meaningful? Would the Africans regard me as a lost brother who had returned?. . . and I wondered, "What does being *African* mean . . . .?"

> Was Africa "primitive"? But what did being "primitive" mean? . . . How much of me was African?

Wright arrived in Africa apparently unencumbered with the Victorian views of his distinguished predecessors: he was a rationalist, with no time for Christianity; an ex-Marxist, who still retained a predilection for materialist analyses; and a foe of the sentimental racism that gave meaning to Crummell's and Blyden's African adventures. But, deprived of this intellectual baggage, he also lacked answers to the one question they could always answer, namely, what am I doing here?

Without Christianity he could not see his visit as the work of providence; he could not say, with Crummell, that the demands that Africa makes on black people everywhere are "a natural call," a "grand and noble work laid out in the Divine Providence." His materialist analyses could offer him the shared experience of racial exploitation as an answer, but that could give him no special reason to be in Africa rather than anywhere else in the non-white colonized world. And his consistent resistance to racial explanations, rooted in "blood," deprived him of the answer that runs through the more than a century of Afro-American thought about Africa, from Crummell to Du Bois and on into the Black Nationalism of the sixties.

Because he has no reason for "being there," Wright's reactions seem to oscillate between condescension and paranoia. "Lock your car and come with me," he orders a taxi driver

> expecting him to demur. But he didn't. I found that that was the only way to get any consideration out of a native.

When he is not in this condescending mood, Wright often meets gestures of friendship with suspicion: the first day in the Gold Coast a salesman in a store unwisely asks Wright whether he knows where his African ancestors came from:

> "Well," I said softly, "you know, you fellows who sold us and the white men who bought us didn't keep any records."

Even laughter and smiles recurrently produce distrust. At his first meeting with Nkrumah:

The Prime Minister threw back his head and laughed. I got used, in time, to that African laughter. It was not caused by mirth, it was a way of indicating that, though they were not going to take you into their confidence, their attitude was not based on anything hostile.

And when Wright met my late great-uncle Otumfuo Sir Osei Agyeman Prempeh II, then king of Ashanti, my distinguished affine obviously made the mistake of smiling once too often:

He was poised, at ease; yet like other men of the Akan race, he smiled *too* quickly; at times I felt his smile was artificial, that he smiled because it was required of him.

Somehow, one feels that in Paris, or Chicago or back home in Mississippi, even Wright might have grasped that a poised old man in a position of power, who smiled his way through dinner, could just be a fellow with good manners.

The prime minister and the king are merely inscrutable; but everywhere he goes, people are trying to cheat him out of his money, or lie to him about their customs.

I found that the African almost invariably underestimated the person with whom he was dealing; he always placed too much confidence in an evasive reply, thinking that if he denied something, then that something ceased to exist. It was childlike.

There are no doubt some who would read this as a parody of colonial discourse, but, as Saunders Redding has observed, Wright lacked "the ironic cast of mind and heart . . . he took all men and the world as he took himself: with grim seriousness." Wright's failure of sympathy mars even the three passages Michael Cooke has recently commended as "brilliant scenes" from a novelistic perspective: the episode set in a Las Palmas whorehouse—amusingly absent from the bowdlerized British edition that presumably went to the colonies; Wright's "feminizing" attempt to purchase a cooking pan from a woman in the street; and the tale of the stolen purse, recounted by his British host in Koforidua. Each evokes from Wright a signal moment of condescension: to a judge of the Nigerian Supreme Court; to African women (all of them, one fears); to the colonizing British who cannot "live side by side with the Africans without becoming infected with the African's religious beliefs."

Wright finally reveals explicitly the structure of assumptions that governs his interpretation of African behavior.

Most of the Africans I've met have been, despite their ready laughter, highly reserved and suspicious men. It would be easy to say that this chronic distrust arose from their centuries-long exploitation by Europeans, but the explanation would not elucidate the total African attitude. They never seem to feel that they have judged a man rightly unless they project some ulterior motive behind his most straightforward conduct. . . . I submit that the African's doubt of strangers, his panic in the face of reality has but peripheral relations to objective reality.

Every word here reads easily as a projection of Wright's own failings. Face to face with Africa, Wright retreated from reason; and his book is the record of a mind closed to the world through which he travelled.

This paranoid hermeneutic reaches its extraordinary climax in Kumasi, my hometown, capital of the "brooding Ashanti," when Wright is discussing the "human sacrifice" which, he has been assured, follows the death of an Ashanti chief. This passage of attempted anthropology invites serious attention, precisely because of the book's analytical pretensions. Subtly, the tale he has been told is transmuted so that, by the end, the killing of *local* people to accompany the king to the "other world" has become a "homicidal attitude toward the stranger." Finally, there passes very close to the surface the thought—reinforced by the fact that Wright had considered entitling the book *Stranger in a Strange Land*—that our author fears that these smiling, inscrutable black men are, in fact, out to kill him.

This interpretation is achieved through an anthropological fantasy, a fantasy incredible by the standards of ethnological speculation on ritual murder.

> If the human sacrifice—and that of animals: bulls, sheep, goats, and chickens—does not represent displaced hate of the living, why then is blood the gift that will appease the dead ancestor? The staunch conviction that the dead ancestor wants blood is their inverted confession of their own lust for blood. So that they feel that by killing a stranger and bathing the bones of an ancestor in the blood of that stranger, the ancestor will, for the time being, hold off haunting them, will leave them in peace.

"Distrust," Wright says of the Ashanti, "is the essence of such a life" and we no longer know if he is speaking of them or of himself.

III

References to the traditional religion of the Gold Coast pervade *Black Power;* religion was obviously central to Wright's reactions. Indeed, as John Reilly has discovered, Wright went along with a request from the readers at Harper and Brothers that he excise from the original manuscript "repeated references to his incredulity at aspects of religious practice." But the references that remain are multitudinous enough; and they have the effect of establishing a massive distance between Wright (and his readers in the West) and the people of the Gold Coast.

Of course, the religious practices of the people Wright meets are certainly strange to him, as they are to most Western readers. But Wright's preface tells us that "the book seeks to provide Western readers with some insight into what is going to happen in Africa," and to do this he must seek to render Africa intelligible. To see Wright's account of traditional religion as governed by his rhetoric of distance is to draw attention to the ways in which he seems studiously to avoid any opportunities to render these admittedly alien habits of thought more familiar.

I was raised in the Ghana that Nkrumah's Gold Coast became. I spent my youth in the landscape and among the people Wright seeks to anatomize; and what strikes me repeatedly is the way that *Black Power* defamiliarizes a world I know. And because, like every African intellectual nowadays, I know my way around the thought-world of the West, I am constantly struck, too, by the missed opportunities for understanding; the points at which a route for the Westerner into the traditional world is barred by Wright's desire not to understand. In *Black Power* there is never any real attempt to render familiar the traditional modes of thought whose unfamiliarity inevitably strike the Western stranger; instead we are constantly deluged with indecipherable signs of "African religion."

Wright's desire for distance is highlighted in an anecdote he retells of his first encounter with a Gold Coast funeral. Early on in his visit Wright hears "sounds of drums, of shouting, of shooting" outside his hotel. He rushes out into the noisy procession and watches a brass coffin borne aloft by a group of men:

> they'd run to a corner, stop, twirl the coffin, then, amidst shouting, singing, chanting, they'd turn and race with the coffin spinning above their heads in another direction.

Unable to keep up with the spinning coffin, Wright gives up trying to follow.

> I . . . stood feeling foolish and helpless in the hot sun, sensing sweat streaming down my face.
> I had understood nothing, nothing. . . . [his ellipsis] . . . My mind reeled at the newness and strangeness of it. Had my ancestors acted like that? And why?

Wright seeks enlightenment from an "African dressed in Western clothes"; and the African offers an elaborate explanation of the beliefs underlying many elements of the scene that has just transpired, asking Wright finally whether he understands.

Wright never answers his informant; at the very moment when he is offered entry to this hermetic world, he turns his back on the guide. "Yes;" he tells *us* (as his informant disappears into the crowd forever), "if you accepted the assumptions all the rest was easy, logical. The African's belief in the other world was concrete, definite."

Wright's narrative draws our attention to the sudden breaking off of dialogue, precisely at the point where he is offered the opportunity to find out whether he has understood. But he goes on to account for his estrangement in these extraordinary words:

> If there was another world, the African was about the only man really believing in it; . . .

You wonder what has happened to the "haints" of his native Mississippi, to the *lares* and *penates* of the European classical world, to Christian Europe's belief in an afterlife. To establish distance, it seems, Wright is willing to address "the Western reader" with a travesty of his own world.

Wright reports that he inserted an advertisement "in a local newspaper asking to buy an out-of-print book, R. S. Rattray's *Ashanti*," the classical ethnography of the region; and he has an extended discussion of J. B. Danquah's *Akan Doctrine of God*. Captain Rattray, a British Colonial Office anthropologist, had written that the Ashanti would

> become better and finer men and women by remaining true Ashanti and retaining a certain pride in their past, and that their greatest hope lies in the future, if they will build upon lines with which the national *sunsum* or soul has been familiar since first they were a people.

And his account renders intelligible much of what Wright seeks to render mysterious.

But Wright will have none of this. His account of Danquah begins with the question how "these strange notions came about" and ends with the remark that the Akan belief in life after death makes their lives "as charged and exciting as the moving tables and floating trumpets in a seance in a dreary London flat." The rhetorical sleight-of-hand here is breathtaking: if these "strange notions" operate in dreary London flats, why is their presence in *Africa* something that needs explaining? The human mystery of religious belief is dressed up as an African mystery: once more the sense of alterity is enforced.

At the end of Wright's exposition of Danquah's *Akan Doctrine of God* we read this one-sentence paragraph:

> I come up for air, to take a deep breath. . . . (his ellipsis)

The ellipsis, here as elsewhere, marks a moment when Wright seems literally to be at a loss for words. The figure implies that he is drowning, sucked down, perhaps, into the primal squalor of Africa. For Wright, as he admits, "the religion of the Akan is not primitive; it is simply terrifying."

Despite his exposure to Rattray's humane anthropological account of the "logic" of Akan traditional religion, Africa is still for Wright, as Crummell put it, "the victim of her heterogeneous idolatries." *Juju*, Gold Coast magic, is as offensive to Wright's rationalism as "Fetishes . . . and devil-worship" were to Crummell's Victorian Christianity. And each is equally a projection of the alienated stranger. The truth is that, though Wright's anthropological reading had prepared his mind for the religions of the Gold Coast, he was unable, when faced with the raw experience, to keep that intellectual apprehension. When he came to write about it, he found himself able to report "African religion" only as yet another mark of his own distance from Africa: "the religion of the Akan" becomes just another device to establish his alienation.

IV

Mary Louise Pratt has recently discussed some of the mechanisms by which a discourse—and, in particular, nineteenth-century travel writing about Africa— renders people alien. In her essay "Scratches on the Face of the Country; or, What Mr. Barrow Saw in the Land of the Bushmen," she observes, for example, that "the people to be othered are homogenized into a collective 'they,' which is distilled even further into an iconic 'he' (the standardized adult male specimen)." Pratt also remarks on the role of certain rhetorical strategies in this process of textual distancing: crucially the "temporal distancing" achieved by what Johannes Fabian has called the "denial of coevalness."

Wright's text is quite overt in the use it makes of just these devices of distancing. There are, for example, regular references to "the African." Even an old-style Ashanti imperialist, convinced that all the worthwhile culture of the region originated with the Akan, would be puzzled by Wright's assumption that learning about

Ga villages, or the burial customs of the Northern Territories entitled one to generalize about the Gold Coast, let alone about the continent. Wright displays ignorance again and again of the significance of terms, like "Twi" or "Akan," which he
uses to characterize languages or "tribes"; and yet this does not seem to matter for
his purposes precisely because, in the end, he only recognizes the people he meets
as "Africans." Subtler distinctions may be mentioned, but only to add authority to
his voice—here is a fellow who knows his Fanti from his Ashanti—not to illuminate the specificities of different human cultures.

There is even a passage where Wright reports "an intuitive impression that
these people were old, old, maybe the oldest people on earth," thus securing a
remarkably explicit temporal distancing; remarkable, because, if this is not a
device of distance, this sentence hardly seems to tell us anything at all.

But the central devices of distance in this text are provided, I believe, not so
much by rhetoric as by two *themes:* one of them, as I have suggested, is religion;
the other, as Pratt would perhaps have predicted, is the African body.

We have been in the Gold Coast only a few hours, travelling along the coast in
a government bus, when Wright looks out of the window to see "a crowd of naked
men, women and children, bathing." This scene is absorbed into "the kaleidoscope
of sea jungle, nudity, mud huts and crowded market places" which "induced in me
a conflict deeper than I was aware of"; and these unfamiliar scenes fill him with "a
mild sense of anxiety." At the first stop,

> I stared down at a bare-breasted young girl who held a huge pan of oranges perched
> atop her head. She saw me studying her and she smiled shyly, obviously accepting her
> semi-nudity as being normal. My eyes went over the crowd and I noticed that most of
> the older women had breasts that were flat and remarkably elongated, some reaching
> twelve or eighteen inches (length, I was later told, was regarded as a symbol of fertility!),
> hanging loosely and flapping as the women moved about . . .

Still, "bit by bit," Wright assures us in an attempt to reestablish narrative poise,
"my eyes became accustomed to the naked bodies."

Yet, next day, Wright's second day in the colony, on his first morning in Accra,
he goes into the city and finds himself the physical anthropologist once more:

> I reached a street corner and paused; coming towards me was a woman nursing a baby
> that was still strapped to her back; the baby's head was thrust under the woman's arm and
> the woman had given the child the long, fleshy, tubelike teat and it was suckling. (There
> are women with breasts so long that they do not bother to give the baby the teat in front
> of them, but simply toss it over the shoulder to the child on their back. . . (his ellipsis)

It is not just breasts that draw Wright's sideways glance: there are "monstrous
umbilical hernias"; girls are "skinny, their black shoulder blades stuck out at sharp
angles"; beggars have "monstrously swollen legs, running sores, limbs broken so
that jagged ends of the healed bones jutted out like blackened sticks"; blind men
have "empty eye sockets [that] yawned wetly, palsied palms extended"; "once or
twice" he sees "women who had induced strange swellings on their skins in order
to beautify themselves."

What is striking in these passages is the way that these bodies alienate by evoking disgust. The umbilical hernias, though monstrous, evoke no pity; the beggars' wounds "moved me not to compassion, but to revulsion"; the strange swellings conspicuously fail in their object, which is to beautify. Even where the bodies are graceful they are strange: "they walked as straight as ramrods, with a slow, slinging motion"; the men who bring the goods to shore in their tiny canoes are "wet glistening black robots."

How are we to read these significant bodies? Each record is of an encounter with a body, an encounter that Wright could not have had in Paris and Chicago. We understand how these bodies have caught his traveller's eye. But in a narrative that shifts erratically between an informational and a subjective register, it is striking how these bodies, even those young breasts, whose openness offers the Western imagination erotic possibilities, remain almost always in the information register. When they do not, the subjective register records them as objects of revulsion.

Indeed, so unerotic is Wright's encounter with the African body that he projects his own de-sexualization:

Undoubtedly these people had, through experiences that had constituted a kind of trial and error, and in response to needs that were alien and obscure to me, chosen some aspect of their lives other than sex upon which to concentrate their passions . . .

It takes a moment to grasp what Wright is here suggesting: that sexual desire means nothing to "the African." We can only wonder where all those filthy children with their "monstrous umbilical hernias" came from.

There is one final, oppressive regularity in Wright's encounter with the African bodyscape: again and again, these African bodies are, above all else, *black.*

We can assume, with Wright, that his readers know that most Africans have black skins. If he is constantly drawing attention to that fact, it is in order to sharpen the central paradox of the book:

I was black and they were black, and my blackness did not help me.

This is a paradox in the root sense: it goes against received opinion. And it is, I think, the fact that he cannot understand the minds behind these black faces— these minds that his culture (though not his official theory) had prepared him to find immediately accessible precisely because of the blackness of the faces—that generates first the defensive condescension and then, in the end, the frank paranoia.

I'm of African descent and I'm in the midst of Africans, yet I cannot tell what they are thinking and feeling.

Saunders Redding, one of Wright's astutest readers, has written of Wright's travels to Africa—and to Paris—as a failed search for a home. Despite his repeated resistance, in this book, as in his other writings, to the view of Africa as the homeland of the Negro—"I stoutly denied the mystic influence of 'race' "—it is hard to resist

Redding's claim that Wright's trip to Africa was yet another quest for a place of his own. When, in the final pages of the book, he tells Nkrumah that "our people must be made to walk, forced draft, into the twentieth century," we do not need to ask *whose* people. Scratch the native son and you'll find the native.

Even Wright's reaction to the pidgin English of the servants in the bungalow Nkrumah had arranged for him reveals an uneasiness about his identity:

> But the pidgin English! I shuddered. I resented it and vowed that I'd never speak it.

This resentment can only mean that this "frightful kind of baby talk" reflects badly on *him*. There is here a palpable anxiety about redescending into the ancestral mire.

Wright had arrived in Africa convinced, so he says, that a shared race gave him no basis for understanding the people he would meet, convinced that he had no basis for identifying with them: and *Black Power* is the record of his resentment that they proved him right. *Black Power*'s desire for distance is Wright's revenge for Africa's rebuff: his exaggeration of the gap between Africa and his Western experience is a response to the gap between his African experience and his African dream.

V

What energy and purpose there is in this book derives from Wright's sense of the importance of what Kwame Nkrumah was doing: in a splendid inversion of the strategy of authentication that Robert Stepto, among others, had identified in the affixed letter of the Afro-American slave narrative, Wright prefaced his book with an authenticating letter from Nkrumah. On the prime minister's letterhead and over his signature we read:

> This is to certify that I have known Mr. Richard Wright for many years, having met him in the United States.

For the first time an Afro-American can seek legitimation from a black man, a black head of government: the gesture underscores the truth in Baldwin's claim that the Afro-American is no longer "at the mercy of the American white man's image of him."

But the text not only begins with a letter *from* Nkrumah, but ends with a letter *to* him. The "response" to the African Prime Minister's note "to whom it may concern" is a long letter to "Dear Kwame." Wright's open letter is not drawn in the cold impersonal language of Nkrumah's *pro forma* note, but forged in the red heat of passion. The rhetorical distance, the disproportion between stimulus and response, between Nkrumah's impassive authorizing pre-text and Wright's final hysterical message to "the unknown African," is a measure of the asymmetry of feeling. Wright needs Nkrumah, needs him as his symbol of hope for black humanity; but all Nkrumah has to offer is a brusque acknowledgment that Wright is a suitable visitor, "to the best of my knowledge and belief."

Wright's letter proposes that the heart of "Africa's" problem is that "the African" has no sharply defined ego, no real individuality:

> there is too much cloudiness in the African mentality, a kind of sodden vagueness that makes for lack of confidence, an absence of focus that renders that mentality incapable of grasping the workaday world. And until confidence is established at the center of African personality, until there is an inner reorganization of that personality, there can be no question of marching from the tribal order to the twentieth century. . . . (his ellipsis)

If Wright cannot penetrate "the African personality," perhaps there is no personality to be penetrated.

And what is Wright's solution to Africa's problems; to the problems of these cloudy and unfocused personalities? "AFRICAN LIFE MUST BE MILITARIZED." Crummell's nineteenth-century vision of an Africa civilized by Christianity is replaced by the twentieth-century's desperate alternative: the protestant soldiers of God have become a rationalist army of progress. There is something simply mad in proposing from Paris, less than a decade after the Second World War, that Nkrumah—like Hitler and Mussolini?—needs the instruments of fascism if the trains of the Gold Coast are to run on time. And in proposing what is, despite his explicit denials, the introduction of the fascist state (uncomfortably suggestive of the totalitarian states that we deplore in Africa thirty years on), in proposing a solution that he acknowledges will appear "hard, cruel," the overwhelming impression Wright leaves is that he needs to punish Africa for failing him: and that its failure is, ironically, that it did just what he had asked of it. Blyden or Crummell may have hated much that they found in Africa, but they knew it was theirs. Deprived of the right, which Crummell or Blyden could have claimed, to take pride and pleasure in Nkrumah's achievement by virtue of race; convinced, against his hopes, that this is a place he does not understand, Wright responds with the fury of the lover spurned.

Chronology of Important Dates

1908	Born Richard Nathaniel Wright, September 4, on Rucker's Plantation, near Natchez, Mississippi, first child of Nathan and Ella Wilson Wright.
1911–12	Family moves to Natchez to live with Wilsons.
1913–14	Family moves to Memphis, Tennessee. Father deserts family, leaving them impoverished.
1916	Mother falls seriously ill amd puts Wright and his brother (Leon Alan, b. 1910) in a Methodist orphanage in Memphis, where they stay for over a month. Wright spends summer in Jackson, Mississippi, before going with mother and brother to Elaine, Arkansas, to live with his aunt, Maggie, and her husband Silas Hoskins.
1917–19	After Hoskins is murdered by whites, family flees to West Helena, Arkansas, and then to Jackson. After several months, they return to West Helena. In 1919, Wright and his family move to Jackson, where they stay until 1925.
1923–24	Wright recalls writing his first short story, "The Voodoo of Hell's Half-Acre." No copies are known to exist.
1925	Graduates from Smith Robertson Junior High School as valedictorian on May 29. Leaves Jackson for Memphis.
1927	Moves to South Side of Chicago, with Aunt Maggie.
1929	Finds job as clerk in a Chicago Post Office.
1933	Joins Chicago branch of the John Reed Club, a national literary organization sponsored by the Communist Party. Writes and submits revolutionary poems to *Left Front*. Elected executive secretary of the Club.
1934	Joins the Communist Party. Publishes poetry in *Left Front, Anvil,* and *New Masses*. Becomes a member of the editorial board of *Left Front*.
1935	Publishes leftist poetry in *Midland Left, New Masses,* and *International Literature*. Begins submitting "Cesspool" to publishers (later retitled *Lawd Today!* by Wright, the novel is rejected repeatedly over the next two years; finally, it is published posthumously in 1963). Publishes important poem about lynching entitled "Between the World and Me" in July–August *Partisan Review*. His first piece of journalism, "Joe Louis Uncovers Dynamite," published in *New Masses*. After severe bout with pneumonia in summer, Wright is hired by the Federal Writers' Project (part of the Works Progress Administration).
1936	Takes active role in South Side Writers' Group. Short story "Big Boy Leaves Home" receives critical attention and praise in mainstream newspapers and journals.

1937   Breaks with the Communist Party in Chicago, basically over the question of his freedom as a writer. Turns down permanent Post Office position to pursue career as a writer in New York City. Becomes Harlem editor of the Communist newspaper *Daily Worker* and writes over 200 articles for it during the year. Publishes "The Ethics of Living Jim Crow—An Autobiographical Sketch" and "Blueprint for Negro Writing." Wright's second novel, *Tarbaby's Dawn,* is rejected by publishers and remains unpublished at present, but his story "Fire and Cloud" wins first prize ($500) among 600 entries in *Story Magazine* contest.

1938   *Uncle Tom's Children: Four Novellas* published in March and widely praised. Wright begins work on new novel; asks Margaret Walker to send him newspaper accounts of the case of Robert Nixon, a young Chicago black man accused of murder (executed in August 1939).

1939   Awarded Guggenheim Fellowship ($2000) in March and resigns from Federal Writers' Project. Finishes *Native Son.* Marries Dhima Rose Meadman in August, with Ralph Ellison as best man. Begins work on new novel, *Little Sister* (it is never finished).

1940   *Native Son* published on March 1 and offered by the Book-of-the-Month Club as one of its two main selections; it sells 215,000 copies in three weeks. Wright delivers talk, "How Bigger Was Born" at Columbia University on March 12. Marriage becomes strained during vacation in Mexico; Wright tours South alone in June and meets with his father. *Uncle Tom's Children: Five Long Stories* reissued with "Bright and Morning Star" added. Starts divorce proceedings.

1941   Receives Spingarn Medal of the National Association for the Advancement of Colored People. Marries Ellen Poplar on March 12. Stage version of *Native Son,* starring Canada Lee and directed by Orson Welles, opens. Begins novel "Black Hope" (never completed). *12 Million Black Voices: A Folk History of the Negro in the United States* published in October. Finishes draft of intended novel entitled "The Man Who Lived Underground." Becomes increasingly interested in psychoanalysis.

1942   Daughter Julia born.

1943   A talk on his experiences with racism at Fisk University, Nashville, Tennessee, leads Wright to begin autobiography *American Hunger,* which he completes in December.

1944   Book-of-the-Month Club accepts only the first section of Wright's autobiography, which describes his Southern experiences; Wright changes title to *Black Boy* (the second section is published as *American Hunger* in 1977). His essay "I Tried to Be a Communist" is published in August–September *Atlantic Monthly.*

1945   *Black Boy: A Record of Childhood and Youth* published in March. Writes long introduction to *Black Metropolis,* a sociological study of black Chicago by Horace Cayton and St. Clair Drake.

1946   Travels to Paris, France, at invitation of the French government.

1947   Returns to New York in January, but soon decides to return to Europe permanently with his family, partially in response to racial hostility in New York. Wright, his wife, and his daughter reach Paris in June.

1949   Daughter Rachel born.

1953   *The Outsider* published in March. Wright travels in the Gold Coast (later the independent country of Ghana).

1954   Novel *Savage Holiday* published. Report on trip to Africa, *Black Power: A Record of Reactions in a Land of Pathos,* published in September.

1955   Travels in Spain and attends conference in Bandung, Indonesia, as a journalist.

1956   Two nonfiction works, *The Color Curtain: A Report on the Bandung Conference* and *Pagan Spain,* an account of Spanish life and culture, published.

1957   *White Man, Listen!,* a collection of essays based on his lectures, published.

1958   Novel *The Long Dream* published in October. Begins work on "Island of Hallucinations," the sequel to *The Long Dream,* set in France (unfinished).

1960   Begins new novel entitled *A Father's Law* (unfinished). Proofreads galleys of a collection of short stories entitled *Eight Men* (published posthumously in 1961). Dies of a heart attack in Paris on November 28.

Notes on Contributors

TIMOTHY DOW ADAMS, a Professor of English at West Virginia University, has published a number of articles on American autobiography. The co-editor of *a/b: Auto/Biography Studies*, he is the author of *Telling Lives in Modern American Autobiography* (1990). His current project is a study of photography and autobiography.

KWAME ANTHONY APPIAH is a Professor in the Department of Philosophy and the Department of Afro-American Studies at Harvard University. His books include *In My Father's House: Africa in the Philosophy of Culture* (1992), *Assertion and Conditionals* (1985), and *For Truth in Semantics* (1986).

MICHAEL ATKINSON teaches literary theory and American literature at the University of Cincinnati. A specialist in mythological, psychological, and reader-response analysis, he has recently finished *The Secret Marriage of Sherlock Holmes and Other Eccentric Readings*, which applies a variety of literary theories to the adventures of the world's first consulting detective.

JERRY H. BRYANT has taught at California State University at Hayward since 1963. He is the author of *The Open Decision: The Contemporary American Novel and Its Intellectual Background* (1970) and various articles on writers such as Ralph Ellison, James Baldwin, Ernest Gaines, and Ishmael Reed.

YOSHINOBU HAKUTANI was born and reared in Japan. Educated in Japan and the United States, he is Professor of English at Kent State University. His many books include *Critical Essays on Richard Wright, Selected Writings of Yone Noguchi: An East-West Literary Assimilation, Young Dreiser: A Critical Study*, and *Selected Magazine Articles of Theodore Dreiser: Life and Art in the American 1890s*, for which he received a *Choice* award in 1987.

ABDUL R. JANMOHAMED is a Professor of English at the University of California, Berkeley. Among his publications are *Alex La Guma: The Literary and Political Functions of Marginality in the Colonial Situation* (1982); *Manichean Aesthetics: The Politics of Literature in Colonial Africa* (1983); and (co-edited with David Lloyd) *The Nature and Context of Minority Discourse* (1990).

KENETH KINNAMON, an acknowledged authority on the life and work of Richard Wright, is Ethel Pumphrey Stephens Professor of English at the University of Arkansas, Fayetteville. Among his books are *The Emergence of Richard Wright* (1972), *A Richard Wright Bibliography: Fifty Years of Criticism and Commentary* (1988), and *New Essays on Native Son* (1990).

TONY MAGISTRALE is an Associate Professor of English at the University of Vermont, Burlington. He has published many essays on American literature, particularly the work of

Flannery O'Connor, Wanda Coleman, and Stephen King. His most recent publication is a volume on King in the Twayne U.S. Authors Series.

JACK B. MOORE is a member of the Department of American Studies, the Department of English, and the Institute on Black Life at the University of South Florida. His scholarly publications include books on W.E.B. Du Bois, Joe DiMaggio, American skinheads, and commercial photography.

ARNOLD RAMPERSAD is Woodrow Wilson Professor of Literature at Princeton University. Among his books are the two-volume *The Life of Langston Hughes* (1986, 1988) and the two-volume, revised Library of America edition (1991) of the works of Richard Wright.

JOHN M. REILLY recently completed six years' service as president of United University Professions, the collective bargaining agent for faculty in the State University of New York. Now a Visiting Professor at Howard University, he is continuing to write about African American genre development.

JOSEPH T. SKERRETT, JR. is Professor of English at the University of Massachusetts at Amherst, where he has taught since 1973. His essays on 20th Century American and African American literature have appeared in *Studies in Short Fiction, Massachusetts Review, American Quarterly*, and elsewhere. Since 1987, he has been editor of *MELUS*, the journal of the Society for the Study of Multi-Ethnic Literature in the United States.

LOUIS TREMAINE is Associate Professor of English and Coordinator of African Studies at the University of Richmond, where his research centers on recent African fiction.

PATRICIA D. WATKINS, formerly an Associate Professor of English and Assistant Dean of the College of Arts and Sciences at Morgan State University, is the author of several essays on American literature.

SHERLEY ANNE WILLIAMS is a Professor of English at the University of California, San Diego. A poet, novelist, and critic, she is author of the highly acclaimed novel *Dessa Rose* (1986), *Give Birth to Brightness: A Thematic Study in Neo-Black Literature* (1972), and two volumes of verse.

Bibliography

The basic tools for a student engaging in further research on Richard Wright include Keneth Kinnamon's *A Richard Wright Bibliography* (1988), Michel Fabre's biography, *The Unfinished Quest of Richard Wright* (1973), and the Library of America's two volumes of Wright's works, *Early Works: Lawd Today!, Uncle Tom's Children, Native Son* and *Later Works: Black Boy (American Hunger), The Outsider*, edited by Arnold Rampersad (1991). Also, several journals have devoted entire issues to Wright criticism: *Callaloo* 9.3 (1986), *CLA Journal* 12.4 (1969), *Mississippi Quarterly: The Journal of Southern Culture* 42.4 (1989), *Negro Digest (Black World)* 18.2 (1968), *New Letters* 38 (1971) [reprinted as *Richard Wright: Impressions and Perspectives*. Ed. David Ray and Robert M. Farnsworth. Ann Arbor: U of Michigan P, 1973], and *Studies in Black Literature* 1.3 (1970). The following consists of highly recommended biographies, bibliographies, and criticism, including book-length critical studies.

Biographies

Fabre, Michel. *The Unfinished Quest of Richard Wright*. Trans. Isabel Barzun. New York: Morrow, 1973.

Gayle, Addison. *Ordeal of a Native Son*. Garden City, NY: Doubleday, 1980.

Walker, Margaret. *Richard Wright: Daemonic Genius*. New York: Warner, 1988.

Webb, Constance. *Richard Wright: A Biography*. New York: Putnam's, 1968.

Williams, John A. *The Most Native of Sons: A Biography of Richard Wright*. Garden City, NY: Doubleday, 1970.

Bibliographies

Davis, Charles T. and Michel Fabre. *Richard Wright: A Primary Bibliography*. Boston: G.K. Hall, 1982.

Fabre, Michel and Edward Margolies. "Richard Wright (1908–1960): A Bibliography." *Bulletin of Bibliography* 24 (1965): 131–133, 137.

Kinnamon, Keneth, et al. *A Richard Wright Bibliography: Fifty Years of Criticism and Commentary 1933–1982*. Westport, CT: Greenwood Press, 1988.

Kinnamon, Keneth. "A Selective Bibliography of Wright Scholarship and Criticism, 1983–1988." *Mississippi Quarterly: The Journal of Southern Culture* 42 (1989): 451–471.

Reilly, John M. "Richard Wright: An Essay in Bibliography." *Resources for American Literary Study* 1 (1971): 131–180.

Book-Length Critical Studies

Abcarian, Richard, ed. *Richard Wright's Native Son: A Critical Handbook*. Belmont, CA: Wadsworth, 1970.

Bakish, David. *Richard Wright*. New York: Ungar, 1973.

Bone, Robert. *Richard Wright*. Minneapolis: U of Minnesota P, 1969.

Brignano, Russell Carl. *Richard Wright: An Introduction to the Man and His Works*. Pittsburgh: U of Pittsburgh P, 1970.

Fabre, Michel. *The World of Richard Wright*. Jackson: U of Mississippi P, 1985.

Felgar, Robert. *Richard Wright*. Boston: Twayne, 1980.

Fishburn, Katherine. *Richard Wright's Hero: The Faces of a Rebel-Victim*. Metuchen, NJ: Scarecrow Press, 1977.

Joyce, Joyce Ann. *Richard Wright's Art of Tragedy*. Iowa City: U of Iowa P, 1986.

Kinnamon, Keneth. *The Emergence of Richard Wright: A Study in Literature and Society*. Urbana: U of Illinois P, 1973.

Margolies, Edward. *The Art of Richard Wright*. Carbondale: Southern Illinois UP, 1969.

McCall, Dan. *The Example of Richard Wright*. New York: Harcourt, Brace and World, 1969.

Miller, Eugene E. *Voice of a Native Son: The Poetics of Richard Wright*. Jackson: UP of Mississippi, 1990.

Other Criticism

Agosta, Lucien L. "Millenial Embrace: The Artistry of Conclusion in Richard Wright's 'Fire and Cloud'." *Studies in Short Fiction* 18 (1981): 121–129.

Baker, Houston A., Jr. "Reassessing (W)right: A Meditation on the Black (W)hole." *Blues, Ideology and Afro-American Literature: A Vernacular Theory*. Chicago: U of Chicago P, 1984. 139–172.

Baker, Houston A., Jr., ed. *Twentieth Century Interpretations of Native Son: A Collection of Critical Essays*. Englewood Cliffs, NJ: Prentice-Hall, 1972.

Baldwin James. "Alas, Poor Richard." *Nobody Knows My Name: More Notes of a Native Son*. New York: Dial, 1961. 200–215.

Baldwin, James. "Many Thousands Gone." *Notes of a Native Son*. Boston: Beacon, 1955. 24–45.

Baldwin, Richard E. "The Creative Vision of *Native Son*." *Massachusetts Review* 14 (1973): 378–390.

Bigsby, C.W.E. "The Self and Society: Richard Wright's Dilemma." *The Second Black Renaissance*. Westport, CT: Greenwood Press, 1980. 54–84.

Blake, Caesar R. "On Richard Wright's *Native Son*." *Rough Justice: Essays on Crime in Literature*. Ed. M.L. Friedland. Toronto: U of Toronto P, 1991. 187–199.

Bloom, Harold, ed. *Bigger Thomas*. New York: Chelsea House, 1990.

Bloom, Harold, ed. *Richard Wright*. New York: Chelsea House, 1987.

Bloom, Harold, ed. *Richard Wright's* Native Son. New York: Chelsea House, 1988.

Blythe, Hal and Charlie Sweet. " 'Yo Mama Don Wear No Drawers': Suspended Sexuality in 'Big Boy Leaves Home'." *Notes on Mississippi Writers* 21.1 (1989): 31–36.

Bolton, H. Philip. "The Role of Paranoia in Richard Wright's *Native Son*." *Kansas Quarterly* 7.3 (1975): 111–124.

Bryant, Earle V. "The Sexualization of Racism in Richard Wright's 'The Man Who Killed a Shadow'." *Black American Literature Forum* 16.3 (1982): 119–121.

Bullock-Kimball, Susanne. "The Modern Minotaur: A Study of Richard Wright's *Native Son*." *Notes on Mississippi Writers* 20.2 (1988): 41–48.

Butler, Robert James. "Wright's Native Son and Two Novels by Zola: A Comparative Study." *Black American Literature Forum* 18.3 (1984): 100–105.

Butterfield, Stephen. Chapter 8 in *Black Autobiography in America*. Amherst: U of Massachusetts P, 1974. 155–179.

Cauley, Anne O. "A Definition of Freedom in the Fiction of Richard Wright." *CLA Journal* 19 (1976): 327–346.

Cobb, Nina Kressner. "Richard Wright: Individualism Reconsidered." *CLA Journal* 21 (1978): 335–354.

Cobb, Nina Kressner. "Richard Wright: Exile and Existentialism." *Phylon* 40 (1979): 362–374.

Coles, Robert A. "Richard Wright's *The Outsider*: A Novel in Transition." *Modern Language Studies* 13.3 (1983): 53–61.

Coles, Robert A. "Richard Wright's Synthesis." *CLA Journal* 31 (1988): 375–393.

Corey, Stephen. "The Avengers in *Light in August* and *Native Son*." *CLA Journal* 23 (1979): 200–212.

Davis, Charles T. "From Experience to Eloquence: Richard Wright's Black Boy as Art." *Chant of Saints: A Gathering of Afro-American Literature, Art, and Scholarship*. Ed. Robert Stepto and Michael Harper. Urbana: U of Illinois P, 1978. 425–439. Reprinted in *Black is the Color of the Cosmos: Essays on Afro-American Literature and Culture, 1942–1981*. Ed. Henry Louis Gates, Jr. New York: Garland, 1982. 281–298.

Davis, Jane. "More Force than Human: Richard Wright's Female Characters." *Obsidian II* 1.3 (1986): 68–83.

Douglas, Robert L. "Religious Orthodoxy in Richard Wright's *Uncle Tom's Children* and *Native Son*." *Griot* 6.1 (1987): 49–54.

Ellison, Ralph. "Richard Wright's Blues." *Shadow and Act*. New York: Vintage, 1964. 77–94.

Ellison, Ralph. "The World and the Jug." *Shadow and Act*. New York: Vintage, 1964. 115–147.

Fleming, Robert E. "O'Neill's *The Hairy Ape* as a Source for *Native Son*." *CLA Journal* 28 (1985): 434–447.

Gallagher, Kathleen. "Bigger's Great Leap to the Figurative." *CLA Journal* 27 (1984): 293–314.

Gibson, Donald, B. "Richard Wright: The Politics of a Lone Marxian." *The Politics of Literary Expression: A Study of Major Black Writers*. Westport, CT: Greenwood Press, 1981. 21–57.

Gibson, Donald, B. "Richard Wright and the Tyranny of Convention." *CLA Journal* 12 (1969): 344–357.

Gilyard, Keith. "The Sociolinguistics of Underground Blues." *Black American Literature Forum* 19.4 (1985): 158–159.

Gross, Barry. "Art and Act: The Example of Richard Wright." *Obsidian* 11.2 (1976): 5–19.

Hakutani, Yoshinobu, ed. *Critical Essays on Richard Wright*. Boston: G.K. Hall & Co., 1982.

Hakutani, Yoshinobu. "Creation of the Self in Richard Wright's *Black Boy*." *Black American Literature Forum* 19.2 (1985): 70–75.

Hamalian, Linda Bearman. "Richard Wright's Use of Epigraphs in *The Long Dream*."

Black American Literature Forum 10.4 (1976): 120–123.

Harris, Trudier. "Ritual Violence and the Formation of an Aesthetic." *Exorcising Blackness: Historical and Literary Lynching and Burning Rituals.* Bloomington: U of Indiana P, 1984. 95–128.

Hoeveler, Diane Long. "Oedipus Agonistes: Mothers and Sons in Richard Wright's Fiction." *Black American Literature Forum* 12.2 (1978): 65–68.

Howard, William. "Richard Wright's Flood Stories and the Great Mississippi River Flood of 1927: Social and Historical Backgrounds." *Southern Literary Journal* 16.2 (1984): 44–62.

Howe, Irving. "Black Boys and Native Sons." *Dissent* 10 (Autumn 1963): 353–368. Reprinted in *A World More Attractive: A View of Modern Literature and Politics.* New York: Horizon, 1963. 98–122.

Jones, Lola E. "Sex and Sexuality in Richard Wright's 'Big Boy Leaves Home'." *Amid Visions and Revisions: Poetry and Criticism on Literature and the Arts.* Ed. B.J. Hollis. Baltimore: Morgan State UP, 1985. 102–108.

Joyce, Joyce Ann. "Style and Meaning in Richard Wright's *Native Son.*" *Black American Literature Forum* 16.3 (1982): 112–115.

Keady, Sylvia H. "Richard Wright's Women Characters and Inequality." *Black American Literature Forum* 10.4 (1976): 124–128.

Kinnamon, Keneth, ed. *New Essays on Native Son.* New York: Cambridge UP, 1990.

Kostelanetz, Richard. "The Politics of Unresolved Quests in the Novels of Richard Wright." *Xavier University Studies* 8 (Spring 1969): 31–64.

Loftis, John E. "Domestic Prey: Richard Wright's Parody of the Hunt Tradition in 'The Man Who Was Almost a Man'." *Studies in Short Fiction* 23 (1986): 437–442.

Macksey, Richard and Frank E. Moorer, eds. *Richard Wright: A Collection of Critical Essays.* Englewood Cliffs, NJ: Prentice-Hall, 1984.

Maduka, Chidi T. "The Revolutionary Hero and Strategies for Survival in Richard Wright's *The Outsider.*" *Presence Africaine: Revue Culturelle du Monde Noir/Cultural Review of the Negro World* 135 (1985): 56–70.

Mayberry, Susan Neal. "Symbols in the Sewer: A Symbolic Renunciation of Symbols in Richard Wright's 'The Man Who Lived Underground'." *South Atlantic Review* 54.1 (1989): 71–83.

McCluskey, John, Jr. "Two-Steppin': Richard Wright's Encounter with Blue-Jazz." *American Literature* 55 (1983): 332–344.

Miller, Eugene E. "Folkloric Aspects of Wright's 'The Man Who Killed a Shadow'." *CLA Journal* 27 (1983): 210–223.

Miller, Eugene E. "Richard Wright and Gertrude Stein." *Black American Literature Forum* 16.3 (1982): 107–112.

Moore, Jack B. "The Art of *Black Power*: Novelistic or Documentary." *Revue Francais d'Etudes Americaines* 12 (February 1987): 79–91.

Moore, Jack B. "*Black Power* Revisited: In Search of Richard Wright." *Mississippi Quarterly: The Journal of Southern Culture* 41.2 (1988): 161–186.

Moore, Jack B. "Richard Wright's Dream of Africa." *Journal of African Studies* 2 (Summer 1975): 231–245.

Moore, Jack B. "The View from the Broom Closet of the Regency Hyatt: Richard Wright as a Southern Writer." *Literature at the Barricades: The American Writer in the 1930s.* Ed. R.F. Bogardus and F. Howard. Alabama: U of Alabama P, 1982. 126–143.

Nash, Charles C. " 'The Man Who Lived Underground': Richard Wright's Parable of the Cave." *Interpretations* 16 (Fall 1985): 62–74.

Reilly, John M., ed. *Richard Wright: The Critical Reception*. New York: Burt Franklin, 1978.

Reilly, John M. "Richard Wright Preaches the Nation: *Twelve Million Black Voices*." *Black American Literature Forum* 16.3 (1982): 116–119.

Reilly, John M. "Richard Wright's Discovery of the Third World." *Minority Voices* 2 (Fall 1978). 47–53

Reilly, John M. "Self-portraits by Richard Wright." *Colorado Quarterly* 20 (Summer 1971): 31–45.

Sadler, Jeffrey. "Split Consciousness in Richard Wright's *Native Son*." *The South Carolina Review* 8.2 (1976): 11–24.

Saunders, James Robert. "The Social Significance of Bigger Thomas." *College Literature* 14.1 (1987): 32–37.

Scruggs, Charles W. "Finding Out About this Mencken: The Impact of *A Book of Prefaces* on Richard Wright." *Menckeniana* 95 (Fall 1985): 1–11.

Scruggs, Charles W. "The Importance of the City in *Native Son*." *Ariel* 9.3 (1978): 37–47.

Siegel, Paul N. "Richard Wright's *Native Son*: The Black Nationalist Revolution in America." *Revolution and the Twentieth-Century Novel*. New York: Monad Press, 1979. 90–104.

Singh, Amritjit. "Richard Wright's *The Outsider*: Existentialist Exemplar or Critique?" *CLA Journal* 27 (1984): 357–370.

Starr, Alvin. "Richard Wright and the Communist Party—The James T. Farrell Factor." *CLA Journal* 21 (1977): 41–50.

Stone, Albert E. "The Childhood of the Artist: Louis Sullivan and Richard Wright." *Autobiographical Occasions and Original Acts: Versions of American Identity from Henry Adams to Nate Shaw*. Philadelphia: U of Pennsylvania P, 1982. 92–148.

Tate, Claudia C. "Christian Existentialism in Richard Wright's *The Outsider*." *CLA Journal* 25 (1982): 371–395.

Thaddeus, Janice. "The Metamorphosis of Richard Wright's *Black Boy*." *American Literature* 57 (1985): 201–214.

Trotman, C. James, ed. *Richard Wright: Myths and Realities*. New York: Garland, 1988.

Walls, Doyle W. "The Clue Undetected in Richard Wright's *Native Son*." *American Literature* 57 (March 1985): 125–128.

Wertham, Frederic. "An Unconscious Determinant in *Native Son*." *Journal of Clinical Psychopathology and Psychotherapy* 6 (1944): 111–115. Reprinted in *Psychoanalysis and Literature*. Ed. Hendrick M. Ruitenbeck. New York: Dutton, 1964. 321–325.